UNBOUNDED CONSCIOUSNESS:
QUALIA, MIND AND SELF

UNBOUNDED CONSCIOUSNESS: QUALIA, MIND AND SELF

MING SINGER
Department of Psychology
University of Canterbury
New Zealand

FREE ASSOCIATION BOOKS / LONDON / NEW YORK

First published in Great Britain 2001 by
Free Association Books
57 Warren Street, London W1T 5NR

www.fa-b.com

Copyright © Ming Singer 2001

The right of Ming Singer to be identified as the author of this work has been asserted by her in accordance with the Copyright, Designs and Patents Act 1988.

ISBN 1-85343-542-2 hbk
ISBN 1-85343-541-4 pbk

A CIP catalogue record for this book is available from the British Library

10 09 08 07 06 05 04 03 02 01

10 9 8 7 6 5 4 3 2 1

Designed, typeset and produced for Free Association Books Ltd by
Chase Publishing Services, Fortescue, Sidmouth, EX10 9QG
Printed in the European Union by TJ International, Padstow, England

For my parents

and

Alan and Alexander

Contents

1 Introduction	1
Qualia defined: the mind–mind problem	2
Qualia in a historical context: the agency–sentience separation	5
Qualia's existence and function	8
Qualia and consciousness: further research directions	12
Consciousness as totality of the conscious and the nonconscious	13
Conceptualizing consciousness in dynamic-systemic terms	16
Methods of enquiry	20
2 A Survey of Philosophical Thoughts on the Mind	25
Classical philosophers' conceptions of the mind	26
Heraclitus and Parmenides	27
Democritus	28
Plato	29
Aristotle	31
The legacies of the classical philosophers on the mind–body and the quanta–qualia problems	33
Descartes' dualism and philosophical responses	35
Rene Descartes	35
Philosophical positions in response to Descartes' mind–body dualism	39
Empirical psychology of the mind	51

3 A Survey of Philosophical Thoughts on the Holistic Subjective Self   53

Heraclitus: unbounded-*psyche* as self   54
Protagoras' human-centred philosophy   55
Classical Greek: a holistic *psyche* dominated by ration   56
The Hellenistic and Roman periods: turning within the self through subjective will (Stoicism) and spiritual faith (neo-Platonism)   57
The Medieval period: reality centred around the external absolute   58
The Renaissance: humanistic focus on the aesthetic and feeling self   60
Romanticism against Enlightenment   61
Self in contemporary philosophy   69

4 Contemporary Models of 'Consciousness'   79

Neurocognitive models of consciousness relevant to qualia   79
    Cognitive models of consciousness   79
    Neurophysiological approach to consciousness   88
Quantum physics and chaos theory in neurophysiological research of consciousness   98
    Appeal to quantum physics   99
    Appeal to chaos theory   113

5 Self as Cognitive Agent and Humanistic Guide   125

Self in the founding psychologies   128
    Wundt's psychology of consciousness and *Volkerpsychologie*: self as 'totality of life processes'   128
    James' adaptational psychology: self as 'stream of consciousness'   130

Freud's psychology of the unconscious: self as
    constituting the conscious and the unconscious
    mind 134
Self after the founding psychologies 137
    Self as cognitive agent 137
    Self as sentient experiencer and humanistic guide 149
Self in contemporary socio-political and cultural-historical
    analyses 158
Key issues in recent self research 161
    Self with an internal versus external focus 161
    Self research: neurophysiological correlates and
        system-dynamic features 163

6 Qualitative Consciousness: Its Existence and Function 165

Dissolving the conceptual separation between qualia
    and non-qualia 167
    Chalmers' information-state model of consciousness 168
    Superposition of qualia and non-qualitative experience:
        a convergent view 172
The function of qualia 179
    Accessing information within mental workspace: qualia
        and the activation of the nonconscious 181
    Mental conclusions: transition between covert parallel
        construction and overt serial manifestation 195

7 An Unbound Mental Workspace 201

A complete notion of consciousness 201
    Undoing the mind bondage: returning to the unbounded
        psyche 202
    Embracing the unconscious: transcending the
        conscious–unconscious divide 204

Multiplicity and self-organization characterize
    consciousness   209
  Multiplicity as a covert property of consciousness   210
  Self-organization as a dynamic process of
    consciousness   213
Method of enquiry into the unbound consciousness   219
  Experimentation and hermeneutics: sense-making in
    tandem   220

Epilogue   225

Bibliography   229

Index   248

1
Introduction

The study of consciousness has been one of the most persistent mental pursuits engaging early philosophers, contemporary scientists, and common folks alike. Despite centuries of intellectual endeavour and a plethora of ascertainable theories and considered opinions, the subject remains enigmatic. As McGinn (1997) puts it, *'Consciousness has ... come to be cast as the fairground coconut of contemporary thought: everyone wants a crack at knocking it'* (p.65). Numerous and varied attempts notwithstanding, the coconut isn't wobbling yet. And according to some, it may never yield to any such human attempts (e.g., McGinn, 1991; Nagel, 1974; Pinker, 1997). However, for most others, regardless of its difficulty, the topic remains fascinating, inviting and perhaps more importantly, resolvable. Indeed, while Chalmers (1996) asserts that *'Consciousness is the biggest mystery. It may be the largest outstanding obstacle in our quest for a scientific understanding of the universe'* (p.xi), his naturalistic information-state theory, at the same time, gives reason to believe that the subject need not remain forever a mystery. Similarly, although Searle (1997) acknowledges that *'This era is at once the most exciting and the most frustrating for the study of consciousness in my intellectual lifetime'* (p.xi), he nonetheless argues that a non-reductionist conceptual framework grounded in 'biological naturalism' can now steer the issue towards a satisfactory solution.

This book pertains to consciousness and in particular, its more puzzling qualitative aspects. It is by no means yet another attempt at cracking the coconut in the sense of proposing a fundamental theory of qualitative consciousness. It represents a rather modest attempt at four specific and related goals: (1) to illuminate the historical reasons as to why qualitative experience has a less than legitimate status of existence in contemporary consciousness research, (2) to justify such sentient experience's irreducibility to its physical correlates, (3) to speculate over its possible functions in life's adaptation, and (4) to suggest conceptual as well as methodological extensions as directions for future research. Next, following a definition of relevant terms, each of these goals is elaborated further.

QUALIA DEFINED: THE MIND–MIND PROBLEM

It has recently been noted that there are in fact two different, albeit related, issues of consciousness within the 'mind–body' problem. The first concerns the relationship between physical and mental events, which can be formulated into the question, 'How can a physical entity give rise to mental events?' This question first arose in times past as human beings observed the natural and 'seemingly given' phenomenon of mental events occurring in their own physical bodies. The philosophical debates over the centuries have been mainly concerned with this issue (i.e., the mind–body problem). Philosophical reflections aside, much of this 'mind–brain' question has however been answered by results from scientific investigations in cognitive and neural-biological sciences. These investigations have shown that consciousness or mental events have physical correlates in the form of neuronal activities in the brain. Thus, in the mental realm, the mind appears to be reducible to physical matters, in much the same way as all compound 'things' in the physical realm are reducible to a small number of primary physical properties.

However, once this first issue in the mind–body problem has been, in a sense, settled, a second related issue comes begging in its own right. The question now becomes, 'How can each mental event have a *qualitative feel* accompanying it?' This question can be rephrased from a subjective first-personal (e.g.,

X's) point of view: 'What is it like to be X?' or 'What does it feel like to be X?' And presumably such questions can only be meaningfully answered by X itself. It is worth noting that Aristotle is perhaps the first philosopher to have phrased the qualitative-feel question in terms of 'What is it like to be X?' In Book 2 (412b) of *De Anima*, Aristotle made the reference to the question of 'What is it like to be an axe?' in the course of asserting his position that the soul is the *essential whatness* of a thing and that *'if this (essential whatness) disappeared from it (the axe), it would have ceased to be an axe, except in name'* (McKeon, 1941, p.556). And largely due to its metaphysical nature, the issue of qualitative-feel lay dormant for many a century before contemporary philosophers were to again ask similar questions including *'what is it like to be a bat?' 'a monkey', 'a Zombie', 'a thermostat'*, or *'a patient affected by unilateral neglect'*, in exploring the nature of consciousness.

This 'first-personal' question of 'What is it like to be X?' is considered by some contemporary philosophers as the harder part of the mind–body problem (e.g., Chalmers, 1996). The qualitative feature of consciousness, generally termed as 'qualia', appears elusive by nature. The term *qualia* (the plural of *quale*) comes from the Latin words *qualis* (meaning 'of what kind or quality'). It was used in contrast to the term *quanta* (the plural of *quantum,* from the Latin word *quantus*, meaning 'of how much or quantity'). The distinction between qualitative (qualia) and non-qualitative (quanta) aspects of consciousness was also traceable to Aristotle's writings as he reflected upon the nature of the *soul* in Book 1 (402a) of *De Anima*,

> we should naturally be led to place in the front rank the study of the soul. The knowledge of the soul admittedly contributes greatly to the advance of truth in general, and, above all, to our understanding of Nature, for the soul is in some sense the principle of animal life ... First, no doubt, it is necessary to determine in which of the 'summa genera' soul lies, what it is ... is it a quale or a quantum ... (McKeon, 1941, pp.535–6).

To capture its full meaning, the word 'qualia' has been interpreted in a variety of ways: it refers to the 'raw feel' (a term coined by Tolman) aspects of consciousness that are 'intrinsic', 'subjective', 'first-personal', 'experiential', 'non-relational', 'qualitative' or 'phenomenal'. In more concrete examples, qualia are subjective experiences such as 'the feel of redness' when a red thing is in view, 'the feel of contentedness or restlessness' at moments or periods in life, 'the joyfulness of joy' or 'the painfulness of pain' when a long-cherished dream is realized or crushed. And as such, it virtually defies objective or third-person observation and hence escapes the standard methods of enquiry as specified by contemporary science.

By contrast, the non-qualitative or 'quantifiable' consciousness has been variously described as being the 'psychological', 'functional', 'intellectual', 'computational', 'third-personal', 'relational', 'factual' or the 'non-phenomenal' aspects (e.g., Dahlbom, 1993). So, while the term qualia seems the best in capturing the essence of the qualitative feel of consciousness, the term nonqualia (quanta) appears most appropriate in denoting all aspects of the mind that are reachable by quantifying science. In this context, although scientific results have shown that 'consciousness' can be reductively accounted for by physical level neural activities, it is only the nonqualia or quantifiable aspects of consciousness that science has so far canvassed. Qualia or the intrinsic and first-personal aspects of consciousness, being outside the scope of science, have remained unaccounted for. Thus the issue surrounding qualia has come to be regarded as the 'hard' part of the traditional mind–body problem. And because it essentially concerns a 'finer-grain' dualism, the issue has also come to be known as the 'mind–mind' problem (Chalmers, 1996, following Jackendoff, 1987).

The qualia–nonqualia distinction has been consistently made in the literature of consciousness. The distinction is similar to Jackendoff's (1987) 'phenomenological mind' (qualia) *versus* 'computational mind' (nonqualia), and Chalmers' (1996) 'phenomenal consciousness' *versus* 'psychological consciousness'. Qualia have also been referred to as 'non-functional consciousness' (Newell, 1992), 'sensory quality' (Rosenthal, 1996), 'phenomenal experience' (Bisiach, 1988), and 'sentient experience' (Pinker, 1997). The term qualia is used consistently in the remainder of this book to denote the qualitative aspects of consciousness. Other terms that are occasionally used in its place include 'raw feel' or 'sentient experience'. The term nonqualia is also used consistently in this book to denote the quantifiable aspects of consciousness. It refers to the same concept as 'psychological consciousness', 'computational mind', or 'access consciousness' (e.g., Bisiach, 1988; Block, 1995; Pinker, 1997).

However, because there is no agreement as to whether qualia are a recognized integral part of mental states, there is a great deal of confusion as to how the term consciousness is used. In contemporary literatures of positivistic philosophy and mainstream psychology that take the prevailing scientific paradigm and thus question the existence of qualia, the term consciousness is typically used to denote non-qualitative mental states to the exclusion of all their qualitative counterparts. It is only in the humanistic literature wherein subjective sentient experience forms its core, that the term consciousness is used to denote mental states in their entirety: both qualia and nonqualia. Many scholars (e.g., Oatley, 1988; Smith, 1997; Wilkes, 1988) have argued that this semantic confusion is no accident and that it is associated with historical shifts in the intellectual *Zeitgeist* that confine all pursuits of knowledge and truth. And this is the first theme that is explored in this book.

QUALIA IN A HISTORICAL CONTEXT: THE AGENCY–SENTIENCE SEPARATION

One of the key themes in this book concerns the inseparability of qualitative and non-qualitative aspects of consciousness. It is argued that human beings are at once cognitive agents and sentient experiencers. The holistic 'living being in its entirety' (best described by the Greek word *psyche,* or its Latin equivalent *spiritus*) thus constitutes both aspects, with their interacting dynamics. The agent and experiencer within us are intricately intertwined in the adaptation of the ever-changing human condition, in the expression of our innermost potentials, as well as in the experiencing of our uniquely authentic phenomenology. As such, an understanding of what it is like to be human requires a clear picture not only of individual agency and sentience aspects, but also the relating dynamics between the two. Given that the study of 'what it is like to be human' is essentially that of human consciousness, it becomes imperative that both the agentic and sentient aspects of human experience be given equal credence in consciousness research.

These two supposedly closely intertwined aspects of consciousness are, however, conceptualized and researched as unrelated independent parts of the mind. In the current intellectual *Zeitgeist*, it is cognitive agency that forms the core definition of humanity, and hence the exclusive subject of consciousness. This is reflected in the research orientation that characterizes contemporary analytic philosophy and mainstream human sciences. Sentience, the equal partner of cognitive agency in all affairs of humanity, has been largely relinquished to the peripheral domains of existential, phenomenological philosophy and humanistic, transpersonal psychology.

This currently prevailing mind–mind division, as part and parcel of the mind–body problem, has been in the making throughout human history. One of the aims of this book is to illuminate the reasons as to why qualia are not granted a legitimate status in contemporary research. This is done through a brief historical survey of the philosophical deliberations on human consciousness. It is hoped that the survey will highlight the point that historical shifts in intellectual paradigms have contributed to the gradual but sure shaping of the current science-over-humanity *Zeitgeist*. The peripheral status of qualia *vis-à-vis* consciousness is but one specific manifestation of this prevailing intellectual climate.

By placing qualia and consciousness in a historical context, it becomes clear that the early pre-Greek notion of a holistic *psyche* denotes the entirety of what it is like to be human. The long historical pursuit of the nature of *psyche* is marked by an unceasing tension resulting from the division between *psyche*'s agency and sentience subsystems. The process of the pursuit captures well Hegel's notion of the 'dialectic' progression (i.e., a self-repeating thesis–antithesis–synthesis cycle) of human historical evolution. Since the early hints of an agency–sentience separation, traceable back to the pre-Socratic philosophers, the pursuit of *psyche* has featured the dialectic battles between the two. In the pre-Socratic period, the battle took place between the theses of 'thinking-as-*psyche*' (Heraclitus, Parmenides) or 'matter-over-mind' (Democritus) and Protagoras' antithesis of human-centred philosophy. In Platonic philosophy, the separation between perishable *Senses* and immortal *Ideas* implicates a sharp discontinuity between sensing and thinking (as reason or ration), with the latter being inaccessible from the former. While Aristotle asserted a close and continuous relationship between the two, he still maintained the thesis of a ration-dominated *psyche*. This thesis focusing on human reason and intellect however triggered off the antitheses of the Hellenistic and Stoic philosophies, which placed individual free will and spiritual faith at the core of *psyche* and hence humanity. In a true dialectic fashion of progression, a synthesis arose out of the tension between intellectual reason and spiritual faith that marked the philosophies of the two halves of the Greek era. During the Medieval period, the works of St Augustine and later Thomas Aquinas represent attempts at such a synthesis.

So the dialectic process pertaining to the agency–sentience separation went on during modernity, which witnessed the tension between Enlightenment and Romanticism. With direct relevance to the qualia–nonqualia issue, the most significant legacy of modernity concerns Descartes' exclusion of the nonconscious from the *psyche*, as well as Hume's subsequent substitution of the holistic feature of the *psyche* ('personal identity' in Hume's term) with associated atomistic units of mental 'ideas'. By modernity's end, the human *psyche* was no longer in its original 'wholesome' state. And amidst such conceptual changes, there have been corresponding changes in both the lexicon and the semantics of words used to denote the notion.

There is little ambiguity in the somewhat antagonistic division in contemporary approaches to consciousness: with cognitive agency being the core of analytic philosophy or empirical psychology, and sentience the focus of their existential and humanistic counterparts. The agency–sentience division has become the norm in contemporary studies of the *psyche,* which by now is an unhappy word in today's academic and common discourse. And in its vast space, new entities like mind and self coexist uneasily waiting to be concisely defined, understood and integrated into a harmony that it once was and perhaps should always be. However, within the Cartesian and Humean tradition, the term mind has been consistently used in positivistic philosophy and psychology to denote *psyche*'s much reduced place, where only the agentic, awared and networked mental states legally reside. Outside this tradition in the humanistic, existential and psychodynamic literatures, the term self (or mind, consciousness) appears to retain *psyche*'s original vast and unbounded state, although the core connotation is more of a sentient experiencer than a controlling agent.

QUALIA'S EXISTENCE AND FUNCTION

The agency–sentience division goes hand in hand with the contemporary debate over the issue of qualia. The debate has focused primarily on the question of whether qualia exist at all, and for those philosophers contented with their existence, the further question of qualia's structure and organization within consciousness. Regarding the first question of existence, philosophers differ in their views. Those taking an 'eliminative materialistic' view to the mind have denied outrightly the very existence of qualia. So to these philosophers there is really no mind–mind problem at all. Other materialistic theorists taking the 'identity' view have regarded qualia as identical to their corresponding non-qualitative mental states and argued that once the latter is understood in terms of its physical correlates at the neuronal level, qualia are automatically understood. Again, to these philosophers there does not appear to be a mind–mind issue that is separate from the first issue of the mind–body problem. Philosophers taking the 'epiphenomenal' view would see qualia as a by-product of mental events in the sense that they are themselves not causal agents of behaviour and hence they possess no 'functional' significance. Theorists in these two latter groups, although not denying qualia's existence, nonetheless trivialize qualia's significance.

Materialistic and epiphenomenal views aside, there exists another view to qualia which not only acknowledges their existence but also further postulates their irreducibility to fundamental neural properties. This non-reductive view has given qualia a 'valid' status within the realm of the mind and consciousness. Once this philosophical position is taken, several issues beg solution. Among the issues arising, the most obvious is the question of the ontological and organizational features of qualia. This is a big question as it almost parallels the primordial and first issue of the 'mind–body' problem that concerns the relationship between the physical and the mental. And the answer to that question requires the building of a whole picture of reality. Taking on precisely this challenge, Chalmers (1996) proposes an information-state model of consciousness that accounts for the ontological and structural features of both qualia and nonqualia. While the model is firmly grounded in positive laws specified by contemporary physical, cognitive and neurobiological sciences, it logically leads to further speculations about reality, that turn out to be consistent with the metaphysical position of panpsychism. Regardless, a philosophical model couched in naturalistic terms is now available for settling parts of the qualia problem: their existence as well as their structural and organizational features.

However, even though qualia's existence and structure can now be accounted for, another key question remains. It is argued that the key issue that needs to be addressed now is a pure 'functional' and 'teleological' one: what functions do qualia serve in the scheme of things? or more precisely, what function can qualia serve for the beings that have them? This is the next key question explored in this book: the question of the reasons for human beings to have qualia or to experience the intrinsic raw feels which accompany our mental thoughts. An answer to this question is demanded by the prevailing scientific and philosophical paradigms of pragmatism and functionalism, which place at centre stage the 'cash value' of any 'concept'. Within these paradigms, for any concept to be 'meaningful' and hence to be a potential candidate for 'truth', it has to serve a causal function. Accordingly, for qualia to be considered as legitimate aspects of consciousness, they would have to play some causal role. And conversely, if qualia do not have a causal function, it cannot logically be an aspect of the human mind. Given this, it is argued that the question of the function of qualia is really an integral part of the 'mind–mind' problem, and that unless the question is answered, there is scant hope for the notion to be taken seriously.

In addressing the issue of qualia's existence and function, the book appeals to the system-dynamic notion of 'superposition' that can denote a concomitant 'both-and' state of existence of fundamental constituents of a dynamic system. In micro quantum systems, it has been suggested that the superpositioned state characterizes the 'particle-wave duality' of the existence of basic particles (e.g., de Broglie, 1930; Heisenberg, 1989). In macro dynamic systems, it has also been argued that 'chaos' and self-organized 'order' coexist and that the seemingly chaotic randomness of systemic processes is 'superimposed upon order' (e.g., Prigogine and Stengers, 1984; Stenger, 1988, 1990). The notion of systems dynamics has been applied to consciousness research from either a quantum (e.g., Bohm, 1986; Hameroff, 1994; Marshall, 1989; Penrose, 1997) or chaos-theoretic (e.g., Freeman, 1994; Hardcastle, 1995) perspective. Extending such an application to the existence of qualia, this book argues that qualitative and non-qualitative consciousness coexists in a 'both-and' superposition. This justification for qualia's existence appears to be consistent with other existing arguments framed in naturalistic terms (e.g., Chalmers, 1996; Searle, 1997).

The proposition of a superpositioned coexistence of the two aspects of consciousness necessarily implies a causal function for qualia. Extending the idea that superposition suggests complementarity (e.g., Zohar and Marshall, 1994), it is argued that the functions of the two aspects of consciousness are also complementary to each other. Given that the function of consciousness in general is well-understood to be the mediating causal agent in life's adaptations, qualia and nonqualia are then to share (complementarily) such an overall function. The specializations of qualia and nonqualia can be made more specific in information processing and system dynamic terms. In those terms, consciousness serves first, to access and activate relevant information and schemas in the 'mental workspace' (Baars, 1988, 1997) for constructing 'mental conclusions' (Marcel, 1983). It then serves to select, from among those constructed mental conclusions, a limited and specific 'privileged' one for conscious expression or 'awareness'. In the ongoing dynamic loops, consciousness further serves the feedback role in relaying the awared conclusions back into the mental workspace for simultaneous and subsequent information processing and conclusion constructing (e.g., Mandler, 1997).

Within this entire scheme of the functioning of consciousness, qualia and nonqualia serve by sharing these functions of schematic activation, conclusion construction as well as information feedback. In a complementary fashion, qualia and nonqualia may serve all these functions with reference to the two complementary domains (i.e., the unconscious and the conscious) within the entire mental workspace. In other words, it is plausible that nonqualia specialize in the activation–construction–feedback functions pertaining primarily to the conscious, whereas qualia perform these functions by invoking primarily the vast nonconscious mental domains. In discussing the mind's information processing functions, Mandler (1997) has pointed out, *'Unconscious representations and processes generate all thoughts and processes, whether or not conscious; the unconscious is where the action is!'* (p.482). While both notions of qualia and the unconscious have been shunned by positivistic paradigms in contemporary enquiries into human consciousness, there seem to be reasons to believe that the mind's actions relating to the unconscious may well be linked to qualia. These reasons are explored later in Chapter 6.

QUALIA AND CONSCIOUSNESS: FURTHER RESEARCH DIRECTIONS

The proposed function of qualia rests on the intimate link between qualitative experience and the nonconscious processes. This presumed link demands that the notion 'consciousness' be clearly redefined to embrace the entire range of the conscious and the nonconscious mind. In other words, for the proposed function of qualia to make sense, the term consciousness needs to denote the entire spectrum of human experience ranging from the sphere of the conscious (the awared) throughout that of the nonconscious. Consciousness in this sense thus identifies with the pre-Cartesian notion of the *psyche* in its entirety.

Consciousness as totality of the conscious and the nonconscious

As mentioned previously, ever since Descartes unseated the nonconscious from the *psyche*, the nonconscious has been ousted from any positivistic enquiry into human consciousness. Instead, it has been consigned to humanistic and psychodynamic domains. However, there is recent evidence suggesting that the notion is taken seriously again by analytic philosophers and neurocognitive scientists. In other words, there are signs that aspects of the nonconscious are being readmitted back into the empiricistic paradigms as a legitimate subject of enquiry. For instance, several recent information processing and computational models of consciousness have rested on the presumptions that the nonconscious exists and that consciousness encompasses a vast realm of the 'unawared': the realm of the 'cognitive unconscious' (e.g., Baars, 1997; Kihlstrom, 1987; Shallice, 1988). The inclusion of this realm of the nonconscious stems from the recognition that, as a causal agent in life's adaptations, consciousness cannot be fully operational without the input from the unconscious. However, as can be expected from the functionalistic stance typically associated with such intellectual paradigms, their admission of the notion 'nonconscious' is only to the extent of its role as cognitive agent. The nonconscious in these computational models pertains only to its cognitive capacity, and hence the term cognitive unconscious.

It is argued that such a limited readmission of the nonconscious, while necessary, is nonetheless insufficient for a fuller understanding of human experience in its entirety. The mind so defined is still, metaphorically speaking, in bondage. To fully understand consciousness and its qualia, this bondage needs to be undone so as to allow the return of the original *psyche*. Thus, the notion 'mind' or 'consciousness' needs to encompass all domains of the nonconscious, in both the Freudian and the

Jungian sense. The key reason for embracing both types of the nonconscious is to do with the 'seriality-capacity' differences between conscious and nonconscious processes (e.g., Mandler, 1992, 1997; Bargh, 1997). As Mandler points out, in contrast to the serial or sequential nature of conscious (awared) processing, nonconscious processes operate in parallel and therefore appear unlimited in capacity.

Mandler (1997) speculates that this may be linked to the 'time-stopping' or 'frame-freezing' feature of various forms of nonconscious mental states. In the neurocognitive science literature that deals primarily with conscious processes, the notion of time has recently received increasing attention. The role of time in conscious processing has been researched from the neurobiological, psychological and computational perspectives (e.g., Rosenbaum and Collyer, 1998). While there exist limited exceptions (e.g., Barnes, 1998), conscious processes at the neurocognitive and behavioural levels appear to be constrained by time and hence are typically characterized by seriality. From a functional viewpoint, a serial or sequential mode of processing constraint by time is also necessary for conscious adaptations. Without such a constraint, conscious processes can cause havoc in our functional adaptations in daily life (e.g., Gregory, 1996; Harrington and Haaland, 1998; Mandler, 1997).

While conscious processes are time-relevant, evidence in the transpersonal and psychodynamics literatures suggests that nonconscious processes are likely to be time-transcendent. It is in this time-transcending fashion that the nonconscious processes pertaining to both the Freudian and the Jungian unconscious may exert their influence in shaping human experience. Through the Freudian unconscious, an individual's no-longer awared early life experiences leave their marks on his/her currently awared mental states. Going beyond, but interacting with, these intrapsychic forces, the workings of the Jungian collective unconscious make manifest the collective human cultural heritage in our present moments of awareness. Viewed in static structural terms, the nonconscious then constitutes mental representations of the non-awared individual and collective history. Viewed in dynamic processing terms, the nonconscious processes, underlying our moment to moment awareness, pertain to the paralleled activation–construction–feedback operations that involve these non-awared representations.

One of the suggestions for future consciousness research concerns bringing back the nonconscious so that the term consciousness can be used consistently to denote *psyche* in its entirety. The return of *psyche* as consciousness in its entirety has at least two significant implications. The first implication is in terms of current related debates over qualia and the self; the other implication concerns the conceptualization and the methodology of further research in human consciousness.

Regarding the first implication for current debates over qualia and the self, defining consciousness in terms of the entirety of *psyche* is necessary for the proposed function of qualia. This helps to settle the central part of the qualia debate. The debate over the notion self is related to the qualia issue in the neurocognitive science literature. Given that this debate also has its roots in the agency–sentience separation, the return of *psyche* in its entirety can also contribute to the resolution of this debate.

Parallel to the recent trend in readmitting the nonconscious back into empiricistic enquiries into consciousness, there appears to be a similar trend in bringing back the pre-Humean notion of the self: the personal identity or 'subjectivity' (Baars, 1997). After centuries of shunning the notion self, analytic philosophers and empirical cognitive scientists have recently paid a greater attention to it. For instance, within the Wittgenstein–Ryle–Quine–Davidson tradition that places linguistic activities at the core of consciousness, Dennett (1991) sees the self as the centre of 'the narrative gravity' and argues that it is the self that 'has access to consciousness'. In empirical cognitive science, recent models of consciousness have carried the explicit presumption that the notion self is a necessary boundary condition for the workings of these models (e.g.,

Johnson-Laird, 1988; Umilta, 1988).

However, as is also the case with the nonconscious, the admission of the notion self has involved only its cognitive agency aspect. The sentient self remains excluded. Self in these computational models pertains only to a cognitive capacity for 'attending to one's own thoughts' or self-reflection. Even though the self takes on a grander role in Baars' workspace model of consciousness, as being the 'behind-the-scene director' in the mental theatre (Baars, 1988, 1997), this grander role accorded the 'self' is still a much restricted one. According to Baars (1997), the director-self is a 'decomposed' and 'better-understood' subset of the holistic self, which is seen as the 'cognitive or brain entity' (p.143). Regardless of the recent effort in including the notion self in cognitive scientific enquiries of the mind, the notion remains a divided and hence an ambiguous one. However, it is argued that with the return of *psyche* in its entirety, the agency–sentience divide with reference to the notion self can also be bridged. And in its complete sense, that embraces both agentic and sentient aspects, the notion self then identifies with *psyche* in its entirety.

The return to *psyche* has a further implication for the conceptualization and methodology of future research in consciousness and its qualitative aspects. The two key suggestions are that consciousness (*psyche* embracing the conscious and the nonconscious) be conceptualized in system-dynamic terms, and that both empirical experimentation and interpretive hermeneutics be used as methods of enquiry.

Conceptualizing consciousness in dynamic-systemic terms

A dynamic-systemic perspective to consciousness is in tune with some key theoretical advances in contemporary physical sciences. There, similar dynamic features of multiplicity and emergence characterize both the micro quantum and the macro complex and chaotic systems. In the quantum realm, even though the progression or evolving trajectory of each particle is governed by the deterministic computational rule (the Schrodinger equation), there is a certain degree of indeterminancy associated with the exact unmanifested state of individual quantum object. Because of this, theories of 'multiplicity' have been proposed to account for the nature of the micro state underlying the manifested reality. Several versions of these theories converge in suggesting that the unmanifested covert state may be conceived as a pool of coexisting potential states. For Schrodinger, the covert state features a 'superposition' of dual-aspects. A multifaceted underlying reality is explicit in Bohm's (1951) 'pilot-wave' notion, the 'splitting- or many-worlds' theories (e.g., DeWitt and Graham, 1973), as well as the 'it-from-bits' (e.g., Wheeler, 1994) and 'one-big-world' interpretations (e.g., Everett, 1973; Chalmers, 1996; Lockwood, 1989).

The idea of covert indeterminancy and multiplicity is also evident in the dynamics of macro chaotic systems. However, such systems also are equipped with a 'free' or 'given' capacity for self-organization (e.g., Kauffman, 1993; Prigogine and Stengers, 1984), and out of which, emergent properties may result. Therefore, both micro quantum and macro chaotic systems share similar dynamic features of covert multiplicity and overt emergence through the system's self-organization capabilities. In scientific terms, emergent properties of complex systems are to be understood in gestalt terms: they are new properties resulting from the combined dynamic interactions among the individual elements of a system. In the context of the gestalt slogan, 'the whole is more than the sum of parts', emergent properties may correspond to the aspect of the 'whole' which is additional to 'the sum of parts'.

These system-dynamic features of unceasing change and self-organization also find parallels in various philosophical perspectives on human condition and potentials. For instance, the idea of change is central to Heralitus' notion of the *psyche* as being constantly changing and 'in flux' (e.g., Allen, 1966). The dynamics of the Humean self (personal identity) was also described in terms of 'a flux of perceptions and feelings' (Reese, 1980, p.519). Such chaos of constant change appears to be contained by a self-organizing 'strange attractor' (e.g., Peat, 1996). The attractor idea is implicit in many philosophical thoughts: it appears as Aristotle's *final cause*, Leibnitz's *monad*, Kant's *noumenon*, the humanistic notions of the proto-self, or Taylor's (1989) 'nature-within'. In analytic philosophy and empirical psychology, the idea of a self-organizing attractor is not inconsistent with the notion of the agentic self as 'the centre of narrative gravity' (Dennett, 1991) or 'behind-the-scene director' (Baars, 1997).

While these ideas of multiplicity and self-organized emergence originate in the first place from physical sciences, there have been attempts at applying the notions to the dynamics of numerous other social and biological systems (e.g., Ayers, 1997; Kauffman, 1993; Stacey, 1995; Zohar and Marshall, 1994). Glimpsing from the research on consciousness as reported in the literatures of the mind and the self, both features of covert multiplicity and overt emergence appear to characterize the mind and self.

In mind research, modularity is the fundamental assumption of computational and connectionist models (Fodor, 1983; Pinker, 1997). Modularity, however, necessarily suggests multiplicity. As such, underlying multiplicity is key to such notions as 'the mind's I' (Hofstadter and Dennett, 1981) or 'society of minds' (Minsky, 1985). Multiplicity aside, computational and connectionist theorists have also spoken of possible emergent properties. For instance, Pinker (1997) suspects that qualia or sentience may be an emergent property of the mind. Referring to sentience, Pinker writes, '*It seems to be an extra quality of some kinds of information access. What we do need is a theory of how the subjective qualities of sentience emerge out of mere information access*' (p.145). In neuroscience, the proposal that mental states are properties emerging from the brain's neural dynamics was made first by Eccles and Sperry. More recently, Crick (1994) stresses the 'scientific' rather than the 'mystical' meaning of the word emergence and proposes that *'complex sensations and behaviours arise in the brain from the interactions of its many parts'* (p.12). Searle (1997) expresses a similar view: *'Consciousness ... is a feature that emerges from certain neuronal activities, we can think of it as an "emergent property" of the brain'* (pp.17–18).

In the self literatures, there is ample evidence suggesting that the dynamics of the self are best characterized by multiplicity and emergence. The idea of multiplicity is central to 'possible selves' (Markus and Kitayama, 1991), 'family of selves' (Cantor and Kilstrom, 1987) and various other notions of subselves (see Lester, 1993–94). These covert multiple selves compete for expression in awareness. The self literature (psychodynamics' in particular) is replete with accounts of the emergent self as being the result of complex underlying dynamics of the competition for expression among the possible covert subselves.

To summarize, covert multiplicity and overt emergence are both distinctive features of the mind and self, and hence of consciousness itself. Because of this, it becomes imperative that the notion consciousness be conceptualized in terms of system dynamics. Such a conceptualization will allow the application of relevant and useful notions from both literatures of micro quantum and macro complex systems. As such, a unified and coherent set of system-dynamic principles can be used in accounting for consciousness in its entirety: from its micro neuronal bases, through its rich yet covert multiplex states, right to the currently manifested states which constitute our moment-to-moment awareness.

It is noted that similar suggestions, albeit more limited in scope, have been made independently in the literatures of the mind and self. For future mind research, Varela, Thompson and Rosch (1992) have explicitly urged combining complex-dynamic systems with the neurocognitive science. Zohar and Marshall (1994) have advocated an integration of the cognitive-computational and the quantum-systemic perspectives. And, there is already a limited literature that has applied either the chaos notions (e.g., Freeman, 1994; Hardcastle, 1996) or the quantum notions (e.g., Eccles, 1989; Hameroff and Penrose, 1996; Hodgson, 1991; Lockwood, 1989; Marshall, 1989; Penrose, 1997) to mind and consciousness. Separately in the literature of the self, the term 'quantum self' (Zohar, 1990) denotes a new conceptualization of the dynamics of the self, in quantum-systemic terms. More recently, Carver and Scheier (1998) also argue for the application of system-dynamic theories to the regulatory processes of the self. Specifically, they have applied chaos as well as catastrophe theories to the dynamics of the regulation of behaviour by the self.

Methods of enquiry

Two suggestions for future consciousness research have been made: to conceptualize the structure of consciousness in terms of the totality of psyche and to view its processes (both micro and macro levels) in terms of complex system dynamics. Such conceptual repositioning necessarily requires shifts in the methods of enquiry. Consciousness research constitutes the exploration of a boundless mental workspace consisting of mental domains (the conscious and the nonconscious) having distinctly different features in terms of seriality and capacity. From a system perspective, the dynamics of mental elements (be it functional mental modules or specific mental states such as sensory qualia) within this unbound workspace are perhaps best described by the quantum idea of superpositioned 'entanglements' (e.g., Shimony, 1997). And emergent properties may result out of such multifaceted and enmeshed interactions among component elements. Working within a computational and connectionist framework, Pinker (1997) has specifically pointed out the intricacies of the interactions among mental modules (or mental organs in Chomsky's term): *'the circuitry underlying a psychological module might be distributed across the brain in a spatially haphazard manner ... Some organs ... interact with the rest ... across a wide-spread, convoluted interface, and cannot be encircled'* (p.31). Similarly, Baars (1997) has also alluded to the complexity of unconscious processes underlying the relationship between conscious qualia and 'unconscious qualia' (p.22), in colour and music perceptions.

The complexity of the dynamics of consciousness occurs not only due to the seriality–capacity differences between conscious and nonconscious processes, but also the bewildering entanglements throughout the entire mental workspace. Given that the standard method of enquiry in empirical sciences (i.e., scientific experimentation) involves the observation of specific mental state by a 'snapshot' approach, the observed state is, in a sense, plucked out of and insulated from the entangled web of interconnections. The combined influences of virtually all contextual particularities, both immediate and distal ones, are left unattended to in this kind of observation. As such, the experimental method by itself would possibly produce a misleading, and certainly incomplete, story (e.g., Carver and Sheirer, 1998; Zohar and Marshall, 1994). The story is possibly misleading because it fails to capture the non-discrete and holistically interconnected nature of human consciousness. It is incomplete as it can not reveal the uniqueness of individual experience that is shaped collectively by each individual's innate endowment and cumulative past history.

Therefore, a fuller understanding of consciousness requires additional methods that can reveal both the wholeness and the uniqueness of human experience. In other words, the cross-sectional 'snapshot' perspective that underpins scientific experimentation needs to be supplemented with an extended dynamic and longitudinal perspective. In this context, an additional and appropriate method appears to be hermeneutic interpretation. As a sense-making strategy, hermeneutics refer to the ongoing interpretive process pertaining to the understanding of the meaning of texts, events or behaviour (e.g., Riser, 1997). Complementing the experimental method, the hermeneutic interpretive method considers subjectivity as an inseparable aspect of any sense-making process, and as such, it always involves self-understanding. Also because hermeneutic interpretation constitutes an ongoing dialectic process of revision, it may result in the further development of one's potentials (e.g., Ozanne, 1999). It is in these contexts that hermeneutics can tap the richness of the ongoing whole, as well as the subjective unique features, of individual experience.

With these overall themes in mind, the plan of the book is briefly outlined as follows. The next two chapters together present a historical review of the agency–sentience separation in philosophy, that is primarily responsible for the mind–body (and hence the mind–mind) problem in the first place. Consistent with the conceptual separation, the literatures of the agentic mind and those of the sentient self are reviewed, respectively, in Chapters 2 and 3. The review in each chapter traces back to the metaphysical deliberations of the first Classical philosophers and ends with the views of contemporary (analytic and humanistic) as well as postmodern deconstruction philosophers. It is noted that despite the arduous efforts of exploring the mind and independently the self, the underlying agency–sentience divide has brought about the seemingly unresolvable mind–mind problem.

Following this survey of philosophical progress, Chapters 4 and 5 together present a review of existing models of consciousness. These models have been proposed rather independently as models of the agentic mind, the agentic self, or the sentient self. Models of consciousness as the agentic mind exist virtually exclusively in the literatures of cognitive neuroscience and cognitive psychology. Models of the agentic self exist typically in the literatures of mainstream psychology and other human sciences. And models of the sentient self are found in the psychodynamic, humanistic and transpersonal psychology literatures. To parallel the philosophical reviews of the mind and self, models of the mind and of the self in these human science literatures are reviewed respectively in Chapters 4 and 5. The review shows that while the agency–sentience separation is still very much the game of the day, there is convergent evidence suggesting a trend for a synergistic agency–sentience synthesis.

Following and building upon existing views of consciousness, Chapter 6 of the book argues for the concomitant existence of qualia and nonqualia by appeal to the system dynamic notion of superposition. It is noted that various existing arguments for the existence of qualitative consciousness converge in suggesting that qualia and nonqualia are simply aspects of the superpositioned consciousness. Having justified qualia's existence, the chapter then turns to the discussion of possible functions of qualia. It is argued that qualia and nonqualia serve the function of life adaptation in a complementary and modularized fashion. While non-qualitative consciousness specializes primarily in processes pertaining to the conscious mental workspace, qualia's complementary functioning concerns primarily the nonconscious mental domain.

For these arguments to make sense, it becomes necessary to make amends to the current limited conceptualization of consciousness. These 'amends' are discussed in Chapter 7. First, a return to the pre-Cartesian notion of the *psyche* is suggested, so that the term consciousness can denote the mental workspace in its entirety: both the conscious and the nonconscious domains. Second, a dynamic-system approach to consciousness research is suggested so that a unified set of scientific and naturalistic principles can be applied to aid its understanding. Third, an equal reliance on the method of scientific experimentation and hermeneutic interpretation is needed to reveal the conscious--nonconscious interactive dynamics. The Epilogue reiterates the theme of bridging the agency–sentience divide.

With this whole picture in mind, the reason then for consciousness to remain a mystery is perhaps not due to our lack of the right 'mind architecture' (McGinn, 1997) or 'cognitive equipment' (Pinker, 1997). Our mind may after all be capable of unveiling its own mystery, if only we could do two things: to redesign a little our mind architecture by freeing up its boundaries, and to utilize all its equipment, experimental and interpretive, in this awe-inspiring bootstrapping task.

2
A Survey of Philosophical Thoughts on the Mind

Anthropological and evolutionary evidence likens human existence in the beginning to that in a 'magic world' (e.g., de Riencourt, 1980). In palaeolithic times, there was no 'psychological' differentiation between human beings and mother nature. Human consciousness was totally immersed in nature and hence was an integral and inseparable part of all existence. As such, consciousness had no limits or boundaries within a vastly interconnected network of nature's manifestations. Human beings' then 'mental' functioning centred around the accepting and decoding of the free-flowing phenomena continuously and automatically displayed in nature. The experiences learned from nature were interpreted in pictorial or symbolic forms and were revered as facts, even though they are called legends and myths in today's lexicon.

However, this 'spirit-man' (or 'magic-man') existence discontinued during neolithic times as a result of the evolutionary change in human's conscious outlook about his own existence. The 'ego' (i.e., 'I' in Latin, meaning the conscious self) started to assert itself by gaining an independent identity from nature and all other manifestations. This is documented in the anthropologist Donald Johanson's study of the drawing on the wall of the Lascaux Cave in the French Dordogne, believed to be the first record of human beings becoming 'aware of the self'. The drawing was traced back to the Cro-Magnon men who inhabited the earth around 15,000 BC. The picture simply shows a 'sticklike' figure (the self) and a palaeolithic hunting scene, which included animals that had already been extinct by the Cro-Magnon time. Johanson suggested that the painter was drawing a scene from the 'mind' and not the then immediate physical surroundings. As the ego separated itself, the interconnected threads that used to weave together all existences in an integral, albeit 'primitive', harmony were gradually cut off. The ego's exercise of its own free will thus set the scene for the further evolution of the conscious and generative mind.

In several early civilizations, the intellectual mind was still not totally isolated from nature itself. There was anthropological evidence of the interconnectedness and unity of human consciousness in the Mayan civilization (in today's South America), in ancient Egyptian times, as well as in some of today's indigenous cultures (e.g., Peat, 1996). However, the persisting evolutionary force that drove the human ego towards the expression of its own free will was unstoppable; this consciousness of fundamental unity in the early civilizations just had to give way to the destined expression of the human being's individual ego mind.

CLASSICAL PHILOSOPHERS' CONCEPTIONS OF THE MIND

In the Classical Greek lexicon, there was no word which could 'even roughly' be translated into today's words 'mind' or 'consciousness' (Wilkes, 1988, p.19). In their place, the term *psyche* was typically used. The Greek word *psyche* stems from the Latin *spiritus* (meaning 'breath'). Given that the Greek word *psyche* is often translated as 'soul', and its Latin counterpart *spiritus* is translated directly as 'spirit', the word *psyche* was used to mean 'breathing or being alive', and to be alive also meant to have a soul or spirit. Therefore, in examining Greek philosophers' conception of the mind, it is necessary to be alert to the fact that these philosophical endeavours were aimed at an understanding and analysis of the human *psyche* as a whole. To the early philosophers, the *psyche* referred to the thinking, feeling, willing and intuiting being in its entirety. However, various analyses gradually but firmly reduced the holistic *psyche* solely to its intellectual functioning.

Heraclitus (540 – 475 BC) and Parmenides (515 – 450 BC)

Early Greek philosophers were the first to reduce the *psyche*'s function to 'reasoning' and 'thinking'. The pre-Socratic philosopher Heraclitus' pursuit of the *psyche* resulted in his asserting that the exercise of the mind in the waking state constitutes human consciousness. Only the products of such mind-exercise are to be treated as facts. The experiences gained from myths or legends were therefore factually meaningless. The status of the 'thinking mind', as distinctively different from that of the holistic mind of the early 'spirit-man', was formally concretized by these early Classical philosophers. Heraclitus believed that all existence is ever changing and is in a constant state of flux (e.g., Allen, 1966; Popkin and Stroll, 1993). In the absence of permanency, a sound 'mind' has to follow what is 'real', and only the conscious world of the waking state, that is 'common to all', is real. To Heraclitus, being rational (as a thinking being) is to hold on to the real and to deny the unreal, such as the dreaming state where each individual is 'in a world of his own' (see Schrodinger, 1958). The 'thinking' mind thus acquired an independent status of its own and separated from the holistic *psyche*.

Parmenides concurred with Heraclitus and went a step further by asserting that thinking and reason *is* the whole of being or psyche. Thus, human existence is by nature intellectual and as such, the only 'substance' of being is rational thoughts. Parmenides' equating of being with thinking has gained him the reputation of being the earliest philosopher of the school of 'substance monism' (Reese, 1980). The school of substance monism in the later mind–body problem embraces all monistic positions asserting that all existence or reality is of one single kind of substance, be it purely mental, purely physical, or in a single state of 'superposition' capable of being consciously realized as either mental or physical. Parmenides' monism thus specifies the substance as the mental property of thoughts. Because the only existing substance constitutes mental ideas rather than physical matter, this school of monism has come to be known as idealism, a term coined later by Leibniz (Reese, 1980).

Democritus (460 – 379 BC)

Also holding a monistic view of reality, Democritus however believed that the primary substance constituting the single reality was physical and materialistic, rather than mental, in nature. Democritus developed the thoughts of his tutor Leucippus on the 'primary constituents' of the single reality and formulated the *atomism* theory. The theory suggested that all existing 'things', animated or inanimated, were made up of the same ultimate or primary entity, the *atom*, which could not be further divided. As *atoms* were regarded as being in constant motion and as being of different size, shape and velocity, this primary entity thus possessed these basic quantitative differences. In this context, it seems that Democritus was the first philosopher to have come close to correctly deciphering the mystery of the physical reality.

Democritus' position on mental thoughts was consistent with his materialistic monism. He believed that the physical body was made up of 'soul atoms'. And because of the constant movement of all atoms, 'thought' or consciousness thus results from the motion of the soul atoms. As such, Democritus taught that *'the soul is to be identified with reason, the thinking and judging part of man'* (Frost, 1962/1989, p.156). Democritus also considered perception or sensation purely as a physical process. It was Democritus who first made the distinction between 'primary qualities' and 'secondary qualities' (Reese, 1980, p.471). The former referred to the sorts of objective or quantitative qualities that things or matter possess (e.g., motion, size, shape, quantity), and the latter referred to the subjective qualities that these things produce in human beings through the senses (e.g., colour, sound, feel or smell). Given that Democritus further asserted that all qualitative differences between 'things' are 'derivative' from their quantitative features, all secondary qualities were then derived from primary qualities (e.g., Allen, 1966).

From here, it seems plausible to make inference about Democritus's view of qualia (if indeed he had one): as all mental events were derivatives of bodily events, they are reducible to the physical and materialistic level. Given that qualia are an aspect of mental events, whatever specific view Democritus would have had of qualia, it would have been one of *materialism.* As such, Democritus' views could be seen as the precursor of later materialism. Later *materialism* of the mind–body problem was to be further divided into three finer categories of *reductivistic, eliminative,* and *epiphenomenal materialism,* according to the position on whether qualia exist as separate entities from non-qualitative mental states.

Plato (428 – 348 BC)

Later Classical philosophers, Plato and his disciple Aristotle, continued in according reason or ration the most pivitol status in human existence. However, their views of the mind–body problem were vastly different. For Plato, there exists two kinds of reality: the reality of the *Senses* (physical and perceivable) and the reality of *Ideas* (mental thought, immaterial and eternal). The dualistic reality of *Sense* and *Idea* is to be found respectively in the physical Body and the immortal Soul. The Soul contains three parts:

Appetite (or Desire), *Will* (or Spirit) and *Reason*. The perfect or ideal state for an individual is a harmonious balance amongst the three parts of the Soul, but with *Reason* having ultimate control over *Appetite* and *Will*. Thus, in Platonism, the mental reality exists independently from the physical reality, with the mental reality being seen as at a higher level than the physical. Within the realm of the mental, reason is superior to other mental thoughts of desire and will. Human beings are then under the overriding control of the mental faculty of *Reason*.

Plato's conception of the reality had obvious implications for the later mind–body problem. Two of Plato's assertions earned him the reputation of being the earliest metaphysical dualist: that there exist two separate realities of the physical body and the conscious mind, and that the mental reality has its 'seat' in the human brain. In the context of the mind–body problem, Plato's dualism can be regarded as a version of *substance dualism* in the sense that the two realities constitute different entities or substances (e.g., Frost, 1962/1989; Reese, 1980; Ross, 1951).

Within the realm of the mind or the reality of the *idea*, it should be noted that the Greek word *idea* means 'image', 'impression' or 'contemplation', which thus denotes all mental thoughts. Even though Plato believed that sensation may provide the first clue to ideas, the separation of thoughts from senses means that the realm of *Idea* was not accessible through the lower and inferior faculty of sensing. This assumed discontinuity, which exists between sense perception and higher mental processes, thus represents the earliest version of a mind–mind dualism: the ideation–sensation duality. However, it should be noted that the qualia–nonqualia duality represents a different kind of mind–mind issue from that of Plato's. This is because qualitative feels can accompany both sensory perception and higher mental thoughts.

Aristotle (384 – 322 BC)

Instead of a dual mental–physical form of reality, Aristotle argued for one unified reality consisting of two inseparable dimensions: the *Substance* (i.e., the essence of what 'a thing' is made of) and the *Form* (i.e., the actual manifestation or specific characteristics of 'a thing'). The *Substance* of a thing contains all its 'potentials', which can be transformed into its actual *Form*. The 'human' reality consists of a body (*Form*) and its coexistence, a soul (*Substance*). Aristotle further postulated that the seat of the soul is the heart rather than the brain. Thus for Aristotle, the single reality has dual (mental and physical) properties, and it can be attained through either the mental faculty of reason or the physical faculty of sense (e.g., Allen, 1966; McKeon, 1941).

Thus, by making the mental (i.e., 'Substance') and the physical ('form') complementary entities within the realm of one single reality, Aristotle reversed Plato's dual reality back to the pre-Platonic notion that only a single reality exists. However, in this regard, Aristotle's monism is different in nature from either the *Idealism* (i.e., mental *Monism*) of Parmendes or the *Materialism* (i.e., physical *Monism*) of Democritus. Given that the single Aristotelian reality consists of both a mental and a physical property, this monistic view of reality thus carries the features of *property dualism*: a single reality having both mental and materialistic properties. As such, the Platonic ideation–sensation dualism was carefully avoided because the single reality presupposes a close and continuous relationship between the two (Reese, 1980, p.136).

Aristotle's sketch of the *Substance* or *soul* deserves further attention. The soul was further divided into three parts: the *nutritive soul* (for sustaining and reproducing its *Form*), the *sensitive soul* (for processing sensations and sensory inputs), and the *rational soul* (consisting of an immortal part of active reason and a mortal passive reason). It is here that Aristotle's version of a mind–mind dualism is found. In constrast to Plato's ideation–sensation dichotomy, Aristotle's dualism is best described as a divide between passive reason and active reason. Aristotle suggested that sense qualities and sensations about the external world are created through the five senses. Such qualities or sensations that are common to more than one sense (i.e., the *common sensibles)* are perceived by the 'common sense', a part of the *sensitive soul*. Here, 'data' from all senses are integrated with those from 'imagination' and 'memory' into a holistic perceptual experience. All these were assumed to take place within the realm of the *sensitive soul*.

The two parts of the *rational soul* (active versus passive soul) are referred to by some as the 'active mind' and the 'passive mind' (e.g., Leahey, 1992, p.59). It is within this realm of the *rational soul* that Aristotle identified the only immortal aspect of the entire being: the active mind (*'nous poietikos'* meaning active reason). The active mind is pure thought and reason which acts upon the rest of the being through the perishable passive mind (*'nous pathetikos'* meaning passive reason). For Aristotle, the active mind is not tied down to the individuated *form*, rather, it is common and identical in all human beings and hence is immortal and imperishable. As such, Aristotle argued in Book I (408b) of *De Anima* that,

> Thinking, loving, and hating are affections not of mind, but of that which has mind, so far as it has it. That is why, when this vehicle decays, memory and love cease; they were activities not of mind, but of the composite which has perished; mind is, no doubt, something more divine and impassible (McKeon, 1941, p.548).

Note that the word mind refers to the active part of the *rational soul*, the collective active mind or active reason. The active reason, being 'pure actuality', is unlike the passive reason which is only 'potentialities' waiting to be actualized by the actions of the active reason. In this context, Aristotle's dualistic mind pertains to the division between the collective active mind and the individuated passive mind.

From here, it seems possible to infer Aristotle's position on qualia, even though there is some debate over this (e.g., Wilkes, 1988). Given that qualia are, by definition, the qualitative properties of subjective and 'individuated' personal experiences, they cannot then belong to the active part of the *rational soul*, which is supposedly identical in every person. By implication then, qualia would have been considered perishable in Aristotle's philosophy. However, this seems to be different from the implications drawn from Plato's thoughts. Given that Plato granted the entire *soul* (as consisting of all desires, passions, will, as well as Reason) the immortal status, in contrast to the perishable senses, it could be said that at least those qualia which accompany such desires, passions and will are also unperishable.

Although Aristotle's views of qualia are not clear, his position on the first part of the mind–body problem appears more definite. By assuming the existence of an immortal part of the *rational soul* (i.e., the active mind), that is separate from the rest of the mortal being, the mental activities associated with the active mind were then irreducible to the physical form. Thus, Aristotle cannot be considered a materialistic reductionist.

The legacies of the Classical philosophers on the mind–body and the quanta–qualia problems

Early Greek philosophy had a profound influence over later Western thought. Their legacies with respect to the mind–body and the mind–mind qualia problems are threefold. First, the fact that humanity is firmly anchored on pure reason essentially shaped the subsequent views of human existence throughout modernity. The extreme focus on reason and intellect thus earned this early philosophical school the name rationalism. The persistency of this focus on reason has eventually led to the study of such notions as reason or ration to become an independent field in its own right: the field of rationality. The emphasis on objective reason to the exclusion of subjective feelings was explicitly evident in the theories of ethics (both the deontological and the teleological schools) (Singer, 1997). The image of a human being, with reason dominating over feelings, has perpetually imprinted on the Western psyche. As such, qualitative feelings are thereafter cast aside as peripherals in all contexts of 'being human'.

Second, the Aristotelian philosophy of 'reason through sensing', which asserts that 'abstract concepts' (reasoning with the mind) began with 'concrete percepts' (observation with the senses), helped pave the way for the development of contemporary science and scientific methods. This presumed intimate relationship between sense data and mental thoughts is foundational to Aristotle's logic. Because reason is achievable through sensing, inductions about reality are first made from sensory experiences, these sense-induced forms of 'knowledge' then become the basis for further deductive reasoning. From here, Aristotle used the word *science* to mean, 'demonstrated knowledge of the causes of things' (Reese, 1980, p.517). Thus science began with the inductive reasoning of sense data.

Aristotle's philosophy had a continuous influence over the steady development of scientific methods throughout the medieval (AD late 500 to 1300) and the Renaissance (AD 1300–1600) periods. Scientific achievements in astronomy and physics reached a peak during the seventeenth-century scientific revolution, which eventually gave rise to Auguste Comte's positivism during the early nineteenth century. As Comte pointed out, the evolution of human intellect begins with theology (i.e., explaining events in terms of acts of God), through metaphysics (i.e., explaining events by appealing to abstract concepts), and finally, to positivism (i.e., explaining events through scientific methods) (Reese, 1980, p.99). Positivism contends that all knowledge can only be studied by the empirical methods of observation and verification. Any proposition remains 'factually meaningless' unless it can be empirically observed and validated. With the 'mind' evolving from a metaphysical to a scientific framework, the notion that reality can only be established through scientific methods of observation and verification is accepted without reservation as an integral part of most contemporary cultures. In this intellectual climate, the notion of the human psyche and all its related qualitative or subjective experiences are rendered factually meaningless, largely as a result of their escaping the scientific methods of enquiry.

Third, the Classical philosophers' thoughts on the differences between the mental and the physical directly shaped the various contemporary perspectives on the mind–body problem. However, roughly beginning with the fall of the Roman Empire (AD late 400s), the advances that Classical philosophers had made in the spheres of both natural science and the human mind were suspended until the end of the Middle Ages. During that time, the churches and their teachings constituted the truth about reality and human existence. It was not until the Renaissance era towards the end of the sixteenth century that some of the themes of classical philosophy reappeared again. The resurgence of the notion of human beings as their own master, with free will and reason, thus set the scene for the formalization of the mind–body dualism in the seventeenth century, largely as the result of the metaphysical views of the French philosopher Rene Descartes.

DESCARTES' DUALISM
AND PHILOSOPHICAL RESPONSES

Rene Descartes (1596–1650)

The substance dualism in Platonism and the Aristotelian notion of pure reason are faithfully reflected in Descartes' infamous phrase, *'cogito, ergo sum'* (i.e., 'I think, therefore I am').

Descartes asserted that the mind and the body are two completely different (created or given) substances or entities and that the prime property of the mind is thought. And contrary to the physical reality which is conceived as an 'extension' of the prime physical properties, there is no extension within the realm of the mind. Therefore, the physical body is extendable with reference to space and time, whereas the mind is not extended and has no need to be (e.g., Copleston, 1993; Descartes, 1980).

In the context of the mind–body problem, Descartes' view on the existence of two different realities closely reflects the Platonic notion of the separation of the mind from the senses. Descartes approached the duality by focusing on the 'empirical' interaction and connection between the two. Many commonly observable phenomena (e.g., the 'phantom limb') suggested that the physical body is closely linked to the thinking mind. In an attempt to resolve the mind–body link, Descartes first speculated that the connection took place somewhere in the nervous system near the base of the brain (the pineal gland). However, unable to resolve the many related mind–body problems which arose from his pineal gland theory, Descartes subsequently conceded that the mind–body connection may just remain as an inexplicable mystery that simply had to be accepted without being comprehended.

Given that thought was not considered extendable, Descartes further posited that everything to be found in the mind is only some form or mode of thought. This led to two significant positions on thought. First, all mental thoughts have the feature of consciousness. As such, the mind denoted only conscious (i.e., awared) mental events; all unconscious events were formally excluded from it. Several recent scholars have used the term 'Cartesian catastrophe' to refer to the legacy of this on the contemporary narrow conception of the mind in terms of only conscious mental activities (e.g., Wilkes, 1988). Wilkes described the catastrophic effects of Descartes' equating mind to conscious awareness as twofold:

First, it forced a schism between 'conscious' and 'non-conscious', compelling virtually everyone thereafter to assess the role of each, and to cast their own theories in terms dictated by the dichotomy. Second, psychology and philosophy were now stuck with two separate realms; and the task for centuries was how to relate them, how to bring them back together again. 'The mind', in other words, was hived-off from the body. We can see the loss this entails by contrasting 'mind' once again with the supplanted term psyche. (p.25)

So, it seems that Descartes' main legacy was to have 'halved' the mind by the criterion of awareness. This ensured that the study of the nonconscious aspects of the human psyche was forever banished from enquiries of the mind. This philosophical conception, which was itself a result of the upsurge of scientism in the seventeenth century, was further reinforced by the continual advancement in science and scientific methods until the present day. In this context, the study of the nonconscious part of the human mind in both the Freudian and the Jungian sense has been met with great scepticism by contemporary mainstream psychology.

The second significant position concerns more directly the qualia issue. Subjective emotions were regarded by Descartes as forms of thought. In *The Passions of the Soul*, Descartes presented his analysis of man's emotional life. He identified six 'passions' as keys to emotion: love, hate, desire (appetite), admiration, happiness and sadness. He concluded that feelings and passions were simply different modes of the thinking substance. Given this, the conscious qualitative experiences of these feelings and passions (the qualia per se), being an integral part of the thoughts themselves, would also be a mode of the thinking substance. However, Descartes' position on the qualia problem is unclear, simply because it is unclear whether such a finer distinction within Descartes' notion of the conscious mind was made at all. This confusion may have led Chalmers (1996, p.12) to argue that, while Descartes may have been partly responsible for conflating the phenomenal (qualia) and the psychological (nonqualia) aspects of the mind, it was difficult to decide whether Descartes in fact identified the mental with the phenomenal (qualia). Despite this confusion, it seems certain that qualia do exist for Descartes. Dennett (1988) noted that Descartes *'never doubted that his conscious experiences had qualia, the properties by which he knew or apprehended them'* (p.42).

One further note concerns the present-day mind–mind problem. Descartes' finer-grain dualism *within* the mind thus pertains to the division between conscious awareness, which was Descartes' 'mind' per se, and all mental events that are not within the realm of conscious awareness. However, Descartes' finer-grain dualism (conscious–nonconscious) is to be distinguished from that of Plato, or Aristotle. For Plato, the substance dualism within the mind pertains to sensation and thought, which were presumed to belong respectively to the two substances of the perishable *sense* and the immortal *idea*. For Aristotle, the finer-grain substance dualism within the mind pertains to the separation of the immortal, collective active mind in the *rational soul* and the individuated passive mind. Given these distinctions, it becomes clear that while the early philosophers have identified many kinds of finer-grain distinctions in dividing the mind within itself, none of them made a distinction between the qualia and nonqualia mind. However, the early philosophers' emphasis on objective reason over subjective mental events, reinforced by later scientific advancements during modernity, eventually led to the present-day qualia debate. However, as there is indeed a time for everything, many centuries were to pass before the qualia question was to be formally posed again. In the sections to follow, the main philosophical reactions to Descartes' views of the mind are reviewed.

Philosophical positions in response to Descartes' mind–body dualism

There were three major categories of response from the seventeenth- and eighteenth-century philosophers to Descartes' mind–body dualistic position: *materialism, idealism, parallelism* (and *neutral monism*). These differed primarily in terms of their positions on the fundamental nature of reality. Briefly described, *materialism* asserts that reality is basically physical rather than mental. This view thus holds that the mind is the physical brain. There are variations within *materialism*. While the most extreme view totally eliminates the mental (*eliminative materialism*), the two moderate views either identify the mental with the physical (*identity materialism*) or regard the mental as a concomitant but insignificant phenomenon that plays no causal function (*epiphenomenal materialism*). In all three variations, the mental is reduced to physical or bodily events.

Idealism asserts that reality is fundamentally mental; the physical, if it exists at all, lies within the mental realm. This view suggests that the physical is a construction of the mind. Both *parallelism* and *neutral monism* reject the view that the mental is reducible to the physical. They also reject Descartes' view that the two exist as separate substances. Instead, both positions hold that there exists only one single reality. While *parallelism* maintains that the single reality exists in a state of 'dual-aspect' (i.e., both mental and physical), *neutral monism* describes the single state as one of 'neutrality' (neither mental or physical, but capable of manifesting itself in either form). In either case, the mind is not reducible to the physical brain. These three perspectives are reviewed separately in more depth in the following sections.

Materialism
The materialistic view on the mind–body problem generally follows Democritus' doctrine of the primacy of matter over

mind. However, the main problem with Descartes' dualism concerns his fundamental position on the nature of reality. By construing the existence of two different realities of a mental substance and a physical or material substance, Descartes thus created the problem of connecting the two. While his own pineal gland theory was unsatisfactory, some of his contemporaries believed that the mental–physical link could be satisfactorily resolved if both realities are seen as consisting of the same physical substance. Thomas Hobbes (1588–1679) advocated this view in response to Descartes' metaphysical view. Hobbes identified parts of the body such as the nerves and limbs with physical matters of strings and wheels. He also rejected totally the Cartesian view of the separate existence of a mental substance, calling it *'the immaterial material'* (Reese, 1980, p.228). Hobbes argued that all mental events can be accounted for by physical or bodily activities, in other words, mental states are reducible to bodily states and the mind is simply the physical brain.

(1) Eliminative materialism
The Hobbesian position had a profound influence over later materialistic views of the mind. Hobbes' extreme notion that the mind is equated to the 'mechanical brain' can be regarded as the precursor of *eliminative materialism:* the most extreme form of the present-day materialistic position on the mind–body and the qualia problems. This eliminative position maintains that all mental events are accounted for by the processing mechanisms of the brain, and that once such mechanisms are understood, all there is to know about the mind or consciousness is known. Since Hobbes, such a thoroughgoing materialistic view of the mind was to re-emerge as J.B. Waston's (1878–1958) empirical psychology, *behaviourism*, where the entire individual is to be understood solely in terms of observable behaviour; mentalistic notions such as consciousness, mind or purpose, were all rendered factually meaningless.

Further into the twentieth century, philosophers of positivism (or empiricism) developed the Hobbesian view that mental events are governed completely by natural laws. Positivistic philosophers took the view that philosophical problems (including that of the mind) can be solved only by methods that model after physical science. Alongside this emphasis on scientific methods, there was also an increasing emphasis on linguistic analysis. According to the positivistic philosophers, because the function of philosophy is to inform about 'facts' of the world through the use of language, it becomes necessary for philosophy to first examine empirically the use of natural language in serving such a function. In the course of such a linguistic analysis, Ludwig Wittgenstein (1889–1951) explored the possibility of a 'private language' and concluded that private properties of language cannot exist because they fail to meet the key criterion of language: there has to be common or social agreement concerning its usage (e.g., Kenny, 1973; Wittgenstein, 1953). Generalizing from private language to private mental states or qualia, Wittgenstein thus believed that the latter also fails to meet the criterion of social agreement and hence are pseudo-concepts that cannot exist as facts. Later positive philosophers took an even stronger stance than Wittgenstein and argued for a 'reductive naturalistic' philosophy based entirely on empiricism and physicalism. Human consciousness, or the mind, is to be analysed and understood solely in terms of the quantifiable and observable bodily events. The mind is thus equated with the physical brain, a mechanical device with no 'ghost' inside (e.g., Ryle, 1949; Quine, 1960).

This *eliminative reductionistic* view of qualia is also held by other contemporary analytic philosophers who take the view that all that there is to the mind is completely reducible to either basic cognitive-processing or neuronal-physiological activities in the brain. And there is nothing else left about the mind beyond such a physical level (e.g., Churchland, 1984, 1989; 1995; Churchland, 1986; Davidson, 1989; Dennett, 1991; Dreske, 1995). The implication of this *eliminative reductionist* position on the mind for the qualia problem is clear: there is not really such a thing as qualia, so the problem does not exist.

(2) Empiricism of Locke, Hume and the identity theories of materialism

While eliminative reductionism can be traced back to the Hobbesian notion of the mind, another less extreme form of materialism (the identity theories) can also be traced back to the Hobbesian era. Philosophers around that time holding the identity view of the mind include John Locke (1632–1704) and David Hume (1711–1776). Unlike Hobbes who was a rationalistic philosopher, both Locke and Hume were the earliest *empiricist* philosophers. The empiricist claim was that mental events can only be understood in terms of observable sensory data. This claim is thus also consistent with the reductionistic approach to the mind. However, unlike Hobbes, neither Locke nor Hume denied the independent existence of the mental states. What they did was simply to reduce them to empirically ascertainable unit or 'ideas'. And as such, the 'half' mind (i.e., the conscious mind) left behind from Descartes was further reduced to atomic bits.

To Locke, mental events could be reduced to a primary unit of 'ideas', which were derived from outward sensory impressions and inward intuitive reflections. As one of the earliest empirical philosophers, Locke emphasized the fundamental role of subjective sensory experiences and introspection in all mental activities. As such, the mind was to be understood in terms of, not reason, but sensing (the 'sensitive knowledge') and intuition (the 'intuitive knowledge'). In contrast to the earlier rationalistic philosophers who emphasized pure reason alone in the acquisition of knowledge, Locke placed a similar emphasis on the inward and subjective experiences (intuiting) as on the outward objective experiences (sensing). As such, Locke (1975) made specific reference to the issue of the possibility of individuals having totally different subjective qualitative experiences when presented with an identical object.

This issue is central to the question of the existence of qualia. Locke's view was that such qualitative experiences genuinely exist and they should not be seen as being 'false', they simply are private and hence are unprovable. Locke's view has attracted a great deal of later debate over qualia (e.g., Chalmers, 1996; Dahlbom, 1993; Marcel and Bisiach, 1988).

Hume expanded on Locke's notion of association of ideas in developing a picture of the entire mind: complex mental events or thoughts are nothing more than associations of simple ideas which are derived from basic sensory impressions. Hume's picture of the 'atomistic' mind was also a direct result of the influence of the seventeenth-century Newtonian physics. The mind was modelled after the then known discrete states of physical reality. Like the physical world, consisting of discrete particles, the mental realm also was believed to be made up of simple forms of sense impressions.

From his atomistic perspective to mental activities, Hume (1975, see also Stroud, 1981) succeeded in formalizing a picture of human beings without a holistic identity or an integrated sense of 'self'. Hume totally denied the existence of the self and argued that it is nothing more than sense perceptions. The holistic sense of self is, according to Hume, nothing but a collection of different perceptions in a perpetual movement. So, the holistic self was reduced to its atomistic parts, connected together according to their resemblance and congruity with one another.

Hume's denial of the existence of an integrating self and the 'atomisation' of the mental states in terms of simple ideas are the direct result of his empiricistic philosophical stance. He was sceptical of the metaphysical position on the existence of either a mental or a physical substance, and the presumed causal relationship between the two. Hume regarded these metaphysical assumptions as the root of Descartes' mind–body problem. Thus, by not making such assumptions, Hume succeeded in avoiding the causality problem of the origin of the mental states or consciousness. Mental events are to be understood through an analysis of the associations among simple ideas, and there is nothing behind such events that 'causes' them.

Turning to the issue of qualia, while Hume rejected all metaphysical notions of a holisitc self or a substance that causes mental events, he also rejected the rationalistic notion of the primacy of reason in mental events. As one of the earliest empiricist philosophers, Hume was also sceptical of the role of reason in attaining true knowledge. He reversed the reason-over-feeling hierarchy inherent in the thinking of the rationalistic philosophers and argued that, *'Reason is, and ought only to be the slave of the passions, and can never pretend to any other office than to serve and obey them'* (cf. Leahey, 1992, p.117). In this context, Hume thus argued for the primacy of subjective experience over disengaged reason.

While Locke and Hume considered subjective and first-personal qualitative experience as a genuine aspect of mental activities, they nonetheless reduced all mental activities to atomistic parts at the level of sensory perceptions. These two key features of the mind, that qualia exist and that they are reducible to physiological activities re-emerged in the present-day *identity* and *representational* perspectives to the mind--body problem. As mentioned before, the *identity* position (e.g., Flanagan, 1992; Lacan, 1996; Lockwood, 1989; Tye, 1995; Van Gulick, 1992), although of a reductive materialistic type, is less extreme than that of *eliminative reductionism.* While eliminative reductionists deny the very existence of qualia, identity theorists assert that qualia exist but as mental states, they are reducible to brain activities. In this view, qualia, 'raw feels' or subjective mental states are real and persistent. However, qualia are expressible in physical terms, as it is the physical representations that actually express their existence.

(3) Darwinian Huxley and epiphenomenal materialism
While *identity theories* assert that qualitative consciousness has an independent existence but is reducible to physical states, another version of materialism, the *epiphenomenalism,* holds

that phenomenal qualia do not have an independent existence. Rather, qualia exist as an artifact or a by-product of the non-phenomenal conscious experience (i.e., nonqualia). The nineteenth-century philosopher Thomas Huxley first expressed this idea (e.g., Popkin and Stroll, 1993). A most ardent proponent of Darwinian evolution theory, Huxley took the extreme mechanistic view which reduces all living beings to biological and organic existence. In this context, Huxley asserted that phenomenal consciousness is the 'effect' of the physical or bodily processes, and as such, it carries no causal significance. As long as the non-phenomenal experience (non-qualia) is explained in physical terms, its dependent (qualia) is automatically accounted for. The epiphenomenal view thus in effect treats qualia as though they do not exist.

Idealism
Hobbes, Locke and Hume reacted to Descartes' dualism of the separate existence of a mental and physical reality by either totally disregarding the mental reality or reducing it to the physical state. Directly opposite to such a *materialistic* reaction to Descartes' dualism was the position of *idealism* which assumes the primacy of the mental, or *ideation,* over physical matter. Just as there exists a range of materialistic positions from the most extreme eliminative to the more moderate epiphenomenal and identity theories, the idealistic positions also vary from the most extreme form, George Berkeley's (1685–1753) *idealistic monism,* to other moderate forms of idealism. Berkeley's extreme monistic idealism asserted that the fundamental reality is purely ideational, mental or phenomenal. In other words, the physical reality does not exist and all the physical properties could be accounted for in terms of the phenomenal or mental substance.

Even though Berkeley's extreme view of the reality lacks scientific credibility, it gave rise to a more moderate idealistic view held by many eighteenth-century Romantic philosophers including Friedrich Hegel (1770–1831) and Joseph Schelling

(1775–1854) (e.g., Leahey, 1992). The philosophy of Romanticism came into being as a revolt against the main empiricistic and reason-dominated philosophy of the Enlightenment era. The Enlightenment period was marked by the Newtonian and Darwinian revolutions in natual sciences. The moderate idealistic view of reality held by the Romantic philosophers does not deny the existence of a physical reality but asserts that its fundamental nature is mental or ideational. More importantly, this Romantic view of reality has significantly different implications for humanity and human existence from that of the Enlightenment philosophy. Romanticism thus places the self at the core of humanity with an emphasis on subjective feeling, intuition, free will, cultural heritage, and the purposefulness of existence. As these views emphasize the holistic and sentient self, rather than the reasoning mind, they are discussed in detail in the next chapter.

Parallelism and neutral monism

In their attempts to resolve the Descartes problem concerning the relationship between the mental and the physical, materialism and idealism did so by either getting rid of one substance or by reducing one to the other. As a third attempt, *parallelism* and *neutral monism* both kept the basic mental–physical dichotomy and rejected the view that either is reducible to the other. However, they did not treat the two as being independent realities of substances or entities. Instead, they posited the existence of only one single reality. For *parallelism*, this single reality has dual mental and physical aspects. For *neutral monism*, this single state is one of neutrality, but is capable of being 'realized' in either the mental or the physical form.

(1) Parallelism or dual-aspect theories

Benedict Spinoza (1632–1677) proposed *Parallelism*. Parallelism contends that there exists one single reality which has both a mental and a physical aspect (the two 'modes of reality' in Spinoza's term) (e.g., Frost, 1962/1989). The two modes parallel, but do not directly interact with each other, in the sense that for each mental event there is a corresponding physical event and vice versa. This single reality appears materialistic and quantifiable when viewed from an objective, external perspective; but when viewed from a subjective, internal point of view, it appears qualitative and mentalistic (e.g., Hampshire, 1962). This philosophical view of reality is often referred to as 'dual-aspect theory', in contrast to the dualistic theories which assume the existence of two separate realities.

Gottfried Wilhelm Leibniz (1646–1716) followed Spinoza's dual-aspect theory. Leibniz's main contribution to later psychological studies of consciousness was through his introduction of the construct of 'apperception': the 'perception' of a weak stimulus typically below the level of conscious awareness. This idea was followed up in later psychophysical research on subliminal perception below the perceptual threshold, or in Gustav Fechner's (1801–87) terms, the 'negative sensations'. The idea was also further developed by Wilhelm Wundt (1832–1900) in his theory of apperception. While apperception has since been interpreted in operational and processing terms, Leibniz's original emphasis was on the soul's self-consciousness. Specifically, Leibniz used the term apperception to denote the *monad*'s (i.e., the soul's) awareness of itself. As this phenomenon took place within the *monad*, or the soul, itself, it was outside the realm of conscious awareness. The introduction of such a notion of apperception carries the presumption of the existence of a realm outside consciousness. Thus Leibniz 'resurrected' the idea of the 'unconscious'. It can be said that since the Cartesian abandonment of the nonconscious events from the 'mind', it was Leibniz who brought the unconscious mind back into the realm of mental states. This paved the way for Sigmund Freud's (1856–1940) psychoanalysis of the unconscious mind (Leahey, 1992, p.107).

In addition to the later influence over Wundt's empirical psychology and Freud's psychoanalysis, Leibniz's philosophy also shaped the metaphysical mind–body position of Immanuel

Kant (1724–1804). Kant's views (e.g., Allison, 1986; Korner, 1955) were a critique of Hume's views of the nature of the mind. As previously mentioned, Hume rejected not only the traditional metaphysical view that there exists a substance which causes mental events; he also rejected the traditional rationalistic notion of reason-over-feeling. However, Kant responded to Hume's scepticism by simultaneously bringing back the metaphysical approach to the mind and by returning philosophy back to the rationalistic position of the supremacy of reason and rationality. Refining the idealistic views of reality, Kant distinguished between a 'noumenal world' (i.e., world of pure experience) and a 'phenomenal world' (i.e., world of sensory experience) (e.g., Frost, 1962/1989; Korner, 1955). *Noumenon* refers to a pre-existing entity of pure experience, which is akin to the Platonic notion of the immutable *idea* or soul. This pure entity is mostly translated into 'the thing-in-itself' or 'the thing-as-it-is' and according to Kant, it 'organises' the external discrete reality in giving rise to a unified phenomenal experience. The *noumenon* therefore plays the role of the 'self'. However, the noumenal realm lies beyond the phenomenal experiences and hence is unattainable. The knowledge that can be attained through introspective examining of subjective experiences is only the knowledge about the phenomenal world.

Kant's metaphysical views of the mind presume both a qualitative intrinsic aspect of 'the-thing-in-itself' and an objective external aspect of the phenomena. Even though Kant brought back the metaphysical notion of the noumena in his account of the mind, he nonetheless noted its limitation: it is unverifiable and unfalsifiable. Because of this, in his *Metaphysical Principles of Natural Science*, Kant greatly stressed the importance of the study of 'phenomenology' through the method of introspection. Therefore, it is here that Kant's philosophy appears to be sitting on the fence between the metaphysical and the scientific. On the one hand, Kant brought back the metaphysical notion of the 'thing-in-itself' (*noume-*

non) which Humean empiricism rejected, and on the other hand, Kant placed a predominant emphasis on Reason as well as on the empirical study of the phenomenal. Despite the potential confusion due to his 'keeping a double set' of ideas (Putnam, 1987, p.42), Kant's contribution to later philosophies of the mind is clear. His notion of 'the-thing-in-itself', similar to Leibniz's apperception (of the *monad*), was adopted and refined by the founder of psychology, Wilhelm Wundt, in his theory of apperception (Leahey, 1992). It is noted that the phrase 'the-thing-in-itself' has been frequently given as one of the defining features of the concept of qualia in recent discussions of the qualia issue.

Due to his 'double' philosophy, Kant also contributed to later empiricism. Kant's emphasis on the use of introspection in the study of phenomenology had a profound influence over phenomenalism in philosophy. The philosophy of phenomenalism asserts that the only attainable knowledge is that which pertains to the phenomenal. The nineteenth-century neo-Kantians followed most aspects of Kant's philosophy that are consistent with 'science', but they dropped his metaphysical notion of the *noumenon* by focusing entirely on his phenomenology (Reese, 1980, p.384).

Overall, the metaphilosophical positions of Spinoza, Leibniz, and Kant had at least three major influences over later views of the mind. First, Spinoza and Leibniz's parallelism paved the way for later developments of the psychophysical laws in empirical psychology. The *psychophysical parallelism* notion in both Gustav Fechner's and Wilhelm Wundt's psychophysical psychology also presumed a dual-aspected reality. Second, Leibniz's resurrenction of the nonconscious mind further paved the way for the Freudian psychoanalysis of the unconscious. Third, the Spinoza–Leibniz–Kantian tradition, by emphasizing the holistic nature of the mind also had a significant influence over later empirical phenomenology and Gestalt psychology.

(2) Neutral monism

While the dual-aspect theory assumes the concomitant existence of the mental and the physical in the single reality, *neutral monism* assumes that the single reality is neither mental nor physical but exists in a state of neutrality. However, this neutral state is capable of being realized in either mode. Such a view was upeld by William James (1842–1910) and Bertrand Russell (1872–1970). Given that reality is neutral, it then has pluralistic possibilities in its realization. In this context, the reality is also seen as having an evolutionary quality capable of growth and development in a progressive manner. This view is reminiscent of that of some idealistic philosophers including Schelling and Hegel. It is interesting to note that this neutral monism position on reality seems to have found a parallel in contemporary physical science. There, some quantum theorists (e.g., Schrodinger) have argued that physical reality exists in a 'superposition' of dual states (wave–particle duality), capable of being realized in either state.

Non-reductive naturalism

The Cartesian mind–body dichotomous notion, which was essentially preserved in parallelism and neutral monism, had a direct influence over the development during the 1940s of non-reductive *naturalism* (e.g., Woodbridge, Cohen and Ernest Nagel). The key premise of non-reductive naturalism is that any account of reality must make the final appeal to primary natural notions such as space or time. However, not all naturally-occurring phenomena can be reduced to primary physical matters, as claimed by materialism. Chief of all the irreducible phenomena pertaining to qualitative aspects of natural experiences includes aesthetics and ethics. The non-reductive naturalistic position, while being strictly consistent with the laws of the natural sciences, does oppose a complete and unqualified reduction to such laws. As such, the non-reductive naturalists consider qualia to be a valid construct central to the study of the conscious mind. It is within this tradition that Chalmers (1996) recently applied Shannon's information theory and proposed a comprehensive information-state model of consciousness in accounting for the origin and organization of qualia.

Chalmers argued that while his model is within the philosophical tradition of dualism, it could also be classified as a dual-aspected monistic theory. Chalmers (1996) pointed out:

> To capture the spirit of the view I advocate, I call it 'naturalistic dualism'... although a view of dualism, it is possible that it could turn out to be a kind of monism. Perhaps the physical and the phenomenal will turn out to be two different aspects of a single encompassing kind ... two aspects of a single kind'. (pp.128–9)

This model will be reviewed later in Chapter 6.

EMPIRICAL PSYCHOLOGY OF THE MIND

Against the background of philosophical approaches to the mind and consciousness, empirical psychology was founded towards the end of the nineteenth century. As mentioned earlier, Locke and Hume's associationistic empiricism paved the way for further applications of human physiology to the study of the mind. Several physiologists including Gall and Broca were instrumental in bridging the gap between physiological events and mental states. The basic belief was that the brain was the material seat for mental events or consciousness. Their work centred around the mapping of different loci in the brain for associated sensory perception and related motor responses. In a similar effort, biologist Bain aimed to unite psychology and physiology by applying both physiological principles and associationist notions to account for the entire range of mental activities including sensing, thinking, emotions and will. The focus was on the physiological foundations of mental events.

This nineteenth-century endeavour in explaining consciousness in biological and physiological terms flourished in the intellectual climate dominated by empiricistic philosophy and

Newtonian physical science, which has persisted since the seventeenth century. Such a materialisitc approach to the enquiry into the mind received further inspiration during the mid-nineteenth century, from Darwin's theory of biological evolution. In that context, the mind was conceptualized in terms of its biological functions of adapting to the environment. This conceptualization further strengthened the link between Humean associationism and output behaviour. And from here, functionalism and behaviourism were to emerge as the main paradigms of empirical psychology.

However, many during that time were already wary of the extreme domination of materialism in the enquiry of human existence. The early psychophysicist (also a neo-Kantian philosopher), Helmholtz warned of the danger of extreme materialism. Helmholtz was committed to the materialist view and opposed to the idealistic position. He argued that materialism is, like idealism, a 'metaphysical hypothesis', and that an extreme form of it can become a 'dogma' which *'hinders the progress of science and, like all dogmas, leads to violent intolerance'* (cf. Leahey, 1992, p.171).

Towards the end of the nineteenth century, psychology was founded as an independent discipline almost simultaneously in Europe by Wilhelm Wundt and in America by William James. While both psychologies started off as a study of consciousness, their approaches were vastly different. Wundt focused on the synthesis of the agentic mind and the sentient self into a holistic conscious experience; whereas James took the modern functionistic perspective and focused on the analysis of the causal role of consciousness. Thus, for Wundt, consciousness is an end in itself; for James, a means to an end. Their work and the subsequent developments of consciousness research within empiricistic psychology are reviewed in Chapter 4. The next chapter turns to the philosophical history of the holistic and sentient self, which parallels that of the analytic and rational mind.

3
A Survey of Philosophical Thoughts on the Holistic Subjective Self

In the course of the long and arduous enquiry into human consciousness, it is the rational aspects of being that have been fostered and preserved. In contrast, the intrinsic sense of sentience appears to have been quite neglected. Although the early Greek philosophers set out in search of the holistic *psyche* (being), they were nonetheless responsible for placing reason alone at the core of the *psyche*. Philosophers in modernity took turns in redefining this holistic *psyche*. In the hands of Descartes, the nonconscious domain of thought and mind was discarded, hence the *psyche* thereafter was comprised solely of 'conscious thoughts'. Yet another reduction of the Descartes' conscious mind was to take place as the result of the Newtonian and Darwinian revolutions in the physical and biological sciences. These developments in the natural sciences had a convergent impact on the emergence of several influential scientific paradigms including Hume's empiricism and Comte's positivism. Hume's empirical associationism formally rejected the existence of a subjective self (in his term, the 'personal identity'). The holistic feature of the remaining conscious mind was therefore discarded. Within this positivistic tradition, the development of Peirce's pragmatism and Dewey's instrumentalism in contemporary philosophy has resulted in further constraints upon the enquiry into consciousness. According to these contemporary schools of thought, any given notion is to be interpreted in terms of its functional consequences. In this context, the Humean atomistic mind is to be accounted for in terms of its covert and overt adaptive functions.

While the dominant intellectual paradigms have been oriented towards the objectification of the *psyche*, other knowledge paradigms that oppose such an orientation have nonetheless continuously existed in the background. These paradigms place a core emphasis on 'humanness' and hence on the holistic sentient self, complete with feeling, free will and purpose. It needs to be noted that the notion of a holistic self *(psyche)* was never called into question before the Cartesian abandonment of the nonconscious mind and the Humean dismissal of an holistic personal identity. Against this background, it is Leibniz and Kant who are responsible for bringing back the holistic sentient self, as both the nonconscious mind and the holistic personal identity are part and parcel of the Leibnizian *monad* and the Kantian *noumenon*. In the present-day literature, the subjects of the holistic sentient self and the nonconscious mind, although outside the mainstream paradigms of scientific enquiry, are still very much the core of the phenomenological, existential, and humanistic paradigms. Before reviewing in detail such contemporary paradigms dealing with the holistic sentient self and consciousness, it is first necessary to take another look at the history of philosophical thought, but this time with an eye on the status of the holistic subjective self accorded by classical and modern philosophers.

Heraclitus: unbounded-*psyche* as self

While Heraclitus was the first philosopher to abstract the 'waking and thinking mind' out of the holistic *psyche*, he nonetheless still held on to the 'misty-time' image of the human *psyche* as an integral and undifferentiated part of the world. According to Hatab (1992), Heraclitus' notion of the *psyche* appears '*to be a unified whole and ... knowledge is discovered within its regions*'. Heraclitus' own description of the *psyche* seems to suggest that it is infinitely vast and deep such that its 'boundaries' can never be found. Despite this early image, Hatab argued that Heraclitus' portrait of the *psyche* is the first to *'anticipate the modern criteria for selfhood'* (p.174). The earliest philosophical notion of the 'unified' self appears to be unbounded and immersed in an infinite reality.

Protagoras' human-centred philosophy

Protagoras opposed Democritus' notions of *atomism* which reduced all things, both living and non-living, to primary physical matters. Democritus' view of reality represented an absolutist and materialistic position in asserting the existence of an objective reality and the supremacy of matter over mind. Against this prevailing view, Protagoras argued for a humanistic and a relativistic view of reality. His man-centred philosophy was well captured by his infamous comment on the then popular scientific method of observation and measurement in the acquisition of knowledge, *Man is the measure of all things: of things that are that they are, and of things that are not that they are not'* (Reese, 1980, p.464). Later Greek philosophers Plato and Aristotle interpreted this saying as indicating a complete relativity of knowledge and truth: that absolute truth did not exist, rather, truth was what each individual perceives to be the case. Protagoras' humanism thus asserted the central role of an individual's own perception and values in determining reality and truth. Because of its total disregard for the scientific methods of observation and measurement prevalent at the time, later Greek philosophers gave Protagoras' school of thoughts the somewhat contemptuous term *Sophism* (meaning 'fallacy'), and called its followers *Sophists*, the Greek word meaning 'one who professes to make man wise'. This man-centred position was also condemned by later philosophers for its lack of clear objective standards for morality. However, Protagoras' approach could be considered as the precursor of later schools of relativism. And more importantly, it is the precursor of later existentialism and humanism, which stand in opposition to all universalistic matter-centred views to reality, truth and humanity.

Classical Greek: a holistic *psyche* dominated by ration

The notion of a holistic self was often credited to Socrates, who believed that the main goal of human existence is to attain the knowledge of the self and hence to 'Know Thyself'. Plato's notion of the immortal *Idea* also reflects a holistic *psyche*. However, Plato's *idea* was divided into three parts which separated the subjective feelings and will (i.e., *appetite* and *will*) from objective Reason. Reason was presumed to play the role of overseeing the other two and to ensure a harmonious balance between the subjective and the objective aspects of the *idea*. Thus, even though the *idea* was 'divided' into separate parts, it still denoted a unitary holistic *psyche*. Referring to this seemingly divided *psyche* as the soul, Charles Taylor (1989) stresses its unitary and holistic feature:

> the soul is ... in principle, one; it is a single locus. The experience of it as comprising a plurality of loci is an experience of error and imperfection. ... The soul 'must' be one if we are to reach our highest in the self-collected understanding of reason, which brings about the harmony and concord of the whole person. (p.120)

For Aristotle, the holistic *psyche* was the *substance*. Within it, there appeared to be two interrelated integrating agents: the *sensitive soul* integrates the sense data of the 'common sensibles', and the *active reason* works on the actualization of the self's potentialities. Again, ration rules over the thinking and feeling self. Therefore, even though the early Classical Greek philosophers placed a great emphasis on objective reason over subjective feelings and will, their picture of the *psyche* remained as an integrated whole.

The Hellenistic and Roman periods: turning within the self through subjective will (Stoicism) and spiritual faith (neo-Platonism)

When the first part of the Classical period ended with the death of Aristotle around 322 BC, Western philosophy entered the latter part of Classicism: the Hellenistic and Roman era which lasted until the fall of the Roman Empire in AD 476. The main philosophical schools of the post-Aristotle Classicism were Stoicism and neo-Platonism. Both schools rejected the earlier ration-over-feeling view of humanity. In contrast to the early philosophers' broad task of attaining ultimate truth and knowledge, the Hellenistic school focused primarily on the more immediate concerns of living and coping with the changing nature of the human condition. They saw that the way to cope was not through attending to such external reality and to make sense of it by sheer rationalization. Rather, the best way to cope was by turning one's attention within oneself through either the intrinsic power of will (the Stoics) or the spiritual power of faith (the neo-Platonists).

The best-known Stoic philosopher, Epictetus (AD 60–138), a slave and cripple, held the belief that all human conditions and potentials are predetermined and that they were not alterable. Because of this, the only way to achieve happiness was to be 'indifferent' to the external world and all happenings within it. According to Epictetus, the chief of human virtues was will-power, and only through that could the individual attain the indifference towards the outer world and hence be set free from it (e.g., Copleston, 1993; Guthrie, 1977; Popkin and Stroll, 1993). Thus the Stoics' emphasis on subjective will-power foreshadows the philosophy of later Romanticism, and in particular, the philosophy of Schopenhauer that places the will at the core of human existence and purpose. However, for the Stoics, the subjective will operates primarily by turning the individual inward so that the person becomes indifferent to the external changing world.

Instead of emphasizing subjective will, the neo-Platonists such as Plotinus (AD 204–279) focused on humanity's spiritual faith. The neo-Platonists resurrected the spiritual aspects of Plato's philosophy, which was inspired by Pythagoras' (570–500 BC) view of the reincarnation of the pure soul. Plotinus believed in the one single divinity, which exists within each individual human soul as the *nous* (i.e., 'reason'). As the *nous* originated from the one single divinity, its ultimate goal was to be reunited with its source. Plotinus and the neo-Platonists believed that this goal could only be achieved through the introspective contemplation of the divinity within one's self and the renunciation of the desires and activities in the external world.

Regarding the holistic self, perhaps the most significant aspect of the Hellenistic philosophy lies in its emphasis on the inner self and the need for turning within and away from the outer world. This notion of 'living within one's inner self' is at the core of the Eastern spiritual and philosophical thoughts. While Western civilization in the two millenniums to follow was to cast humanity virtualy exclusively in terms of the external world, the calls for turning inward to the inner self were nonetheless frequently voiced (e.g., Tarnas, 1991; Taylor, 1989). Again, because such calls are against the persistent scientific and empiricistic *Zeitgeist*, they have remained largely in the background unheard. However, in the immediate ensuing years, the Hellenistic emphasis on the inner self appeared to have been temporarily suspended by Medieval philosophy's conception of a separate Absolute (God) existing outside the individual self.

The Medieval period: reality centred around the external absolute

The Medieval period started from AD 476, with its first part, the Dark Ages, ending at the turn of the first millennium and its second part, Scholasticism, lasting till the end of the thirteenth century. The church teachings of Christianity dominated the intellectual climate of the time when knowledge or truth was synthesized with religion and theology. It is generally regarded that the work of St Augustine (AD 354–430) marks the beginning of Medieval philosophy. St Augustine synthesized the Platonic philosophy of the existence of an immortal *idea* and Christian theology in asserting the existence of an eternal *idea* in the eternal God. While the Platonic *ideas* of 'good' and 'truth' were regarded as the innate essence of human beings, St Augustine considered them to be the nature of the eternal *idea* 'God'. Further, while for Plato, the attainment of good and truth was through education and the exercise of Reason, for St Augustine, it was through self-introspection. Hence, while Plato believed in seeking truth in and from the external world, St Augustine asked, '*Do not go outward; return within yourself. In the inward man dwells truth*' (cf. Taylor, 1989, p.129). As such, intellectual reason was to take an inferior place to religious faith in the seeking of the truth, and this was well-captured by his famous saying, '*I believe in order to understand*' (Reese, 1980, p.40).

The best-known scholastic philosopher, St Thomas Aquinas (1225–1274) synthesized Aristotle's philosophy with Christian faith. It has often been said that Aquinas' philosophy represents the height of the philosophical synthesis of knowledge, God and humanity. This kind of a grand synthesis of intellectual reason and religious faith thus characterizes the philosophy of the Medieval period. Following Aristotle's empiricism, Aquinas believed that knowledge, the truth of God and hence the essence of humanity, could only be attained indirectly through senses and sensory images. Reason played an important, albeit lesser, part than faith in the attainment of knowledge. Aquinas believed that individuals differed in the extent to which the exercise of reason alone could achieve true knowledge. Beyond individual differences, there is an ultimate limit for everyone that reason could achieve; the full attainment of knowledge beyond that limit requires faith. Therefore, Aquinas believed that while reason and faith, hence philosophy and religion, are complementary to each other, they would remain separate beyond a certain point. It is here that the philosophy of Aquinas has its greatest impact on the later separation of philosophy and theology. A significant consequence for the conception of the self is that its supposedly holisitic and integral nature was seriously challenged: the intellectual reasoning self was to be sharply distinguished from the intuitive believing self. With further influences from the advancements in physical and biological sciences, the reasoning self was to be accorded the sole legitimate status within humanity, a status which the intuitive and sentient self was to be deprived of.

The Renaissance: humanistic focus on the aesthetic and feeling self

After the theology-dominated philosophy of the Medieval period, the early man-centred philosophy was revived during the Renaissance. This period lasted from the fourteenth century through to the sixteenth century. However, instead of creating new conceptualizations of nature and humanity, as did the early naturalistic and humanistic philosophers, the expertise of the Renaissance philosophers such as Francesco Petrarch (1304–1374) and Desiderius Erasmus (1467–1536) was more of a maintanence kind. Specifically, these philosophers revived and maintained not only the early humanistic philosophers' emphasis on the relative nature of truth, but also the naturalistic philosophers' notion of education in attaining knowledge. Regarding the former, Erasmus believed that there are pluralistic perspectives to truth. And despite the then intellectual climate that was clouded by the bitter division between Protestant Christianity and Roman Catholicism, Erasmus remained committed to the relativistic position.

In terms of maintaining the value of learning which Plato and Aristotle greatly stressed, the Renaissance philosophers, particularly Petrarch, rediscovered the writings of early Greek philosophers and fostered the learning of such writings. With the restrictive church-dominated values behind them, the early man-centred values found expressions through activities of ordinary life such as literature and visual arts. Therefore, a significant consequence of the Renaissance for humanity was that, through its emphasis on arts and beauty, the subjective aspects of the aesthetic, feeling, and sentient self were duly fostered. In this context, the Renaissance philosophers thus continued the early Humanists' role in paving the way for later contemporary existentialist and humanistic thoughts.

Romanticism against Enlightenment

The word 'Enlightenment' is used to describe the philosophical climate dominated by reason and science in eighteenth-century Europe. Following Locke's empiricism, the Enlightenment philosophers were much influenced by the Newtonian model of a mechanistic physical reality. Because Enlightenment philosophers subscribed to the view that empiricistic reason and scientific methods are the only tools in the attainment of truth and reality, the period is also referred to as the Age of Reason. The Enlightenment philosophers' materialistic view of humanity was evident in Hume's application of the atomistic model in physics to mental reality. Consistent with this view, Hume denied the existence of a holisitc subjective Self (in his words, the 'personal identity') and accounted for the integration of the Self in terms of the associative principles of resemblance and congruence. The philosophers of Romanticism revolted against the Enlightenment view of the world and humanity.

Against sheer reason, Romantic philosophers' views of both reality and humanity are idealistic. Their views of the physical reality are consistent with the Berkeley and Spinoza–Leibniz traditions that reject the Newtonian mechanistic model and, instead, emphasize the 'consciousness' of nature itself.

Similarly for humanity, Romantic philosophers rejected the Enlightenment view that mental events can be adequately represented in terms of atomistic associations. Rather, they placed a core emphasis on the holisitc and sentient nature of the self. In sum, their views of humanity could be characterized by an emphasis on (1) the holistic and sentient self, (2) the heart's intuitive feelings (3) cultural heritages such as myth and language, (4) subjective free will and volition, (5) the purposefulness of human existence. The following is a summary of these key features of the philosophy of Romanticism.

A 'self-conscious' physical reality

Many idealistic philosophers in Romanticism took the *panpsychism* view to physical reality. They considered the physical reality as being alive, possessing a soul, and hence is conscious. This vitalist view of reality implicitly assumes that reality itself is 'teleological' or 'purposeful'. For instance, Joseph Schelling referred the physical reality to 'visible intelligence'. His *objective idealism* saw nature as a set of 'selves', which develops and evolves towards consciousness. Friedrich Hegel took on this idea and developed an extremely complex notion of the evolution of the universe. Hegel's notion of *absolute idealism* referred to the existence of an 'absolute mind' which is central to the evolving process of the world's history: the history itself is the manifestation of the striving of this absolute mind towards the goal of 'self-realisation' and intelligibility (e.g., Weiss, 1974). While not all Romantic philosophers subscribe to panpsychism, many others share this view (e.g., Fichte, Goethe, Schleiermacher and Schlegel).

This panpsychism view that the physical reality has a mind or consciousness has been shared by some positivistic philosophers including Whitehead. Whitehead's notion of 'protomentality' explicitly suggests a mentalistic ontology for the physical reality. In contemporary philosophy, Abner Shimony (1997) has revived Whitehead's protomental idea and integrated it with concepts from quantum physics in producing a new 'modernised Whiteheadianism'. Shimony cautiously concluded that:

> According to Whitehead, something like mentality is pervasive throughout nature, but high-level mentality is contingent upon the evolution of special hospitable complexes of occasions. The capacity for a system to actualise potentialities, thereby modifying the linear dynamics of quantum mechanics, may be pervasive in nature ... (p.158)

Other well-known recent adpatations of such a panpsychism idea include Thomas Nagel's (1979) 'proto-mental properties' and David Bohm's (1986) 'proto-conscious properties' at the quantum level.

Adopting a non-reductive naturalistic approach to consciousness, Chalmers' recent (1996) information-state model may also carry an implicit assumption of panpsychism. As Chalmers writes, *'But I hope to have said enough to show that we ought to take the possibility of some sort of panpsychism seriously'* (p.299). And towards the end of the book, he comments further about this possibility he raised, *'this is initially counterintuitive, but the counterintuitiveness disappears with time. I am unsure whether the view is true or false, but it is at least intellectually appealing, and on reflection it is not too crazy to be acceptable'* (p.357).

A holistic integrating self

Despite his predominantly rationalistic approach, Immanuel Kant's metaphysical philosophy is widely considered as marking the beginning of Romanticism (e.g., Leahey, 1992). Trained in the Leibnizian tradition, Kant opposed Hume's atomistic view of the mental world. As mentioned in the previous chapter, Kant's metaphysical view of humanity involves a pre-existing pure entity, the *noumenon* ('the thing-in-itself' or 'the thing-as-it-is') that integrates the discrete external reality into a unified phenomenal experience. The *noumenon* therefore plays the role of the holistic self or *psyche*. Kant's conception of the *noumenon* is similar to the Platonic notion of the immortal *Idea*. Because of this, Kant's metaphysical philosophy is seen as the foundation for later similar positions positing the existence of a non-reductive, subjective and unifying self. In reviving the notion of a holistic integrating self, Kant believed that there can be no knowledge without a 'knower'. Therefore, the existence of an integrating knower is necessary in serving as *'a focal point to which we may refer our conscious experience'* (Frost, 1962/1989, p.168).

The revival of a holistic sentient self in Romanticism has a further significant implication for the nonconscious mental states. Following Leibniz, Kant believed that the realm of the mind is vast and that only a small part of it lies within conscious awareness with the remaining part belonging to nonconsciousness. To many other Romantic philosophers such as Schopenhauer, Schelling and Hartmann, the unconscious is mankind's collective heritage throughout its entire history. And as such, the unconscious is seen as the 'irrational or primitive' force within the domain of the holistic self, which drives the individual towards conscious fulfilment and actualization. The Romantic philosophers' conception of the unconscious is similar to Carl Jung's collective unconscious, as both refer to the collection of ideas from the individual's entire evolutionary history. It is however, different from Sigmund Freud's unconscious mind, as the latter constitutes only the repressed mental ideas from the individual's early childhood experience. This aspect of the Romantic philosophy is discussed further in relation to its emphasis on cultural heritage.

Heart's feelings and intuitions over mind's reason
While Enlightenment philosophers in general emphasized the mind's agentic and reasoning aspect, some of them also had doubts about the excessive focus on reason in the enquiry of human nature and existence. Locke and Hume are a few examples. As mentioned in the previous chapter, Locke never

denied the existence of a private subjective self. While Hume denied the existence of a holistic self, he nonetheless clearly expressed the view that subjective feelings should rule over reason rather than the other way round. So, even though the holistic self did not exist for Hume, he still considered subjective feelings to be more critical than objective reason for human experience.

A similar heart-over-reason view was also expressed by other accomplished Enlightenment scientists. The well-known mathematician Blaise Pascal (1623–1662) strongly opposed the Cartesian rationalistic approach to human reality. He distinguished between two mental operations in knowledge acquisition: 'the spirit of geometry' and 'the spirit of finesse'. The former operation involved procedures of logical reasoning whereas the latter, workings of intuitive feelings. Pascale claimed that the heart's intuition may have the power to reach realms beyond those that the reasoning power of the mind is ever capable of. He also believed that the knowledge of God could only be attained by the intuitive feelings of the heart and not through the intellectual reasoning of the mind (e.g., Reese, 1980). Pascale's sketch of the human condition was also a precursor of later existentialism, such as that of Kierkegaard and Sartre. Pascale saw man as living an unbearable and contradictory existence. On the one hand, it is but a frail reed that is infinitely small; on the other hand, because it is a 'thinking reed' capable of knowing its own conditions, so man is at the same time infinitely great. However, man is unable to resolve this paradox of its own existence through reason. And according to Pascale, the only way to get out of this situation was through either God's grace or the heart's intuitive workings.

Another Romantic philosopher, Jean-Jacques Rousseau (1712–1778) argued that in advanced civilizations, it is scientific and artistic achievements, and not virtues or morality, which typically command high rewards. However, he believed that science and arts are not essential for humanity. Rather, an individual could lead a worthy life by following the innate goodness of the heart (e.g., Taylor, 1989). Thus, echoing Pascale's claim that the heart has intuition that is more powerful than reason, Rousseau argued that the heart has goodness which is more valuable than reason. His point that one needs to attend to the feelings of the heart in cultivating the innate goodness captures the essence of an ethic grounded in intrinsic moral character rather than extrinsic ethical rules.

Cultural heritages (myth, language) over reason
A Pascale contemporary, Giovanni Batista Vico (1668–1744) also strongly opposed the prevailing reason- and science-based approach to humanity in philosophy. Vico's objection focused primarily on the exclusion of human historical and cultural heritage from such an approach. According to Vico, it was human historical and cultural heritages, rather than natural environmental features, that can provide the source for a true understanding of human experience. As the history of mankind evolves from the 'theocratic' age of gods and heroes to the 'rational' age of man, the records of such evolvement could be found in either the mythology or the languages inherent in each culture. Vico thus asserted the value of studying myths and languages in the understanding of human nature and consciousness.

Johann G. Herder (1744–1803), together with Vico, are generally considered the earliest forefathers of nineteenth-century Romanticism. Like Vico, Herder believed that language, myths and other aspects of history and culture are natural expressions of human intellect and emotions, hence they are essential for the understanding of humanity. The combined influence of Vico and Herder is not only evident in the Romanticism movement against the Age of Reason, it is also obvious in later philosophies that stress the importance of the collective cultural heritage in human experience. Among the major developments along this tradition are Wilhem Wundt's *Volkerpsychologie*, Carl Jung's notion of the collective unconscious and Rudolf Steiner's *Anthroposophy.* Specifically, Joseph Campbell's analysis of mythology for the understanding of the progression and purpose of human existence can also be seen as being within the Vico–Herder tradition.

Along with his emphasis on cultural heritages, Herder was also typical of a Romanticist in holding the feeling-over-reason view. His saying, *'I feel, so I am'* has been contrasted with Descartes' *'I think, therefore I am'* (Leahey, 1992, p.135).

Expressivism of self and freedom of subjective will and volition

Against the objective reasoning mind of Enlightenment, the sentient integrating self of Romanticism is eager to manifest and express itself. As such, Romanticism also represents the 'Expressivist Turn' in modern philosophy (Taylor, 1989). The notion of self-expressiveness originates from the idealistic and the dual-aspect Romantic philosophers. These philosophers reacted to Descartes' dualism by asserting that it is the ideational rather than the materialistic that is fundamental to reality. As such, both individual beings and nature itself are seen as alive and constantly unfolding and growing toward a state of perfection. Specifically, Leibniz believed that the *monad* (i.e., the proto or primary unit of being) 'mirrors', and hence preserves, the entire essence of nature itself. The *monad* was then considered as the core of the subjective self, which possesses the will-power to perfect as well as to express itself. This feature of self-expressiveness was best summarized by Friedrich Von Schlegel (1772–1829) in his characterization of the spirit of Romanticism. Schlegel saw Romanticism as the free expression of individual personality, free from the domination of the objective and the materialistic. The Romantic notion of the need for the intrinsic self to find outward manifestations had a profound influence over later existentialism. Existentialists believe that each individual being is marked by his/her own originality and uniqueness, and hence existence means living up to one's own authenticity.

The freedom of self-expression requires the power of the will. So, against the lifeless mind of Locke (the *tabula rasa*) which passively received incoming stimuli, the Romantic philosophers believed in an active mind with its own volition and motivating power. However, for the early Romantic philosopher Kant, will was clearly identified with reason and it was practical reason itself (Reese, 1980, p.626). Later, the notion of free will became the core of the being in the philosophy of Arthur Schopenhauer (1788–1860). Schopenhauer had been trained in the Greek tradition but was later profoundly influenced by the Eastern philosophy of Buddhism (Frost, 1962/1989). Schopenhauer's discussion of the will focused on the lifetime process of 'liberation', a key notion of Buddhism and Eastern Spiritual teachings. According to Schopenhauer, an individual's will constitutes his/her entire mental or *noumenal* reality. One's 'wilful' pursuits of instinctual desires bring about pain and suffering. As a result, one needs to liberate oneself from such predicaments. However, the liberation process itself also requires the exercise of the will. The process involves the many stages of contemplating the divine, appreciating aesthetics, renunciating desires and exercising compassion. The end of liberation is marked by the 'negation' of the individual will. Therefore, the will is responsible for both the creation and the liberation of one's suffering. As suffering and liberation feature the entirety of human existence and experience (a key thesis of Buddhism), the will then naturally takes the centre stage of the being in Schopenhauer's philosophy.

Purposefulness of existence
The philosophy of romanticism is closely related to self-expressiveness and it is also characterized by the affirmation of the purpose of existence. For most Romantic philosophers, the purpose of existence appears to accord with the ideas of the Greek philosophers. The Aristotelian notion of the *final cause* of all motions implies that the purpose of existence is to attain the final

state of perfection through the gradual unfolding of one's innate potentialities. In the case of an acorn growing into an oak tree, the process itself is one of unfolding and is always attracted and drawn towards the final state of perfection. Aristotle further referred to the ultimate final cause of all final causes as the *'unmoved mover'* (or God). The purpose of all existence is then to strive to achieve this ultimate state of perfection. In the Pythagoras–Plato–Plotinus tradition, the Plotinus' notion of *nous* denotes the individual soul, with the essence of the Divine being its nature. The purpose of existence is for the individual soul to go through the gradual process of unfolding its inner essence of perfection. The Leibnizian construct of the *monad* closely resembles the *nous* as the individual soul. For Kant, the noumenal realm of pure reason transcends sense experience and understanding. Kant's idea of the transcendental Absolute Whole (e.g., Allison, 1986; Frost, 1962/1989) denotes an all-encompassing principle of ultimate unity. Kant's notion was taken to the extreme by later Romantic philosophers. Both the subjective idealism of Fichte and the absolute idealism of Hegel presuppose an ultimate transcendental world spirit that exists independently of the individual self. The purpose of existence is for the development and unfolding of the individual spirit towards identity and unity with the essence of the divine world spirit. For Hegel, the ultimate purpose for each individual is the realization of this fundamental unity of self within the transcendent world spirit. To sum, Romantic philosophers' views of the purposefulness of life appear to be remarkably convergent. They all seem to rest upon the assumption of a final perfected state towards which all existences are drawn.

Self in contemporary philosophy

The dominant schools of contemporary philosophy include analytic philosophy in the positivistic tradition of Enlightenment and existential philosophy in the humanistic tradition of Romanticism. Analytic philosophers regard all metaphysical notions as unscientific and meaningless. The metaphysical notion of the self is therefore either rejected or neglected in analytic philosophy. However, the core theses of Romantic philosophy are still upheld by the contemporary philosophy of existentialism.

Two major shifts in contemporary philosophy have taken place during the last few decades, which have profound and far-reaching consequences for all intellectual disciplines. The shifts are 'the linguistic turn' (Smith, 1997, p.859) and the deconstructionism movement (see Popkin and Stroll, 1993). Within the positivistic and analytic paradigm, the linguistic turn came about in close association with the thoughts of Whitehead, Russell, and Wittgenstein. The deconstructionism movement has in a sense given rise to 'pluralism' and multiple forms of 'truth'. Both of these related conceptual shifts have had a dramatic influence over the notion of self.

Self in existential or humanistic philosophy

The main concern of existentialism is with the individual self, the meaning and purpose of the self's existence, the predicament of the self, as well as the self's most distinctive property, freedom of choice. For Soren Kierkegaard (1813–1855), 'truth' (or 'good') cannot be objectified as it does not exist as an external reality (as had been assumed in modern philosophy). Truth in essence is 'subjectivity' that can only be attained through each individual self's free will and choices. As such, before the choice for an enlightened existence is made, the individual self is in a state of total 'ignorance', incapable of escaping the human predicament of an anguished existence. That each individual self is born with *'angst'*, and that its transcendence could be attained through the free will of the self, are the two central themes of existential philosophy.

According to Kierkegaard, the process of transcendence through choice involves three levels of self-growth from the initial stages of the aesthetic and the ethical to the final stage of religious faith. The aesthetic level of existence is characterized by engaging fully in obtaining maximal pleasure from the finite external world. The self may enter the ethical level of existence through the realization of, and a conviction to, the ethical obligations required by relating to the world. An ethical existence thus involves a self-determination in moving away from a finite existence, fully engaging in the external reality, towards a life in the infinite eternity of the internal reality. Taylor (1989) accounts for Kierkegaard's 'ethical man' thus: *'In choosing myself, I become what I really am, a self with an infinite dimension. We choose our real selves; we become for the first time true selves. And this lifts us out of despair. Or rather, what we now despair of is the merely finite'* (p.450). Kierkegaard's solution to the anguished plight of existence lies with the final level of religious faith. This level of existence requires the choice of a personal belief and a life in the subjective certainty of faith, even though this may demand an 'irrational' suspension of beliefs at the ethical level.

While Kierkegaard placed the final solution to man's trapped existence in religious faith, other existential philosophers have emphasized the self's freedom in making personal choices. By subscribing to Kierkegaard's thesis of individual freedom in making choices but dismissing his solution through faith in God, Friedrich Nietzsche (1844–1900) has earned himself the status of a true 'humanistic' existentialist. However, Nietzsche's atheistic and nihilistic stance in declaring the death of God and in rejecting an inner source of reality has also paved the way for the development of later deconstructionism. While it is typical to trace the postmodern nihilism and the emptying or 'disappearing' of the self to Nietzsche (e.g., Smith, 1997; Zohar and Marshall, 1994), it is important to note that Nietzsche's solution to the human plight is through the individual self's 'will to power'. The individual strives towards overcoming the limits of the self by actualizing all his/her potentials. Through self-will, human beings can achieve in the future the ideal embodied in the 'Superman'. Nietzsche's superman is a fully actualized human person with an authentic will and a 'master morality' of self-affirmation (e.g., Frost, 1962/1989; Nietzsche, 1968; Reese, 1980; Smith, 1997).

The notions of the perennial and inescapable *angst* and the freedom of will and choice are the core to Heidegger and Sartre's existentialism. Both emphasize that human existence simply means 'being there' and 'being authentic'. An individual's realization that being is embraced by 'nothingness' thus forces one to choose a way of existence that is authentically one's own (e.g., Satre, 1956, 1959). Accordingly, man is but a *'noughting nought'* who wills to negate the nothingness of reality by creating an authentic way of existence for itself.

Self in analytic or positivistic philosophy

Ever since Descartes and Hume abandoned respectively the notions of the nonconscious mind and a holistic self, modern positivistic philosophers and contemporary analytic philosophers have followed that tradition. However, it is worth noting that many of them also rejected the extreme mechanistic approach to the mind and acknowledged the role of the self in the understanding of humanity. Among modern philosophers, the metaphysical philosopher Immanual Kant is a clear example. Auguste Comte (1798–1857), the founder of positivism, held the view that while reason is the key to progress, a 'religion of humanity' that brings together reason and feeling is to be the ultimate 'crown' of the positivist and empiricistic progress (Reese, 1980). The later Enlightenment philosopher, John Stuart Mill (1806–1873) also rejected the Humean atomistic view and emphasized the romanticistic notion of the development of an autonomous self.

Among contemporary positivistic philosophers, Alfred North Whitehead (1861–1947), the teacher of Bertrand Russell and co-author of *Principia Mathematica*, is well known for being the most influential defender of the metaphysical view of the mind. Although Whitehead advocated a natural philosophy, he firmly believed that the mind and human values are outside the scope of the philosophy of science and can only be understood within a metaphysical framework. Whitehead accounted for human perception in terms of two modes: 'causal efficacy' and 'presentational immediacy'. The mode of causal efficacy is characterized by time, as past experiences with any external objects always shape present perceptual experiences. The mode of presentational immediacy is characterized by space as immediate spatial contexts also contribute to present perceptual awareness. Whitehead's metaphysical propositions include the notion of the 'primordial nature of a Supreme being' or God, who is actively involved in all processes of the world. This accounts for the fact that the world never runs out of 'possibilities'. Whitehead rejects all pure mechanistic and empiricistic accounts of humanity and argues that his version of humanity is not a philosophy of science, but 'a philosophy of organism' (e.g., Frost, 1962/1989; Shimony, 1997).

As mentioned before, for Russell, the knowledge 'by acquaintance' is considered as certain whereas that 'by description' is uncertain. In other words, direct experiences or sense-data and awareness of self are certain and already known to us. As such, the self is not distinguishable from the thoughts, images and feelings of experiences (Russell, 1967). Furthermore, Russell made the distinction between two aspects of the self: one 'finite and particular' and the other, 'infinite and universal'. While the former appears to be centred around the individual self and its functioning, the latter transcends both the immediate self and space–time. This universal self is described thus:

> In thought, it rises above the life of the senses, seeking always what is general and open to all men. In desire and will, it aims simply at the good, without regarding the good as mine or yours. In feelings, it gives love to all, not to those who further the purpose of the self. Unlike the finite self, it is impartial; its impartiality leads to truth in thought, justice in action, and universal love in feeling. (cf. Taylor, 1989, p.408)

Therefore, it seems that while Russell's finite self pertains primarily to the agentic self, his notion of the infinite self is what humanistic philosophers and psychodynamic theorists refer to as the 'higher self' or 'unity self' that acts as an integrative humanistic guide.

(1) Self and the linguistic turn in positivistic philosophy
Through the works of Russell (and Whitehead) and his student Wittgenstein, the enterprise of philosophy has turned into the enterprise of language. According to Russell, natural language possesses similar sets of logic as mathematics. Russell's mathematical logic refers to the relations of propositions (e.g., if A, then B). The basic structure of linguistic propositions in natural language is similar to that of mathematical propositions. Therefore, the meaning and the nature of linguistic propositions can be analysed and clarified via the same logical process as in mathematical reasoning. Wittgenstein further argued that philosophical endeavours are simply a battle against the 'bewitchment of our intelligence' by means of language (Wittgenstein, 1953).

This philosophy-as-science-and-language theme takes a firm hold of contemporary philosophical thought in three distinguishable schools. It was initially reflected in the works of logical positivists of the Vienna Circle in the 1920s and 1930s. These Continental European philosophers and mathematicians (e.g., Carnap, Feigl, Godel, Schrodinger) worked on the 'purification' of philosophy by applying the rigour of scientific and mathematical logic to the analysis of philosophical problems. Their goals were twofold: getting rid of the metaphysical elements in philosophy and establishing philosophy as a study of the 'logic of science'.

Following the logical positivists, the philosophy-as-language theme continued in the works of the British Oxbridge scholars known as natural or ordinary language philosophers (e.g., Austin, Hare). These philosophers believed that philosophical problems cannot be tackled successfully unless the tool (i.e., linguistic statements and utterances) of solving such problems is properly understood. Therefore, their work centred on detailed empirical analysis of sentences and utterances in natural language so as to discover their true meanings and functions in communication. The philosophy as logic-of-science theme with a focus on language is also found in the works of the present-day positivistic and analytic philosophers outside Europe such as Quine, Davidson, Churchland, Rorty and Dennett. The earlier European influence (philosophy as science and language), coupled with the prevailing intellectual emphasis in North America on pragmatism and functionalism, has led many of these philosophers to subscribe to an eliminative reductionist approach to the study of human mind and consciousness.

The linguistic turn has had a profound impact on the notion of self. Self in this entire framework is reduced to a 'linguistic game' played in the public or social arena (Wittgenstein). Self as a holistic entity certainly does not exist *within* the individual person for Wittgenstein, as linguistic games can only have meaning when members of a social or communal group share them. As such, there can be no 'private speech'. Dennett (1978, 1983, 1991) follows the positivistic emphasis on language and sees the self as 'the centre of narrative gravity', and it is this self that has 'access' to consciousness. Dennett accounts for the holistic nature of the self in connectionist terms. He argues that a sense of unity of a dynamic system (the brain as modules or neural nets) comes about naturally as each and every one of its component bits does its own thing. Dennett (1983) describes the holistic functioning of consciousness in terms of functional modularity:

> break the whole (processing) system down into subsystems, little homunculi. Each one is a specialist, each one does a little bit of the work. Out of their cooperative endeavors emerge the whole activities of the whole system ... The subsystems don't individually reproduce the talents of the whole. (p.78)

As such, the notion self is not completely rejected, rather, it is seen as an emergent property of the dynamics of the neural networks. Dennett himself admits that the self so defined is but another form of a metaphysical concept: a concept that is 'unscientifically mentalistic'.

Self in postmodern philosophy: the deconstructionist turn

Associated with the turn towards a focus on science and language, the philosophical enterprise took on another major shift: from one that aims to find the meaning of existence to one that centres on deconstructing such aims. Popkin and Stroll (1993) have put it this way:

> The search for ultimate meaning that has been the central feature of Western philosophy since its beginnings is no longer viable. From Descartes to Husserl and Heidegger, the search has become more and more centered in subjectivity, without reaching ultimate meaning or ultimate certitude. What one can now do is 'deconstruct' philosophy ... (p.313)

Partly due to the 'failings' of the existential and humanistic philosophers' endeavours to 'understand' the meaning of existence, the shift to deconstructionism is also partly the result of the general philosophy as-science-and-language movement. The main goal of science concerns finding 'causal explanations' of observed events or behaviour. The focus is on causal explanations rather than 'understanding meanings'. It was in that larger context of the goal of science that philosophers (especially those of the natural language school) turned their attention to the analysis of linguistic behaviour and language itself in order to 'explain' the functions of utterances and statements.

The linguistic turn naturally leads to the deconstruction of the traditional and grander goal of philosophy. Deconstructionism has been mostly associated with the theory of Jacques Derrida (1978). Recently, Smith (1997) has clearly set out the relationship between the linguistic turn and Derrida's work. Smith argued that since the end of the 1970s, there have been general intellectual attempts to reanalyse all subjects in human sciences (e.g., the self, the family, cultural values, history, art) from the perspective of 'the self-referential character of language'. According to Smith, these attempts carry the underlying assumption that:

> language ... signifies yet more language, not some outside world that can be specified apart from language. Derrida's writings sustained this argument through the method of deconstruction, a dazzling display of how every attempt to transcend language only rephrases language. (Smith, 1997, p.859)

The most profound influence of deconstructionism over the conceptualization of the self and personhood can perhaps be see in the works of the French psychoanalyst Jacques Lacan (Bowie, 1991). According to Lacan, the structure of the self can be revealed through the linguistic system. Lacan's analysis of the self focuses on the unconscious which he sees as a 'de-centred' or externalized 'object of analysis'. The self or the unconscious is not the active agent that analyses; instead, it is the object of the analysis. Language is the tool that can be used in the analysis of this external object: the unconscious or the self.

The implication of Lacan's work for the conceptualization of the self is twofold: first, the self that is traditionally seen as an active cognitive agent and humanistic guide, is now *'something signified by particular self-reflective uses of language'* or a *'form of words'* (Smith, 1997, p.862). This self-as-words thesis reflects Wittgenstein's influence and is later mirrored in Dennett's view of self as the 'centre of linguistic gravity'. Second, the self is now cast out from the interior intrapersonal realm to the exterior social and interpersonal domain. Therefore, the exteriorization of a traditional inner self can be seen as yet another consequence of the deconstructionist movement in postmodern philosophy.

The foregoing analysis of the self in the light of the history within philosophy suggests an 'inner-to-outer' (or 'internal-to-external', 'intrinsic-to-extrinsic) shift in its conceptualization. This same shift is also evident from both the surveys of the psychological literature and the socio-political and cultural-historical theories of the self. Chapter 5 presents these surveys that would further illuminate the meaning of selfhood in contemporary times.

4
Contemporary Models of 'Consciousness'

Given that the empirical approaches to consciousness have focused almost exclusively on the nonqualia aspect of consciousness, with but a few recent exceptions, virtually all existing models of consciousness within the fields of cognitive science and neuroscience pertain to the nonqualia mind. However, those recent exceptions have attempted to account for qualia within the empirical framework of functionalism by taking either an information-processing or a neural-network approach. These models are reviewed next.

NEUROCOGNITIVE MODELS OF CONSCIOUSNESS RELEVANT TO QUALIA

In this section, the cognitive information-processing models of consciousness are reviewed first. Constraints of the information-processing approach are then identified. Following this, the neurophysiological approach to consciousness and its constraints are reviewed. Recent applications of quantum and chaos notions to consciousness research are also examined.

Cognitive models of consciousness

In cognitive science, models of consciousness have aimed to explain consciousness by locating or mapping various experiences onto the 'architectural structure' or 'contents' of the information flow within an information-processing system. This approach is typically based on the premise that 'the computer is the last metaphor for the mind' (Johnson-Laird, 1988, p.367) which suggests that a comprehensive model of consciousness is only possible in information-processing and computational terms. Hence to understand consciousness in its entirety, what needs to be done is to unveil the step-by-step procedures or algorithms that the brain, as the ultimate computer, obeys in carrying out its computational functions.

While early processing models conceptualized consciousness as a product of multi-level serial or sequential analyses, recent computational models depict conscious experience as a result of parallel distributed analyses taking place simultaneously at various loci in the brain. This assumption of a parallel distributed mode of processing is consistent with, and hence reflects, the connectionist or neural net dynamics at the micro neuronal level of information processing.

However, the majority of these information-processing models of consciousness have been predominantly concerned with cognitive and nonqualia aspects of consciousness such as perceptual awareness or awareness of other functional processing. Only a few recent ones have explicitly aimed to account for a wider range of consciousness by including specific sets of qualia and unconscious aspects. In the following sections, several of these recent models which have significant implications for qualia and the unconscious are briefly reviewed. The common underlying problems that constrain such models in providing a satisfactory account for these aspects of consciousness are then identified.

Shallice's (1988) model:
a 'coherent pattern of shared control'
In the process of ascertaining the most plausible presumption about consciousness upon which to build a general processing theory, Shallice started by exploring first the feasibility of assuming consciousness as 'one' fundamental phenomenological concept. Resting on this assumption, he then explored

whether there exists a correspondence between different types of conscious experiences and the properties of the information-processing system. To do so, Shallice constructed a list of the different types or 'properties' of consciousness. These properties can be broadly categorized into (a) the 'conscious' (aware) experiences most typically understood as exemplars of consciousness, (b) qualia-obvious conscious experiences such as 'the state of knowing' or 'the state of doubt', and (c) the 'cognitive unconscious' phenomena which were discovered in cognitive and neuropsychological research, such as 'blindsight' (Weiskrantz, 1986) and 'subliminal' perception under masking (Marcel, 1983). Shallice thus considers both the qualia-obvious and cognitive unconscious experiences as the *explanada* of consciousness.

Shallice argued that, if consciousness is conceptualized as one uniformed experience, it may not be possible to find a single correspondence or mapping between conscious experiences and the processing system. Having reached the conclusion, Shallice proposed two alternative possible solutions for achieving a satisfactory model of consciousness. One possibility would require that consciousness be conceptualized as a multifaceted construct consisting of a number of 'sub varieties', with each modelled as operating through separate processing mechanisms. The other possibility would require that the information-processing system be conceptualized as a more complicated network of multiple, rather than one single, high-level central processor. Specifically, either model would posit the existence of these features: (1) a number of high-level processors, (2) a large number of low-level processors, and (3) an overall coherent pattern of control.

The high-level processors include a Contention scheduling processor (for selection of mental schema or performing scripts), a Supervisory system (for modulating and assisting operations of contention scheduling), and a number of subsidiary processors such as the language and the episodic memory processor. Each of these high-level processors had access to, and control over, a large set of other processors. In contrast, each of the large number of low-level processors had access to only a limited number of other fellow processors. In addition, an overall coherent pattern of control also exists for the activation and inhibition of the operations of all subsystems. According to Shallice, this 'coherent shared control' may be the basis for consciousness. The 'content' of consciousness then corresponds to the 'information flow' between the control subsystems and all the rest of the cognitive system.

Johnson-Laird's (1983, 1988) computational model: a 'self-aware' top-level operating system

While Shallice proposed a multiple-top-level-control model, Johnson-Laird persisted with a single-top-level-control model. However, for this to work, one precondition would have to be met: that this top-level operating system would have to have the potential for self-awareness. Johnson-Laird's list of the *explananda* of consciousness consists of four 'problems' of consciousness: (1) the problem of *awareness* (dealing with the conscious–unconscious divide), (2) the problem of *control* (to do with emotion or will), (3) the problem of *self-awareness* (dealing with the holistic and the recursive nature of self-referenced awareness), and (4) that of *intention* (dealing with goal-directed mental representations). All these are related to the key problems associated with qualitative conscious experiences. Johnson-Laird's computational model has two key assumptions about the 'computational architecture of the mind'. First, the brain constitutes a hierarchy of parallel information processors with the highest level processor, the *operating system*, being the 'source' of conscious experiences. Second, this top information processor (the operating system) has its own unique set of operations different from all lower-level processors. Chief of all its operations are its accessibility to a model operational programme of itself and its capacity of recursively embedding operational subprogrammes within subprogrammes. According to Johnson-Laird, it is this top operating system's potential capacity for 'self-awareness' that gives rise to consciousness. Self-awareness depends on a recursive embedding of subprogrammes containing the 'self', which are accessible 'in parallel' to the central operating system.

The idea that the top-level controlling processor needs to be self-aware or to be in a state of 'the mind in control of the mind' has become a necessary condition for most other computational models. This is also obvious in Umilta's (1988) model which assumes that consciousness 'utilizes' attention to exert its functions in controlling cognitive processing towards an 'intended goal', however, 'self-awareness' has to be a necessary condition for the top control processor to be fully operational.

Baars' global-workspace model (1988; 1997): a 'theatre metaphor' for conscious experience

Baars constructed the global-workspace model of consciousness explicitly around a theatre metaphor. The contents of conscious experience or awareness are likened to the players on the lit-up stage. These players play out the scenes under the direction of several behind-the-scenes executive operators. The audience of the play, outside the spotlight, silently watches the play and receives the messages conveyed in the play. Specifically, the global workspace or the theatre model of consciousness has several key features. First, the behind-the-scenes operators including the 'director' (i.e., the observer self) and the contextual operators (e.g., elements of the cognitive unconscious). The director performs executive functions and the contextual operators set the context of the conscious experience. Second, the unconscious 'audience' constitutes 'a vast array of intelligent, unconscious mechanisms', which include automatic routines (e.g., eye movements) and semantic memory network (e.g., lexicon, beliefs of world or of self). Third, the working memory serves to receive conscious input, to control inner speech and to utilize mental image. Fourth, the 'contents' of experience compete among themselves for access to the lit-up part of the stage (attention or awareness). These contents include ideas (e.g., imagined idea, intuitions) and inputs from outer senses and inner senses (e.g., visual image or imagined feelings).

The notions of the cognitive unconscious and the observer self in Baars' model deserve further attention. Both serve as behind-the-scene operators, with elements in the cognitive unconscious as contextual operators and the observer self as the executive director of the entire play. Regarding the cognitive unconscious, its status appears to be more central in the theatre models than in other computational models. However, it is only one aspect of the unconscious that is considered legitimate in the theatre model: the cognitive unconscious or the causal agentic aspect of the unconscious mind.

Similarly, the notion of the self has also been given a more central focus in the Baars model. Here, the observer self acts as the chief director that gives the overall unifying context to conscious experience. Without the director self, the play itself would lose its overall coherence and integration. However, Baars has specifically pointed out that as the behind-the-scene director of consciousness, the self is different from the common usage of the term in its holistic sense (as *psyche*, both a cognitive agent and a humanistic guide). Instead, the director self is a 'decomposed' subset of the holistic self which Baars referred to as a collection of 'cognitive or brain entities' (p.143). In this sense, the self that Baars stresses in this model pertains primarily to its role as a cognitive agent.

However, focusing specifically on the notion of subjectivity (the subjective sense of self), Baars (1996) went further in emphasizing the necessary role of the self in understanding consciousness. He advocated a resurrection of the notion of the observing self by analysing and identifying the close links between consciousness and subjectivity (Baars used the term to mean 'sense of self' or 'selfhood'). Baars argues that the two notions are intimately linked because (1) consciousness is 'generally accompanied by' a subjective sense of self, (2) the qualitative and non-qualitative (cognitive) aspects of conscious experience 'interpenetrate' each other, (3) there is causal interaction between these two aspects of consciousness, (4) the contents of consciousness and a sense of self appear to be orthogonal constructs which always coexist, although they do not always covary, (5) either consciousness or the self is generally seen as 'that to which I have access'. Based on this evidence of close links between consciousness and self, Baars asked the readers to consult his/her own experience to confirm the links:

> But is it real consciousness, with real subjectivity? What else would it be? A clever imitation? Nature is not in the habit of creating two mirror-image phenomena, one for real functioning, the other just for a private show. The 'easy' and 'hard' parts of mental functioning are merely two different aspects of the same thing. (p.215)

Here, Baars identifies the agentic or cognitive aspects of consciousness with subjectivity (self) and considers the two as the dual aspects of the same phenomenon.

Constraints of the cognitive approach to consciousness and qualia

Although these recent models have aimed at embracing many of the 'cognitive unconscious' experiences as well as qualia-obvious experiences such as free will or intention, they are only concerned with the 'functional' or 'relational' aspects of such experiences in that these experiences were treated as 'cognitive agents': free will as a motivating agent and intention as a goal-directed planning agent. As such, the subjective first-personal aspects of these qualia-related conscious experiences have not been addressed. Indeed, Umilta (1988) may have had these subjective aspects in mind when commenting that, *'Whereas other aspects of consciousness may be epiphenomenal, the specific conscious experience that accompanies control is not epiphenomenal and has very important effects on human information processing*' (p.334). So it seems that so long as the controlling aspects of consciousness are the focus of a model of consciousness (as has to be the case within a functional framework), the first-personal aspects are excluded, by definition and necessity, or else treated as non-causal epiphenomena.

This exclusion was also explicit in Shallice's work. On the one hand, Shallice's (1988) model aimed to embrace all varieties of conscious experience in '... *its fundamental sense, namely implying either "feels" or "is aware"*...' (p.310). In his list of the dealt properties of consciousness, some qualia properties such as 'feelings', 'the state of knowing' or 'the state of doubt' were included. But on the other hand, Shallice wrote, '... *a concept like "qualia", which is itself subject to extensive philosophical debate ... will be ignored*' (p.311). Therefore, despite the aim of explaining consciousness in its fundamental and all-embracing sense, Shallice's model did not address the first-personal or intrinsic qualia aspects of consciousness. Again, this can be seen in the light of the Umilta comment, which pinpoints one key problem of the functionalistic approach to consciousness: only those properties of conscious experiences that can be cast in a functional sense as controlling agents of behaviour, are counted as *explananda* of any model of consciousness. Other properties of conscious experiences in their first-personal, non-relational sense (i.e., qualia) are not acknowledged within that framework.

Furthermore, to account for these limited 'cognitive aspects' of qualia-obvious experiences and the 'cognitive unconscious', it has become necessary for these top-down-central-processor models to carry the presumption that the central processor has to have the potential capability of being aware of itself. It is noted that this sense of self-awareness simply involves a reflexive self-referencing capacity, which is much narrower in scope than what the notion of self-awareness typically entails. The notion of 'self' is also needed for the theatre models. In the context of the Baars model, the 'self' is a decomposed subset of the commonly-understood holistic self (the cognitive or brain entities), although as already mentioned, Baars (1996) separately concludes that consciousness and self are aspects of the 'same thing'. Regardless of the proportion of the holistic self that is needed, the fact remains that a metaphysical notion of 'the ghost in the machine' or 'the homunculus' is after all indispensable for a materialistic and functional account of consciousness.

In addition to such a conceptual constraint imposed by the notions of the unconscious and self, the cognitive or information-processing approach to consciousness is further constrained by its methodology. Specifically, the cognitive approach to consciousness is paradoxically dependent on subjective 'introspective' reporting, or accounts of conscious experience. The subjective measurement which features in cognitive research differs from the objective recording of neuronal activities or the direct observation of cortical activation patterns in neurophysiological approaches to consciousness. Here, Shallice's (1988) reference to the 'ghost in the machine' problem of the cognitive approach is relevant. He conceded that:

> Clearly the fields must remain intellectually incomplete unless they can explain how experiential terms like 'see', 'remember', 'guess' 'dream', 'image', and so on are understood and used by the entity whose behaviour is being explained through mechanistic models. (pp.307–8)

A related methodological constraint of the cognitive approach to consciousness concerns its inability to capture the 'continuity' or 'the flow' of consciousness (both nonqualia and qualia) by the discrete measurements (or 'snapshots') taken in the laboratory. Shallice (1993) clearly identified the problem as, *'when one is "in doubt" ... or "miserable" it seems inappropriate to view the experience as corresponding to the state of the cognitive system over a few hundred milliseconds'* (p.326). A similar criticism has been made by others (e.g., Carver and Scheier, 1998; Dennett and Kinsbourne, 1992, Hardcastle, 1995).

To sum up, it appears that for the cognitive computational models to work well in modelling consciousness, several allowances would have to be made. Conceptually, those top-down models would have to allow for the inclusion of aspects of the notion self (ghost, homunculus). Specifically, for it to account for qualitative aspects of consciousness, the functional models would have to anchor themselves on the notion of a 'self-aware self' (e.g., Johnson-Laird, 1988; Oatley, 1988; Umilta, 1988). Even then, some cognitive scientists hold the view that qualia may well be beyond the reach of such a functional and pure-scientific paradigm (e.g., Bisiach, 1988; Oatley, 1988). Methodologically, the cognitive approach would need the input of neurophysiological data in order to model consciousness as a continual, coherent and integral phenomenon (e.g., Baars, 1997; Hardcastle, 1995; Norman and Shallice, 1988).

Neurophysiological approach to consciousness

Research in neuroscience adopts a micro-analytic approach in exploring the fundamental neurophysiological mechanism associated with consciousness. During the last decade or so, neurophysiological studies of consciousness have benefited greatly from major breakthroughs in theory and method. Conceptually, two notions of system dynamics have been applied to neuronal activities: 'parallel distributed processing' (Rumelhart et al., 1986) and 'chaos-coherence' in neuronal oscillations (e.g., Freeman, 1987, 1994; Hardcastle, 1995; Hameroff and Penrose, 1996). Technologically, the developments of multiple-simultaneous single-cell-unit recordings, the multi-channel EEG recordings, as well as the various scanning techniques (PET, CAT and MRI) have helped in recording neuronal activity patterns in larger network units and neural assemblies.

There are at least two related questions pertaining to the neurophysiological mechanisms underlying conscious experience. First, how are lower-level neuronal activities combined in giving rise to a sense of integrated conscious experience? And second, where in the brain do neural activities take place which correspond to various features of a conscious experience? While the two questions are intimately related, the former focuses on the issue of 'binding' together various neural activities occurring at different cerebral loci in producing a coherent conscious experience. In contrast, the latter question centres more around 'locating' or 'mapping' specific neural assemblies or systems associated with each conscious experience.

The 'binding' problem
Recent research literature relating to both issues of the locating and binding of conscious experience derives much inspiration from the ground-breaking finding that all neurones activated by the same stimulus in the perceptual field co-operatively synchronize their firings by exhibiting a 'phase locked' oscillatory pattern at a frequency within the 'gamma range' with an average around 40 Hz (times/sec). This synchronized neural firing pattern is observed across all neural nets or neural assemblies sharing the same receptive perceptual field, even though these neural groups are located in distinctively different cortical areas. For instance, the 40 Hz synchronized firing was evident in the olfactory cortical systems in cats, and rats (e.g., Adrian, 1942; Freeman et al., 1988), in the visual and auditory cortices in cats and rabbits (e.g., Basar et al., 1987). Using magnetic field tomography, such synchronized neural oscillations have also been observed in human primary motor and sensory cortices (see Hardcastle, 1995 for a review).

Many neuroscientists believe that such correlated oscillations are the underlying neural mechanism for binding together different areas of cortical activation into one integrated conscious experience (e.g., Eckhorn et al., 1988; Edelman, 1989; Llinas and Ribary, 1992). Building upon the 40-Hz correlated oscillation found in the visual cortical system in cats, Crick and Koch (1990) suggest that this oscillatory pattern forms the neural correlate of visual awareness and consciousness in their paper 'Towards a neurophysiological theory of consciousness'. More specifically, Crick and Koch focused on visual perception and working memory and explored the way different aspects of perceptual information (e.g., location or shape) are combined into an integral whole in memory. It was found that while the neural representations of these different aspects of a stimulus are separate, neurons belonging to the same representations however share a common frequency (the Gamma range between 35 and 75 Hz) in their oscillations in the visual cortex and related areas. This common-frequency oscillation then allows the different aspects of the neural representations to be bound together for further processing and storage in memory. Crick and Koch argued that the common-frequency oscillations may be the fundamental neurophysiological mechanism for psychological functions such as perception and memory.

However, this 'solution' to the binding problem is still a subject of some controversy. There are three sources of criticism. First, experimental data have shown that synchronized oscillations can be present in a wide range of unrelated mental activities; they can also be absent from cells having similar receptive perceptual fields (see Tovee, 1998). Because of these inconsistencies, Hardcastle (1995, p.209) argues that such coherent oscillations may be the necessary, but not sufficient, condition for feature binding.

Second, even though it is generally agreed that 40 Hz synchronized firing is involved in the binding process, the question remains as to whether binding for a unified conscious experience 'requires' single-cell-level activities. One reason for questioning the importance of binding at the single cell level pertains to the problem with generalizing the coherent activities observed from a relatively small proportion of neurones to the entire neural assemblies having the same perceptual fields. As Hardcastle (1995) noted, there are 'tens of thousands of cells in each visual column' (p.116) and that the currently available recording techniques can only capture 'about ten percent of the cells in any column' (p.122).

Third, recent research into the speed of information processing in visual cortices suggests that there is a high probability of chance synchrony. According to Tovee (1998, also Golledge et al., 1996), the probability of coincident firing for two neurons discharging with an average of 40 Hz is around 0.96 within 600msec. This and related findings have cast doubt on the temporal binding hypothesis (e.g., Engel et al., 1997). In this context, temporal oscillatory synchrony may either be an artifact or a partial solution to the binding problem (for a review, see Tovee, 1998).

Because of these problems, several theorists have argued for conceptualizing the binding process at a higher level of network systems (e.g., Freeman and Baird, 1987). According to Tovee (1998), binding (of visual features) may be closely related to the fact that information is processed in a 'pyramidal' or convergent fashion. Given the anatomical evidence for a 'considerable reconvergence of information' in the higher cortical areas, *coherent representations of objects could plausibly be brought about by physical convergence of the information at higher levels of the system*' (p.135). Independently, Hardcastle (1995) also advocates a system-level solution to feature binding, 'If entire cortical regions are considered to be one network system acting as a single resonating unit, then single-cell oscillations as a vehicle for separately uniting disparate feature-bits with previous memories ... would be unnecessary. Instead, a higher level statistical aggregate of firing neurones would be all that is needed ...' (p.130).

This systemic view to the binding problem is discussed further, later in this chapter, in the context of the application of chaos theory to neurobiological modelling of consciousness.

Mapping or locating conscious experience

Regarding the issue of mapping or locating consciousness, there appear to be three proposals concerning the exact location of conscious experience. One view was put forward by Crick in his book (1994), *The astonishing hypothesis: the scientific search for the soul*. After reviewing relevant neurophysiological evidence on the visual perceptual systems, Crick postulated that each level of visual processing is coordinated by a single region in the thalamus. The thalamus, located immediately below the cerebral cortex and above the core areas of the brain stem, is the central relay station of the brain. The two symmetrical thalami in each cerebral hemisphere have in them the major sensory and motor nerve tracks that carry input information for processing in the cortices and output information for related motor actions. Crick postulated that through the thalamus-cortex connections, there exists a thalamo-cortico-thalamic reverberatory circuit which essentially 'embodies' very short-term memory. Crick argues that because conscious awareness involves such short-term memory, an understanding of the nature of consciousness would require more research into the neural psychological processes associated with the thalamus-cortex reverberatory system.

The thalamus is also considered the seat of awareness and conscious experience by Baars (1997; also Baars and Newman, 1994). However, based on a wide range of neurological evidence from brain damaged patients, EEG recordings and PET scans, Baars (1997) argues that the reticular formation, located about an inch below the thalamus in the core of the brainstem, together with the intralamina nuclei or the ILN cells inside each thalamus are the exact location for waking consciousness. Also extending from the idea that the 40 Hz synchronized neural firing is the basis for binding similar but separately located neural responses into a coherent conscious experience, Baars postulates that the ILN of the thalamus and the reticular nuclei work together in generating the coordinated

40 Hz oscillations for binding. These postulates form the neurophysiological basis for Baars' theatre or global workspace model of consciousness discussed earlier.

Apart from the thalamus and reticular formation, the hippocampus has been considered by other neuroscientists as the location for conscious experience. As the hippocampus is a higher-order structure at the top-level of the hierarchy in sensory processing, it is concerned with the temporary store (in accessible form) of long-term memory. It has been found (Squire and Zola-Morgan, 1991) that such a memory system in monkeys consists of a reciprocal input loop from various cortical areas through the perihinal and parahippocampal cortices, via the entorhinal cortex into the hippocampus. This neural pathway appears to be a 'reentrant loop' which, according to the Nobel Prize winner Gerald Edelman (1989; 1992), involves neural circuits going back and forth until the necessary threshold of conscious activity is reached. Edelman argues that such a reentrant oscillatory loop resembles or corresponds to a conscious experience. More specifically, this 'higher-order consciousness model' that Edelman proposed is an attempt to account for the origin of higher-order consciousness including the concept of self. By mapping various psychological or functional states of consciousness onto corresponding neurophysiological loci centring around the hippocampus, the model postulates that incoming perceptual information interacts with current internal states of the self, as well as relevant 'value-category' memory from previous experiences, in giving rise to 'primary consciousness'.

A similar line of reasoning which also results in locating conscious experience in the hippocampus is found in Hardcastle (1995). However, central to Hardcastle's reasoning is another notion: 'chaos' in complex changing or dynamic systems. Following Freeman's application of chaos theory to the changing pattern of EEG recordings of neural activation (e.g., Freeman, 1987; 1994), Hardcastle also argues that the oscillatory patterns that neural assemblies display over time can be conceptualized as being the 'computation' of the neural system. In this context, consciousness is seen as 'system-dynamic oscillations'. This feature of Hardcastle's model will be discussed later in relation to recent applications of quantum physics to neurophysiological activation corresponding to conscious experience.

Regardless of the basis of the conceptual framework, consciousness is located in the hippocampus. Hardcastle argues that there is no reason to distinguish conscious perceptions from the use of explicit semantic memory (SE system) in interpreting input sense data (either from external senses or internally generated mental images). This is based on existing neurophysiological evidence showing that (1) 40 Hz oscillations were largest in the hippocampal areas in which the p3 waveform was also most pronounced, (2) activation of the SE memory system depends largely on the hippocampus, and (3) the p3 wave is connected to the activation of the SE memory system. Given these neurophysiological links among the locations of the 40 Hz oscillations and the p3 waveforms, and the activation of the SE system, consciousness, according to Hardcastle, is just the activation of the SE system, which depends primarily on the hippocampus region.

Constraints of the neurophysiological approach to consciousness and qualia

The main concern of neurophysiological research is almost exclusively about the psychological or functional aspect of consciousness (nonqualia), rather than the phenomenal, intrinsic or experiential aspect of consciousness (qualia). For instance, Crick's (1994) 'astonishing hypothesis' of consciousness was his answer to a *'scientific search for the soul'*. Taking a radical reductivistic position, the astonishing hypothesis contends that *'all aspects of the brain's behaviour are due to the activities of neurones'*, and that there is no homunculus or a 'separate "I" ', or a 'soul' inside the brain machine. In conclusion, Crick also speculates on the brain seat for free will, which together with intentionality, beliefs, or emotion form the core of the recent mind–mind qualia debate. Based on data from brain injury and the 'alien-hand' syndrome related to one's will-power in controlling motor behaviour, Crick (1994) argues that free will is 'located in or near the anterior cingulate sulcus' (p.268).

However, it needs to be noted that Crick also acknowledges that throughout the discussion of the hypothesis, no mention was made about *'the most puzzling problem of all ... qualia ... except to brush it to one side and hope for the best ...'* (p.256). And while rejecting conventional religious views of the soul by advocating a purely scientific search for it, Crick nonetheless admits that *'It is certainly possible that there may be aspects of consciousness, such as qualia, that science will not be able to explain. We have learned to live with such limitations in the past ... and we may have to live with them again'* (p.258).

Koch, Crick's co-worker on the theory of the 40 Hz oscillation as neural mechanism for binding, holds a similar view. Given that such common-frequency oscillations are responsible for the binding of different informations into an integrated whole that gives rise to psychological and functional consciousness (e.g., visual perception), it is logical to ask whether the same neurophysiological mechanism also underlies subjective or phenomenal consciousness. However, Koch (cited in Chalmers, 1996, p.116) maintains that their theory applies to functional consciousness and that it would be a 'huge jump' to extend a materialistic- or matter-level explanation to account for intrinsic phenomenal states such as feelings and emotions. He also speculated that such subjective phenomenal states (or qualia) 'may not have a scientific solution'.

Similarly, Edelman's (1989; 1992) higher-level model is also one of psychological or functional consciousness, even though it aims at accounting for the notion of self. As far as phenomenal or subjective experiential consciousness is concerned, Edelman specifically pointed out that the model was in fact built with the implicit assumption that qualia exist in human beings. It is through individuals' reporting of such subjectively experienced qualia that a scientific investigation of consciousness is made possible. Edelman (1992) writes: '*it is sensible to assume that, just as in ourselves, qualia exist in other conscious human beings, whether they are considered as scientific observers or as subjects ...*' (p.115). Therefore, while providing a neurophysiological account for functional consciousness, Edelman's model does not explain the phenomenal, intrinsic or experiential aspect of consciousness, even though its implicit assumption is that qualia exist.

Hardcastle went a step further by including subjective first-personal conscious experiences as an integral part of her theory of consciousness. Taking a naturalistic stance, Hardcastle draws an analogy between qualia and the construct 'time'. She argues that even though time, as a natural temporary state, is not entirely 'third-personal' or objective, in the sense that it is frame or context relative, the notion 'time' can still be accounted for in a third-personal and objective language, as is the case in Einstein's theory. Likewise, even though aspects of qualitative experience may be first-personal and inaccessible from a third-person perspective, it is still possible for objective science to capture such subjective experience. Hardcastle (1995) writes:

> Theoretically, we could use these third person accounts and our knowledge of what it is like to have qualitative experiences to 'derive' what other experiences must be like by putting out brains in similar configurations. A combination of third person descriptions and ostension seems to be all we need .... (p.18)

Her 'SE model' of consciousness described before thus reduces all conscious experience, including the 'first-personal' ones, to the neuronal level. However, Hardcastle did acknowledge that not all our common notions of consciousness (e.g., motives) can be decomposed in the physical system, and that her theory does not account for 'some well respected facts about conscious experience' such as individual differences among qualia (p.193).

While most neuroscientists take the reductionist view of consciousness and hence its qualitative aspects, others consider consciousness as a higher-order property that emerges from lower-level neural activities. The two Nobel Prize laureates Roger Sperry and Sir John Eccles seem to be holding such a view. Based on his work on the split-brain patients, Sperry (1977, 1992) proposed the non-reductive 'emergence' view of consciousness and argued that consciousness emerges as a result of the complex interactions among lower-level neuronal or brain activities. The subjective properties of consciousness, or qualia, as emergent properties, also play a causal role of the highest-level central controller. Because consciousness is an emergent property, it is not to be seen as an epiphenomenon, or other insignificant correlate of brain processes; nor it is to be reduced to or identified with those lower-level neural events which give rise to it in the first place. Instead, Sperry (1977) considered consciousness as a dynamic emergent property of brain activity and as an *'active integral part of the cerebral process itself, exerting potent causal effects in the interplay of cerebral operations ... the subjective properties seen to exert control over the biophysical and chemical activities at subordinate levels'* (p.117).

Sir John Eccles is known for his proposal of a 'non-physical consciousness' in 'filling in' the causal gaps in physical or brain processes. Taking a dualistic position, Eccles advocated putting qualia 'out of the neuronal circuits' and argued that a 'divine providence' operates over and above the matter-level: the neuronal activities (e.g., Eccles, 1989). Despite the many criticisms towards the dualistic nature of the argument, Eccles' emergent position is consistent with the application of quantum physics to consciousness. This feature of the theory will be discussed later in this chapter.

Therefore, it seems that neuroscientists hold diverse views regarding the existence of qualia. While the micro-level postulates of the neurophysiological approach are capable of explaining psychological or functional aspects of consciousness, they are, with the cognitive processing models, inadequate in accounting for the subjective qualitative aspects of consciousness.

QUANTUM PHYSICS AND CHAOS THEORY IN NEUROPHYSIOLOGICAL RESEARCH OF CONSCIOUSNESS

Recent neurophysiological approaches to consciousness have appealed to quantum physics as well as chaos theory. The rationale for such an appeal seems apparent. The functional units of the nervous system, the neurons, are simply cells which conduct nerve impulses in the form of electric signals. Living cells are composed of various types of molecules which in turn are made up of atoms. As quantum physics describes the micro-level behaviour of atomic and subatomic particles, it seems to be a logical starting point for a fundamental understanding of neuronal activities. At a larger scale, quantum physics also explains the macro-level state of coherence; it may therefore be useful in accounting for the large-scale overall unity associated with conscious experience.

Chaos theory refers to a study, in both qualitative and quantitative terms, of complex aperiodical behaviour in deterministic non-linear systems. Given that the brain can be seen as a multi-levelled dynamic system, the chaos notions may also be useful in the understanding of its activities at both the micro-level individual neurones and the macro-level cortical systems. In the context of the neurophysiology of consciousness, the appeal to quantum physics or chaos theory thus carries a larger implication for unifying the dynamic processes underlying mind and matter.

Appeal to quantum physics

Before discussing the application of quantum notions to consciousness, it becomes necessary to briefly sketch the key features of quantum physics that are relevant to such an application.

The term quantum physics originates from Max Planck's theory that all forms of energy (heat, sound or light) are radiated and exist as small separate and discrete units rather than as a continuous and inseparable entity. These discrete units are termed quanta (from the Latin word 'how much'). The theory also posits that any change in energy state can only be described by a discrete unit of value with no possible value in between such basic units. The energy state within the quantum realm thus changes in non-continuous quantum 'leaps'. Planck's theory was applied by Einstein to the behaviour of light. He proved that light also travels and exists in discrete units (photons). Independently, Bohr also proved Planck's theory in the realm of matter and atoms by demonstrating that, in atoms, energy is released or absorbed through electrons jumping from one orbit to another around the atom's nucleus.

The structures of quantum particles aside, two key issues of quantum mechanics are directly relevant to the application of quantum notions to neuronal activities in the brain: The first concerns the behaviour of individual particles and the predictability of its trajectory. The second issue concerns the relationship between individual quantum particles and the interactive pattern among them.

Behaviour of individual quantum particles
The behaviour of each individual particle can be described in terms of several dimensions including its *position*, *momentum* (the particle's motion which depends on its mass and velocity) or *spin* (i.e., the particle's intrinsic angular rotation along three axes of space). The measurement of these various dimensions

pertains to the quantum measurement problem. Central to this problem are the *Schrodinger equation* for the quantum wave function, *the collapse postulate*, and Heisenberg's *uncertainty principle* (for a review of the quantum measurement problem, see Bell, 1988; Casti, 1990; Everett, 1973).

According to the widely accepted Copenhagen interpretation of quantum mechanics, the exact position or movement of an individual particle cannot be predicted with complete certainty by any physical equations. The equations can however determine the *probability* of finding the moving particle within a unit space. In making such a probabilistic prediction for an experiment designed to measure, for instance, a particle's position, the experimenter needs to find out the 'wave function' (i.e., a mathematical quantity indicative of probability) for this specific experimental condition by solving the Schrodinger equation. This equation is a linear differential equation which determines the dynamics of a system evolving with time. The Schrodinger equation thus gives a probabilistic estimate of the outcome of the actual measurement in the experiment, in this case, the position of the particle. According to the Schrodinger equation, most dynamic systems would evolve with time into a 'superposition' of many, sometimes mutually exclusive, states. This superpositioned state is thus a state of *potentials* and *probabilities.* Schrodinger further speculates that the physical reality in the quantum realm itself exists in such a superposition: whenever the reality is not 'disturbed' by any act of measurement, it appears to be in a state of 'wave of potentialities'. Any quantum object is simultaneously a particle and a wave, and is both 'here and there' in space (e.g., Zohar and Marshall, 1994). This point concerning the meaning and interpretation of the Schrodinger equation of the wave function will be returned to later. While the validity of the equation in predicting almost all attributes of quantum objects and their changing dynamics over time is firmly established by experimental results (e.g., Casti, 1995), Schrodinger's interpretation of the meaning of the equation in terms of the underlying quantum reality itself is not without criticism. Many other alternative interpretations have been proposed (e.g., Bohr, 1934; Bohm, 1951, 1980; Everett, 1973).

While the Schrodinger equation gives the probability of an experimental outcome, the *collapse postulate* states that such a probabilistic superposition would breakdown or 'collapse' into a single actualized state whenever the measurement is actually taken. In the above experiment measuring the particle's position, the Schrodinger wave function only gives the probability of finding the particle in a unit space; the particle still could be 'simultaneously existing' anywhere in space and time. However, the moment the measurement is actually made, the wave function or the superposition of 'all positions of the particle' collapses or condenses into a state of a definite position in space. Any act of measurement in the quantum realm is further constrained by Heisenberg's uncertainty principle. According to Heisenberg, the very process of observation or measurement in the quantum world would itself change the object which is being observed or measured. As a result, at this micro level, one cannot measure simultaneously two or more of the attributes of a quantum particle, be it the particle's spin-position, or its position-momentum. Because of this, there is always a degree of uncertainty or indeterminacy associated with individual particles at the quantum level.

Interaction and 'binding' among quantum objects

In the quantum realm, objects appear to be constantly interacting with one another. The evidence of the relationship and binding among quantum objects comes from several sources.

(1) Standard model of particle physics

This model refers to a set of theories that summarize existing empirical evidence on quantum particles and the interacting forces that bind these particles together. Regarding the binding forces, the model states that there exist in the universe four types of forces that bind objects together: *the weak nuclear force, the strong nuclear force, the electromagnetic force* and *the gravitational force*. While the first two nuclear forces are found only in the quantum realm within the nucleus of each atom, the latter two forces operate outside the atomic nuclei at both the micro and macro physical realms. Specifically, within the atom's nucleus, the *weak nuclear force* binds the nucleus together, hence controls the gradual process of radioactive decay. All particles within the nucleus (i.e., quarks, protons and neutrons) are bound together by the *strong nuclear force*. Outside the atom's nuclei, the *electromagnetic force* binds the orbiting electrons to atoms, as well as binding atoms together to form *molecules*. The *gravitational force* binds all masses to one another.

The origin of some of these binding forces has also been specified in the gauge theories of the Standard Model. The gauge theories assert that the electromagnetic, the weak and the strong nuclear forces are the result of the exchange of particles, called the gauge bosons. The gauge bosons that are exchanged to create the electromagnetic force are photons and those that are exchanged to generate the weak and strong nuclear forces are respectively the W and Z particles and the gluons. All these gauge boson particles have been observed in experiments (see Stenger, 1990).

(2) 'Photon bunching' effect
The photons are particles of light. They are the gauge bosons through whose exchange the electromagnetic force is generated. In the experiment showing the photon-bunching effect (e.g., Loudon, 1983), a beam of light or photons is fired towards a measuring screen. Instead of arriving as single photon particles hitting the screen, the photons arrived in small clustered bunches hitting the screen at different intervals. This finding suggests that photons (as boson particles) have a natural tendency to interact closely and bind with one another.

(3) The quantum 'non-locality' effect

Sometimes called the 'instantaneous action at a distance' in quantum physics, the non-locality effect refers to an effect without a known local cause. It was Einstein who first demonstrated that the mathematical equations of quantum physics lead to the prediction of such instantaneous or non-local effects. For a 'local effect' to occur, communications between the two particles would require codes transmitted faster than the speed of light. Even though Einstein thought that this prediction was 'ghostly and absurd', together with Podolsky and Rosen, they proposed a thought experiment to test this prediction (see Stenger, 1990). In the proposal, two particles (protons) were separated from a common source and travelled to opposite directions in space. According to the prediction, measuring the position or momentum of one particle would simultaneously 'collapse the wave function of the other' or 'fix' those attributes of the other particle. This idea was taken up by David Bohm (1951), who suggested that instead of measuring the positions or momentum of the quantum particle, the dependent measure should be the spin dimension (the intrinsic angular momentum). Working from such a design, John Bell calculated the quantitative correlation between the two measures of the spins of two particles, and showed that the correlation was greater than any other theory of 'local' or 'real' variables could potentially predict (d'Espagnat, 1989; Redhead, 1987). Bell's theorem was experimentally tested by Aspect et al. (see Stenger, 1990) with light beams of photons. When the measurement of the spin component of one photon along one axis was taken, the state of the spin of the other photon was found to be automatically determined. The quantum non-locality effect was therefore empirically observed.

While the above quantum effect is non-local along the spatial dimension (two previously entangled photons separated in space), a similar quantum effect has also been observed with reference to the dimension of time. Here, two separate photons from two different sources of laser beams were fired, at different times, onto a detection screen through an open slit in a barrier in front of the screen. The wave-like interference pattern observed on the detection screen suggested that the two photons arrived at the screen simultaneously despite the time lag in the start of their 'travel' (Bohm, 1980). A similar effect was observed with the same photon travelling through a reflected barrier with an equal chance of either going through the barrier to reach directly the detection screen, or being reflected off and forced to travel a much longer indirect route before reaching the same detection screen. The observed wave-like interference pattern on the screen again suggested a temporal non-locality effect (cf. Zohar and Marshall, 1994). These quantum non-locality effects thus seem to be operating beyond the constraints of both space and time. This has lead many to argue that the un-interfered reality, or the reality undisturbed by any acts of measurement, is likely to exist in a state of a superposition whereby there appears to be no separation among quantum objects within it. The entire state of reality can be characterized by a non-discrete and holistic continuum.

(4) The Bose-Einstein condensate
The Bose-Einstein condensate (BEC) refers to a quantum system with its component particles showing the highest level of synchronized binding and hence the BEC is considered the most coherent of all dynamic systems (e.g., Hey and Walters, 1987; Marshall, 1989). Within a BEC, all the parts (bosons) in this system are in a state of total synchrony: seen as particles, the bosons completely 'overlap' with one another and appear to be one single unified particle; seen as waves, the phases of the component waves also entangle and lock together to appear as one single wave (the boson unified field). Examples of BECs include dynamic systems like laser beams, superconductors, and pulsars (neutron stars). These physical systems typically exist in a state of isolation insulated from any environmental entanglements. They are also extremely low in temperature (a superconductor may be below $-300°$ F).

In neuroscience, research into conscious experience has appealed to the BEC process as a possible solution to the global binding problem (the apparent coherence and unity of conscious experience). This kind of research focuses on the search for similar synchronizing phase transitions in the neural excitatory oscillations. Many have argued that coherent neural firings (a similar BEC state) in the brain are the basis for binding and conscious experience (e.g., Frohlich, 1986; Hameroff and Penrose, 1996; Marshall, 1989).

(5) The wave-merging interaction between two quantum systems
Given that any quantum object or system can be viewed from either its particle or its wave aspect, the interaction between such systems could also be examined from either the particle or the wave perspective. The above three sources (a, b, and c) of interactions or binds between two quantum objects are observed when they are seen as particles. However, examined from their wave-like property, when two quantum systems are brought together, their respective wave functions tend to merge and become phase-entangled. Through the synchronization of oscillations, a new coherent wave function emerges as a result of the wave-merging. The most complete form of the entanglement of wave functions is observed when two BEC systems are brought together. A recent experiment using laser beams as BECs has shown that when two BECs (trapped laser beams) come into contact with each other, the observed interference pattern is only possible 'if each BEC's atoms co-operated to form a single coherent wave, with the overall atom wave of one BEC interfering with the atom wave of the other condensate' (Andrews et al., 1997).

The emergence of a new wave function as a result of the interaction between two BEC systems also has significant implications for neuroscientific research into consciousness modelling. If neural firing processes corresponding to conscious experience indeed involve phase transitions into a synchronized oscillatory pattern, akin to the quantum process underlying the BEC state, then there is ground to further speculate that whenever multiple BECs meet, a new co-opted oscillatory pattern would emerge. The meeting of such BECs may operate at various levels. At the individual neuronal level or the basic neural net or neural assembly level, the wave-merging process may correspond to component-binding in corresponding perceptual or sensory experience. At higher levels, the emergence process could underlie other unified conscious experiences, including the sense of self.

Application of quantum notions to neuroscientific research into consciousness

Both the quantum rules that govern individual particles (its wave functions) and the interaction among them seem to be applicable to the neuroscientific approach to consciousness. However, to apply quantum notions this way, it becomes necessary to demonstrate that the dynamics of the neural processes corresponding to conscious experience resemble the fundamental quantum effects including the collapsing of wave function as well as the tendency towards quantum coherence.

It appears that both types of quantum effects (wave function collapsing and BEC-type coherence) have found parallels in the dynamics of the brain. Many have speculated that conscious experience may involve the collapsing of wave functions at both the level of individual neurones (e.g., Hameroff, 1994; Hameroff and Penrose, 1996; Hodgson, 1988; Lockwood, 1989; Stapp, 1993) and the level of the brain's two hemispheres (Nunn et al., cited in Zohar and Marshall, 1994). Furthermore, researchers in neuroscience have appealed to quantum coherence process in order to solve their version of the binding problem pertaining to conscious experience. To this end, neuroscientists have looked for similar synchronized neuronal activities leading to the coherent state similar to a Bose-Einstein condensate found in dynamic physical systems (e.g., Frohlich and Kremer, 1983).

(1) Neural activities akin to quantum collapsing of wave function
Neuroscientists have speculated on the exact locations where such quantum wave-function-collapsing effects might take place in the brain. Several loci have been proposed. First, Gol'danskii et al. (cf. Zohar and Marshall, 1994; p.55) suggest that such effects take place in the ion channels (protein molecules) lining the membrane walls of each individual neurone. Second, following the quantum physicist Margenau's (1984) suggestion that the mind is analogous to a quantum 'probability field', Eccles proposed the *microsite hypothesis*. The hypothesis specifies the presynaptic vesicular grids within each neural axon as the site for the quantum collapsing effect (Eccles, 1989). Third, Hameroff (1994) suggests that quantum collapses occur in the cytoskeletal microtubules in individual neurones. The proposed quantum effect involves the dynamics of the conformational state of the tubulins (the protein molecules within the microtubules) (Hameroff and Penrose, 1996; Penrose, 1994, 1997).

The *cause* of wave function collapse is related to the loci of quantum collapsing effects in the neural dynamics. In the quantum realm, although physicists still debate whether the uninterfered (by acts of measurement) reality exists in a state of 'nothingness' (Bohr and the Copenhagen interpretation) or a 'superposition' of all wave functions (Schrodinger interpretation), for those advocating the superposition view, several proposals are already made as to the *cause* of the collapse of this indeterminate state. One proposal states that the superpositioned state will collapse into a definite position whenever a 'measurement' is taken (e.g., Wigner, 1961). Therefore, the very action of measurement itself, regardless of the type of measuring tool, would make manifest the state of the object being measured. Another proposal argues that it is gravity that causes the collapse of the wave function (Penrose, 1987, 1989, 1997). The third proposal is that the wave function simply collapses spontaneously and it can happen at any time without any known external cause (e.g., Bell, 1988). Therefore the wave function seems to collapse either due to a known external cause or spontaneously without known cause.

In neuronal activities in the brain, two similar causes of collapse have been distinguished by Penrose (1997; also Hameroff, 1998; Hameroff and Penrose, 1996): 'subjective collapse' with a known external cause; and 'objective collapse' without a known cause.

(i) 'Subjective collapse' or 'subjective reduction' (SR) In quantum physics, among the various suggested measuring tools that cause wave function to collapse is 'consciousness' itself (e.g., Wigner, 1961). Following on from this, some neuroscientists argue that an independent 'conscious self' (an 'intentional state', a 'mental unit' or 'a psychon') causes the quantum collapsing effects in the brain (e.g., Eccles, 1989). In other words, the awaring self here acts as the 'measuring tool' which causes the collapsing of superpositioned wave functions within the neurones. This kind of external cause is referred to by Penrose (1997; also Hameroff and Penrose, 1996) as subjective collapse, or reduction (SR) in the brain.

(ii) 'Objective reduction' or objective collapse (OR) In contrast to the external SR cause, Hameroff and Penrose (1996) proposed that an internal and naturally-occurring process can also cause the superpositioned neuronal state to collapse: the orchestrated objective reduction (OR) process taking place in the tubulins, in the brain's cytoskeletal microtubules. Unlike the SR, whose occurrence requires that the system (brain) interacts with an external measuring tool, the OR is a 'self-collapse' mechanism inside the neurones. The OR can occur spontaneously without the interference from any outside agent (i.e., measuring tool of any kind). The occurrence of OR is due to the natural force of quantum gravity (Hameroff, 1998; Penrose, 1997). Penrose (1997; also Hameroff and Penrose, 1996) argues that this automatic kind of collapse within the tubulin itself

constitutes the non-computational or non-algorithmic aspect of consciousness.

The above speculations on the collapse of wave functions are at the level of individual neurons. At the larger-scale level of cerebral hemispheres, recent experimental evidence suggests that an act of measurement has the effect of altering respondents' conscious experience, as indicated by the EEG patterns. In the Nunn et al.'s experiment (cited in Zohar and Marshall, 1994, pp.57–8), respondents were required to attend to two 'left-hemisphere' tasks of number discrimination and button-pressing with the 'right' thumb. They were presented with single digits and required to respond by pressing a button whenever the single digit presented was 2, 5 or 8. Respondents' EEG patterns were recorded from both hemispheres. However, although the electrodes were attached to both hemispheres, the respondents had no knowledge as to whether the electrodes were switched on for the measurement. The hypothesis tested was that, if the neural firing activities in the brain are quantum phenomenon, they would be collapsed by any act of measurement (in this case, the EEG recording). Here, as far as the respondents are concerned, the electrodes are attached to both hemispheres; they had no idea that the actual recording from either hemisphere was controlled by the experimenter.

The results showed that respondents' task performance (number discrimination as indicated by the right hand's button-pressing response) was altered by the act of measuring EEGs. These 'left-hemisphere' tasks were significantly impaired when EEGs were recorded only from the right hemisphere; the tasks were however enhanced by the recording taken from the left hemisphere. Given that the collapsing of superpositioned wave functions is associated with 'moments' of consciousness (or 'conscious now') (e.g., Hameroff and Penrose, 1996), collapsing of the wave function of the right hemisphere would 'tune' respondents to right-hemisphere-related conscious tasks. In this study, the right-hemisphere task was 'listening to the background music', which is irrelevant to the two 'left-hemisphere' experimental tasks. It is likely that because of this divided and competitive attention, the experimental tasks themselves were impaired. On the other hand, when the act of measurement took place in the left hemisphere, it collapsed its superpositioned wave functions and fostered neural activities in that hemisphere and the corresponding experimental tasks were consequently enhanced.

Given that respondents were totally unaware of the actual recording from one specific side of the brain, these results were taken to mean that the act of measurement has a significant effect on altering task-evoked brain activities. By implication then, the results are indicative of the quantum nature of neuronal activities underlying conscious experience.

(2) Neural activities resembling quantum BEC-type coherence
As mentioned earlier, the BECs in the quantum realm are not only isolated from environmental interference (trapped gas or laser beams), but they also are at an extremely low temperature. These criteria have been the stumbling blocks in the search for coherent BEC-like activities outside the quantum realm, such as in the living biological cells of a normal body, or in the brain neurones. Despite the difficulties, there is evidence suggesting that synchronized oscillations exist in three levels of neuronal structures. First, at the minutest level, oscillatory coherence (with GHz frequencies) is observed with protein molecules or ion channels in the membranes of each individual neurone. Second, at the intermediate level, coherent oscillations (with gamma range 35–75 Hz frequencies) are observed with small neural assemblies (up to around 150 cells) by using multiple unit recordings. Third, at the global level, such synchronized oscillations are also observed with tens of thousands of neurones by the EEG recordings.

(i) GHz coherent oscillations of protein molecules inside individual neurones In each single neurone or nerve cell, there are around 10 million protein molecules (or ion channels) lining the

membrane walls. A single protein molecule may be composed of tens of thousands of atoms. Thus a logical starting place to look for quantum effects at the minutest level of biological cells seems to be within the protein molecules. Frohlich (1986) postulates that coherent neural firing akin to the formation of BECs may be found in the cell walls of individual neurones in biological tissues. Specifically, the individual protein molecules in the living cell membranes have vibrating dipoles (with + and − charge at each end) which emit tiny electromagnetic waves. These waves oscillate within the microwave frequency range (GHz between 10^9 and 10^{11} Hz). According to Frohlich, each oscillating molecule behaves like a 'pump system': when no excitatory energy is present, the molecule dipoles are 'out of phase' with no coherent pattern in their oscillations. However, when the neurone is excited through energy inputs, these dipoles go through a phase transition which gradually leads to the most synchronized oscillatory pattern akin to the BEC state in dynamic physical systems.

Experimental evidence from recent biophysical research has shown that such a quantum-like coherent oscillation state exists in protein molecules or ion channels in biological cells (Genberg et al., 1991; also cf. Zohar and Marshall, 1994, for Del Giudice et al., 1989 and Gol'danskii et al., 1984). Furthermore, other bioscientists have found that living cells may have the same coherent oscillation pattern, but the oscillation frequencies are even higher than those within the microwave range: they are within the visible light range (around 10^{15} Hz). This finding was seen as evidence of the transfer of photons (light particles) in living cell membranes (cf. Zohar and Marshall, 1994, p.52, for Popp, 1988 and Inaba, 1989). These experimental findings taken together thus suggest that quantum-like BEC coherence is evident in the protein molecules inside the cell membranes of individual neurones.

(ii) Gamma range coherent oscillations of sets of neurones having similar perceptual fields Research using micro

electrodes for recordings of single-neurone firings has shown that sets of individual neurones sharing the same perceptual field progress to oscillate in unison (e.g., Eckhorn et al., 1989; Llinas and Ribary, 1992; Stryker, 1989). The observed coherent oscillations of bundles of individual neurones also resemble the coherent BEC state. Generating from these limited sets of individual neurone synchronizations, many have argued that the observed coherence may form the basis for the binding of components of the perceptual 'bits' in giving rise to a unified conscious experience (e.g., Crick and Koch, 1990). However, as mentioned earlier, problems with such a solution to binding arise not only from the inconsistencies in related findings (e.g., Gray et al., 1989) or 'coherence by coincidence' (e.g., Tovee, 1998), but also from the question of generalizing from such a limited number of neurones to all neurones in the entire neural assemblies having the same perceptual fields (Hardcastle, 1995). Because of this, many neuroscientists have turned to a larger-order coherence at the level of cortical systems co-involved in various conscious experiences (e.g., Tovee, 1998).

(iii) Coherent oscillations from EEG recordings This larger-order coherence has been observed with EEG recordings. Given that one electrode records electric field potentials produced by several tens of millions of neurones (Crick, 1994), EEG recordings allow for the comparison of oscillatory patterns of cortical systems associated with distinctive mental activities. When recordings are taken from the whole surface of various cortical systems, coherent oscillations within the gamma range have also been observed. For instance, the EEG from the entire surface of the olfactory cortex in rabbits shows a coherent oscillatory pattern during odour recognition (see Hardcastle, 1995 for a review). Similar coherent stimulus-evoked EEG wave patterns are observed in other sensory and motor cortical systems (e.g., Basar et al., 1987; Freeman and Barrie, 1994).

Such system-oscillation coherence is suggestive of the idea that these large-order cortical systems can be conceptualized as coherent quantum systems, like the Bose-Einstein Condensates. Generalizing from here, the entire brain can be seen as composed of many of these systems. At an even larger scale, the dynamics of the entire brain itself may resemble those of a BEC system (e.g., Marshall, 1989). And in this context, consciousness may be seen as the result of coherent system-dynamic oscillations.

Appeal to chaos theory

Chaos (or nonlinear dynamic system) theory concerns the use of simple mathematical rules in describing the phase transformations of nonlinear dynamic systems. The behaviours of these systems, although seemingly random, are however governed by underlying simple deterministic rules. Examples of nonlinear dynamic systems embrace a wide range of thermodynamic, numerical, biological, or social systems.

The Mandelbrot set (Mandelbrot, 1982) represents a chaotic *number* system. The deterministic rule is the equation

$$Z_k = Z_{(k-1)}^2 + C$$

where (i) $k = 1, 2, ...$, (ii) $Z(0) = 0$, and (iii) C is a complex number in the form of $x + yi$ (i is the square root of -1).

Starting the equation calculation with $k = 1$: $Z_1 = 0 + C = C$. Thus for every C value (with pairs of any real numbers x and y), there is a different 'dynamic system' of the series of Z_k values ($\{Z_k\}$ sequence) determined by the equation. In such an iterative number system, each $\{Z_k\}$ sequence forms a 'trajectory' of that particular 'dynamic system' (the system created by that C value) in the two-dimensional plane. For some chosen Cs (e.g., $x = 0$ and $y = -0.5$: $C = -0.5i$), the trajectories of the corresponding $\{Z_k\}$ sequences will remain 'bounded' within a finite area in the complex number plane. For other chosen Cs (e.g., when $x = 2$ and $y = 0$: $C = 2$), the trajectories of the $\{Z_k\}$ sequences will diverge to infinity (unbounded).

The trajectories of the $\{Z_k\}$ sequences are either bounded within a closed region of the complex plane, or else unbounded. Accordingly, the C numbers that start off the different $\{Z_k\}$ trajectories can be classified into two mutually exclusive number sets. The Mandelbrot set consists of all the C numbers with corresponding $\{Z_k\}$ sequences that remain bounded. The second set (its complement) consists of all other C numbers corresponding to $\{Z_k\}$ sequences that go off to infinity.

The pattern of all trajectories for all C number systems can be more clearly seen when they are represented on the two-dimensional complex plane. The resultant plot is the famous Mandelbrot set (for details of the mathematics of the Mandelbrot set, see Casti, 1995; Gleick, 1987; Mandelbrot, 1982; Peitgen et al., 1992; Penrose, 1989; Schroeder, 1991). The *boundary* between the two complementary sets has been the focus of attention of chaos theorists. This boundary area represents the complicated transitional area in the two-dimensional phase space between total 'order' (all $\{Z_k\}$ sequences ending up with real number values) and total 'disorder' or chaos (all $\{Z_k\}$ sequences diverging to infinity). It is in this context that the boundary area is evocatively referred to as the 'edge of chaos'. It is also within this boundary area where both order and disorder are intricately and inseparably intertwined that the key features of dynamic systems are found. The key features are: 'nonlinearity' (and related notion of 'sensitivity to initial conditions'), 'emergence' (and the related notions of 'iteration of simple algorithm', 'variability and 'peaked potentiality'), as well as 'self-organization' (and related notions of 'bifurcation', 'attractor' and 'period-doubling').

Nonlinearity (sensitivity to initial conditions)
The relationships among key variables of a dynamic system are typically nonlinear. The iterative quadratic equation governing the Mandelbrot set is an example of a dynamic numerical system. The relationship between the value of the system variable (Z_k) and the control parameters (x, y, or C) of the

number system is nonlinear. In such a system, a very small change in the control parameter variables can make a big difference in the value of the system variable (the value Z_k can be either a small real number or a number diverging to infinity). The mapping of the Mandelbrot set shows this clearly in terms of the fractal pattern in its fine boundary areas. In these areas (the edge of chaos), there exists a complex mix of C numbers belonging to either the Mandelbrot set or outside it. This suggests that extremely close 'neighbouring' C systems can have a totally different trajectory pattern, with one C system having a bounded trajectory while its close neighbour C system (with ever smaller change in the x or y values) going off to infinity. Therefore, in this chaotic number system, the system's evolutionary process is said to be sensitive to 'initial' conditions.

This feature of nonlinearity and sensitivity to initial values of the parameter variables is also evident in other dynamic systems including thermodynamic systems (e.g., Newston, 1994) and social psychological systems (e.g., Ayers, 1997; Carver and Scheier, 1998; Vallacher and Nowak, 1997).

Emergence (iteration of simple algorithms, variability, peaked potentiality)

In the Mandelbrot set, each dynamic number system is created by following the same single mathematical rule of a power function, with reiteration. The implication is that a simple set of deterministic rules governing a dynamic system can set off an extremely complex pattern of behaviour (in the shape of the ever-finer fractals in the boundary region of the set). The Mandelbrot set demonstrates this in numbers. According to Mandelbrot (1982), this phenomenon (simplicity leading to complexity) is observable in a great number of other non-mathematical events including water dripping from a tap, earthquake patterns, stock-market fluctuations, evolution and extinction of species. In each of these phenomena, a simple deterministic rule with feedback loops governs the progression;

as each phenomenon evolves, unexpected and 'self-similar' patterns of complexity somehow *emerge*. Thus, with the help of an inbuilt feedback mechanism, the simple act of repeating the simple rule seems to bring about the emergence of unexpected (unpredictable) new features (patterns). In nonlinear iterative systems, such emergent new features are from the *'intrinsic dynamics of the system itself without the need for an external imposition on the system'* (Goldstein, 1997, p.126). It is precisely this feature of a chaotic system that seems to run counter to a key assumption of science: that determinism is necessary for prediction and predictability. However, given that a chaotic system is obviously one that is determined but not predictable, the chaos notions appear to have a significant implication for distinguishing determinism and predictability (e.g., Ayers, 1997; Tinsley, 1993).

The emergence of new patterns out of repeated iterations of simple deterministic rules seems to be closely associated with increased variability in behaviours of the dynamic system. The increased variability may lead to dramatic qualitative reorganization of the system in terms of the emergence of a new 'order'. In the evolutionary progression of a dynamic system, the idea that heightened variability precedes emergence of a higher-level new order has been widely observed in relation to sudden qualitative phase transitions, or bifurcations in a system. In this transitional phase, the dynamic system displays complex behaviours that vary and alternate between 'order' and 'disorder'. In the Mandelbrot number system, this variability is manifested in the fractal pattern in the boundary region.

Related to increased variability is the notion of 'peaked potentiality'. The work on the behaviours of a dynamic system at the edge of chaos suggests that the system's potential may reach its peak at these points of its evolution (e.g., Lewin, 1992; Waldrop, 1992). In experiments of computer cellular automata performed by Packard and Langton at the Santa Fe Institute, it has been shown that a dynamic system's information processing and storage capacities would reach a maximal level when the system is at the edge of total disorder, or at the order/chaos border. Other experimental data have however been inconsistent regarding the peaking of potentiality at the border (see Coveny and Highfield, 1995; Horgan, 1996).

Although the question of whether a dynamic system reaches its peak potential at the border of order and disorder is unresolved, the system seems to display a greater variability in its behaviour at these points. Such heightened variability may lead to either total chaos or the emergence of a new order. In either case, the system undergoes a phase transition (or bifurcation) from the state of 'existing order' to a new state (chaos or new order). The emergence of a new state in the evolution of dynamic systems is closely linked to the notion of the 'self-organization' of such systems.

Self-organization (attractor, period-doubling)

Another key feature of dynamic systems at the boundary between stability and chaos (i.e., order and disorder) concerns signs of self-organization (e.g., Prigogine and Stengers, 1984). The signs of self-organization can be described either in qualitative terms (e.g., bifurcations or transitions between attractors) or in quantitative terms (e.g., power laws). The attractor or the fractal structure is an example of a qualitative sign of self-organization. In the two-dimensional map of the Mandelbrot set, the central core area can be seen as one vicinity in the complex plane where certain trajectories of the $\{Z_k\}$ sequences are 'attracted' to converge. In the boundary regions of the set, the fractal structure reveals directly the patterns of self-organization around the attractors. This sign of self-organization in the highly 'ordered' fractal structure emerges more clearly with each greater scale of magnification of the border of the set. The pattern appears 'self-similar' (Casti, 1995, p.230) and yet never quite repeats itself.

Qualitative descriptions aside, there exist quantitative power laws that govern the evolution of the dynamic system within the boundary between order and chaos. The nonlinear laws specify the rate of phase transitions. In other words, these power laws govern the progression of the system from an earlier state of total stability (or order) to a new state of either complete chaos (or entropy, disorder) or a new order. Examples of order to entropy transition are found in thermodynamics and avalanches. One such quantitative law is Feigenbaum's (1978) *law of period doubling*. According to Feigenbaum, the rate of transition from order to turbulence in dynamic systems follows a power law (2^x). Experimental evidence supportive of the period doubling law has been obtained in thermodynamic systems including turbulence observed in fluid and heated liquid helium (e.g., Swinney, 1983). Independently in the simulation of avalanches, Bak's (e.g., Bak and Chen, 1991) notion of *self-organized criticality* is associated with a similar process. Using an analogy involving sandpiles and avalanches caused by adding grains of sand on top of existing piles, Bak proposes that the relationship between the frequency and size of the avalanches follows an inverse power law. However, experimental testings of Bak's sandpile hypothesis have been inconsistent (see Nagel, 1992).

In addition to the order–entropy transition, power laws seem to also govern the evolution of dynamic systems from an earlier order to a new order. While the above order–entropy transition requires input from an external environment (i.e., additional heat or sand grains), the transition from order to a new order typically requires no such input. In this sense, self-organization of dynamic systems takes place 'intrinsically' in a 'closed' system. The emergence of a new state of order is generated internally within the closed system. Kauffman (1993, 1995) refers to this intrinsically generated self-organization as an 'order for free'. Using Von Neumann's (1966) idea of cellular automata and computer simulation, Fredkin first developed the simple algorithm that eventually leads to self-reproduction. The algorithm determines the 'on' or 'off' state of a pixel (a grid cell on the computer screen): a pixel is kept on in the next generation if and only if an odd number of the four nondiagonal neighbours of that pixel is currently on (see Gardner, 1971; Poundstone, 1985). Repeated iterations of this simple deterministic algorithm result in a new order: the system will reproduce four copies of itself every (2^1, 2^2, 2^3 etc.) cycles. The rate of self-reproduction thus follows a power law. The quantitative rule governing this progression thus resembles that leading to chaotic behaviour in physical dynamic systems. Similar power laws appear to underlie other cellular automations which simulate the features of intrinsic emergence and self-organization in biological evolution including Conway's 'Game of Life' (Berlekamp et al., 1982; Stenger, 1990) and Langton's *Artificial life* (Langton, 1989; Langton et al., 1992).

Application of chaos notions to biological and social systems
In the application of chaos notions to biological evolution, many have argued that (in addition to the deterministic evolutionary rules encoded in the genes) the features of emergence, sensitivity to initial conditions and self-organization also are necessary to the biological evolutionary process. Here, biological organisms are seen as complex adaptive systems. For instance, the *symbiogenesis* notion proposed by Margulis (1993; Margulis and Sagan, 1995) may be seen as an example of such an application. Aspired by Lovelock's Gaia hypothesis, Margulis conceptualizes the earth as an ecosystem consisting of small ecosystems. Symbiogenesis suggests that long-term symbiosis within the ecosystems in the evolutionary process can lead to the emergence of new forms of life. It has been pointed out that the notion of self-organized criticality may play a role in symbiogenesis (Smolin, in Brockman, 1996, p.143).

The theoretical biologist Kauffman's (1993, 1995) notion of 'order for free' (self-organization without external input) is an example of the direct application of chaos notions to biological evolution. Kauffman argues for the 'coevolution' of complex systems. He applies the idea that complex adaptive systems can achieve peak potentiality at points within the edge of chaos, and suggests that complex biological systems coevolve and work together in getting themselves to the edge of chaos, where they are capable of achieving maximal levels of adaptivity. Through such a self-organized process, new features can emerge from these coevolving systems.

Biological evolution aside, chaos notions have also been applied to biological functioning including the electrical activities in the cardiac cells (e.g., Glass and Mackey, 1988). In human subjects receiving psychotherapy, it has been found that subjects' cardiac responses associated with personally significant events show the nonlinear features of chaos (Reidbord and Redington, 1992).

In addition to biological systems, chaos notions are also relevant in understanding social psychological systems. For instance, in the developmental literature of children's acquisition of new cognitions and skills, a greater variability of behaviour typically precedes the gaining and emergence of new insights or adaptive strategies (e.g., Cavanaugh and McGuire, 1994; Goldin-Meadow and Alibali, 1995; Kelso, 1995; Siegler, 1994; Thelen, 1995; van Geert, 1994). Variability also precedes phase transitions associated with a variety of phenomena in social psychology (e.g., Vallacher and Nowak, 1997; Carver and Scheier, 1998). Other key notions of chaotic systems (including the emergence of fractal structure, intrinsic self-organization, and phase transitions) have also been applied to the descriptions of human movements (e.g., Newston, 1994), the emergence of group behaviour norms or public opinion (e.g., Latane, Nowak and Lie, 1994; Nowak et al., 1990), the evolution of altruistic behaviour (e.g., Messick and Liebrand, 1995), social judgement and close interpersonal relationship (e.g., Vallacher and Nowak, 1997). Chaos notions have recently been applied to areas within the psychology of emotion as well as cognition (e.g., Combs et al., 1994; Finke and Bettle, 1996).

The application of dynamic system notions is also evident in the study of large-scale or macro human systems such as economic, organizational and management systems (e.g.,

Broekstra, 1998; Levy, 1994; Stacey, 1991, 1995). However, because of the problem associated with quantification and measurement in such macro social systems, these applications are largely qualitative and descriptive, hence they fall into the categories of *metaphorical* or *analogical* applications, rather than the quantitative *practical* application of chaos theory (Ayers, 1997).

Application of chaos notions to neurophysiological research into consciousness

The application of chaos notions to the brain and conscious processes is at both the levels of the individual neurone and larger neural assemblies. Mandell (1985) argues that biologists should conceptualize not only protein molecules as dynamic systems, capable of phase transitions, but also the EEG patterns. Stadler and Kruse (1994) also argue for a reconceptualization of neuronal processing in terms of chaotic system dynamics involving both features of emergence and self-organization around strange attractors. Empirically, nonlinear analyses of the EEG waveforms or event-provoked potentials reveal chaotic patterns in neuronal activities (e.g., Basar, 1990; Elbert and Rockstroh, 1987; Roschke and Aldenhoff, 1992).

With specific reference to consciousness modelling, neuroscientists have searched for the pattern of chaos (e.g., feedback, emergence and self-organization) at the level of neural assemblies and cortical subsystems which co-specialize in various perceptual and cognitive functions. By treating large aggregates of neurones in the brain as units of dynamic systems, researchers in consciousness have looked for chaotic patterns associated with the computations of such large-scale neural systems. At this level, the processing feature of *feedback* and the related feature of *emergence* characteristic of chaotic physical systems are also present in neural-system computations. Specifically, recall that in the Mandelbrot set, the deterministic algorithm requires that each result of the computation (at any particular point in the entire dynamic process) becomes part of the 'initial condition' for the immediate next computation. Such iterative feedback loops consequently lead to the emergence of unexpected and complex new features characterizing the Mandelbrot set. In cortical systems responsible for conscious experiences, there exists a parallel in the collective activities of neural nets. Various studies have shown that any new perceptual experience or learning would register an effect on the overall stable pattern of neural oscillations established from previous learning, by changing that pattern. For instance, Freeman (see Hardcastle, 1995 for a review) has shown that a stable *contour plot* pattern (based on the EEG taken from the olfactory cortex of rabbits) emerges after the rabbit has learned to recognize the scent of sawdust. However, this contour plot pattern of sawdust scent changed significantly after the rabbit learned to recognize other odours such as the smell of banana. The findings thus suggest the existence of an iterative feedback and re-entrant process at the neuronal level, which corresponds to each new stimulus input (change in external control parameters). As such, computations of neural aggregates may also be described by system dynamics characteristic of the phenomenon of chaos.

However, contour plots provide only qualitative descriptions of the pattern of chaos; quantitative proof of chaos can only come from empirical evidence showing that the conscious-experience-evoked bifurcation process occurring in neural systems also follows a nonlinear equation. Freeman has formulated such a mathematical formula (a nonlinear differential equation) to approximate neural-net bifurcation dynamics associated with conscious experiences such as learning and memory. However, the equation fails to predict reliably the corresponding EEG waveforms. Although the quantitative proof still awaits confirmation, based on the cumulative qualitative evidence, Freeman (1987) has argued for the conceptualization of information oscillatory patterns in terms of a bifurcating path between stable 'attractor' states. In this context, the cortex is seen as consisting of various interconnected complex dynamic systems. Consciousness is then defined in terms of such system-dynamic oscillations (Hardcastle, 1995).

Although the application of chaos notions to brain and consciousness research is at its beginning stage, there is increasing evidence suggesting that chaotic dynamics may characterize neuronal activities in the brain (see Ayers, 1997; Barton, 1994; Basar, 1990). Such an application has at least two significant consequences for research into consciousness. The first concerns the notion of 'time'. It has been argued that conscious (awared) and nonconscious mental processes differ primarily in terms of seriality and parallelism (Mandler, 1997) and that the main function of consciousness is to fit a 'parallel mind to a serial world' (Bargh, 1997). The dimension of time clearly is relevant to the serial–parallel distinction. Independently in the recent dynamic system literature, van Geert (1997) points out, *'the most important thing about dynamic systems theory, however, is that it reinstalls a major phenomenal dimension into our scientific theorizing, namely, time.'* (p.151). As such, conceptualizing consciousness in dynamic system terms appears necessary. The importance of the dimension of time in consciousness research is discussed later in Chapters 6 and 7.

A second significant consequence of conceptualizing conscious experience in terms of emergent coherent-system-oscillations in complex dynamic systems concerns the 'binding' issue. Hardcastle (1995) explains this significant implication for the seemingly irresolvable binding problem thus: *'we do not have to understand binding in terms of single cell interactions; instead, it could be a property inherent in our brain's "higher level" oscillations'* (p.131). To conceptualize conscious experiences as products of higher-level system dynamics allows for the application of other notions of chaos to consciousness. The theoretical implications are many-fold. For instance, can the evolution of consciousness be indeed an 'emergent' property of the brain which uses deterministic computational rules? Many scholars working on the ontology of consciousness have already made similar speculations (e.g., Eccles, 1989; Hameroff, 1998; Penrose, 1997; Sperry, 1977). However, it is important to note that most of these scholars made the speculation as a result of their application of quantum notions to consciousness. Therefore, it seems that a convergent prediction can be made from either quantum physics or chaos theory. Other convergent predictions for consciousness from either the quantum or the chaos perspective are discussed later in the book.

5
Self as Cognitive Agent and Humanistic Guide

In the history of the enquiry into consciousness, the notion of self has undergone several changes. In Classical times, it was the holistic *psyche,* of which the thinking mind was a faculty. There was no agency–sentience separation, and hence the self was both a cognitive adapting agent and a sentient humanistic guide. However, Descartes' exclusion of the unconscious from the holistic *psyche* paved the way for empiricist Hume's sceptical denial of the existence of a holistic self (Hume's own term, 'personal identity'). The remaining Humean self, defined by the associationistic principles of congruency and resemblance, features primarily psyche's cognitive agency aspect. The Idealistic and Romantic philosophers, revolting against this reduction, brought back the notion of an integral self, but they went to the other extreme by defining the 'self' virtually solely in terms of *psyche*'s sentient aspect.

Self as a cognitive agent appears to have primarily an external and extrinsic orientation. Its key function concerns the individual's relationship with the outer world and his/her adaptations to the interpersonal and physical surroundings. Self as a humanistic guide, on the other hand, has more of an internal and intrinsic orientation. Its main function pertains to the individual's relationship with his/her inner world and related adjustments in the intrapersonal and psychical environment. However, the underlying dynamics of the agentic and the sentient aspects of the self are inseparable, as the person progresses in life constantly striving for and moving towards a state of equilibrium, both within and without. With the agentic and sentient self interacting constantly in controlling and shaping the process of 'becoming', the desired harmonious state of 'being' is achieved transiently in-between and often, for fleeting moments. Viewed this way, human experience or consciousness simply constitutes the cyclic dynamics of becoming and being, with both the agentic and guiding self being part and parcel of the dynamics of an entire lifespan.

However, the self is not only able to achieve brief harmonious states of being periodically, it is capable of attaining a more permanent state of being through its own transcendence. This self-transcendent state is referred to as 'unity consciousness' in the literatures of psychodynamics and humanistic psychology. The ancestry of this psychological conceptualization of a higher 'state of being' can be traced along its philosophical roots to the early Heraclitus notion of the one unified and unbounded *psyche* within which all exists. Self's unity level of consciousness was also explicit in the Romantic philosophers' notion of the 'nature within' as the integrating source inside each individual self (e.g., Taylor, 1989). It is also the same notion that the analytic philosopher Russell referred to as the infinite or universal self, discussed in Chapter 3.

This transcendent state of the self thus lies beyond the agency–sentience divide. Throughout the dynamics of life and experience, it remains as an actualizable potential lying dormant within each individual self. Its actualization however, seems to be an entirely individual and subjective affair. A transcended self represents a perfected sense of harmony within which the agent and experiencer, having both been accredited, are now embedded in one new and larger reality that emerges out of the transcendence. And in this larger reality, the self acquires a new purpose of existence. It is oriented inwardly for the maintenance of this transcendence: being becomes an end in itself and no longer a means to an outwardly extrinsic end. Most importantly, it is in this unified state of being that the transcended self becomes one's own humanistic guide.

Self-transcendence therefore concerns the potential development of selfhood and consciousness in an intrinsic and teleological sense. Given that human development and evolution necessarily require a reference to time, the humanistic and psychodynamic models that deal with self-transcendence are necessarily longitudinal and macro-phenomenological by nature. In contrast, the neural network models (discussed in the previous chapter) and the social cognitive models of the self (discussed later in this chapter) take a normative 'cross-sectional' stance by approaching consciousness from a micro 'snapshot' perspective without a significant reference to the time factor. In addition, these models are concerned primarily with the functional and instrumental ends of adaptation in an extrinsic sense. Given these seemingly incompatible features between the humanistic and cognitive models of consciousness, it is little wonder that some psychologists have posed the question of whether it is *'an accident or an artifact that the same term "consciousness" is applied to them all?'* (Shallice, 1988, p.326).

The rest of the chapter presents a survey of the notion of self in the psychological and human science literatures. The survey starts with the three founding psychologies of Wundt, James and Freud. It is noted that the notion self was an integral part of the study of the *structure* of consciousness for all three psychologies. Although the agency–sentience separation was evident, both Wundt and Freud tried to place a similar emphasis on each aspect of the self in their approaches. However, the developments in psychology after the founding schools have significantly shifted the research focus of the self. The striving for psychology to become a pure science has pushed further the separation of the two aspects of the self. As a result, self as a cognitive agent and a sentient experiencer have been studied in isolated and diverse fields of contemporary psychology and human sciences. These contemporary approaches to the self are also reviewed.

SELF IN THE FOUNDING PSYCHOLOGIES

The nineteenth-century endeavour of explaining consciousness in biological and physiological terms flourished in the prevailing intellectual climate dominated by empiricistic philosophy, Newtonian physical science, and Darwinian biological evolution. It was in this *Zeitgeist* that the discipline of psychology was founded towards the end of that century. Three psychologies were founded independently and almost simultaneously in Europe by Wilhelm Wundt and Sigmund Freud, and in America by a group of 'Social Darwinian' philosophers led by William James. While all three were primarily a study of the human mind and consciousness, their approaches were vastly different. Wundt approached it from the traditional philosophical perspective of rationalism by focusing on the synthesis of holistic conscious experiences. Freud approached the mind from the psychoanalytic perspective and focused on the unconscious mind. James, however, took the modern perspective of pragmatism by focusing on the analysis of the functional role of conscious experiences.

Wundt's psychology of consciousness and *Volkerpsychologie*: self as 'totality of life processes'

William Wundt (1832–1900) specified two main tasks for psychology: first, to investigate the *'life processes'* (i.e., consciousness), and second, to understand *'the totality of life processes'*; it was expected that such endeavors may perhaps help to *'mediate a total comprehension of human existence'* (Wundt, 1873, p.157). Wundt applied physiological principles and the experimental method of introspection in the investigation of consciousness. The conceptual basis for his experimental method, the principle of *psychophysical parallelism*, stems from the Leibnizian tradition. Wundt referred to the psychical and the physical side of experience as inner versus outer experience. However, '*the expressions outer experience and inner experience do not indicate different objects, but different points of view from which we take up the consideration and scientific treatment of a unitary experience*' (Wundt, 1907, p.2). In studying consciousness, it is the 'unitary' nature of experiences that was the focus of Wundt's psychology.

This relates to the second task of understanding the 'totality of life processes'. Wundt (1896) considered the holistic 'self' to be 'the unity of volition' as well as the 'universal control of our mental life which it renders possible'. Following Leibniz, Wundt believed that *apperception* plays the unifying and integrating role of the self, in giving rise to a synthesized and unitary subjective conscious experience. So, an analysis of apperception becomes the necessary first step for an understanding of the totality of consciousness.

However, given that Wundt's philosophy of human existence was much influenced by that of Romanticism (especially Vico and Herder), he was fully aware that the 'totality of consciousness' can only be partially understood through an analysis of apperception at the level of the individual self. To gain a fuller understanding, it is necessary to go beyond each individual Self by exploring the collective historical and cultural heritages of human evolution. Therefore, Wundt argued that the study of *Volkerpsychologie* was essential, as it deals with the influence of collective human activities, such as language and mythology, on the individual mind and self. Wundt's *Volkerpsychologie* thus deals with the aspects of the mind which are '*inexplicable in terms merely of individual consciousness*' (Wundt, 1916, p.3). As such, consciousness (or life processes), for Wundt, is not different from the holistic being or Self. To understand consciousness requires not only to analyse experiences in their '*immediate form*' but also to know '*their relations to all the other contents of the experience of the knowing subject*' (Wundt, 1907, p.365). Therefore, by emphasizing the viewpoint of the 'knowing self', Wundt places a core emphasis on the 'synthetic' as well as the 'intrinsic' nature of consciousness.

James' adaptational psychology: self as 'stream of consciousness'

Just as *parallelism* significantly affected later developments in Wundtian psychology and hence the mind and qualia issues, *neutral monism* also had a profound influence over the development of William James' (1842–1910) empirical psychology. Although James' philosophical heritage can be traced back to empirical associationists like Locke, Hume and Mill, it was Charles Sanders Peirce's (1839–1914) philosophical pragmatism and Herbert Spencer's (1820–1903) Social Darwinism that had the most obvious impact on his utilitarian and functional approach to the mind and consciousness. Philosophical pragmatism came into being during the late nineteenth century in America as a result of the dissatisfaction with traditional philosophy's lack of practical social value. Peirce's pragmatism was originally a theory of knowledge that asserted that the meaning of an idea is determined by its pragmatic consequences or effects. James applied such a notion of 'deriving meaning from utility' to the understanding of the mind and consciousness. He argued that consciousness is not an entity as often assumed in metaphysical philosophy; rather, consciousness serves a functional role and thus has pragmatic consequences for the individual. But what kind of function or what kind of pragmatic value does consciousness have? Here, James' views were influenced by Spencer's Social Darwinism which regarded human beings as biological organisms striving to adapt to an ever-changing natural world so as to meet the fitness criterion for its survival. Adopting this view, James argued that the pragmatic utility of the mind or consciousness is in guiding the individual's adaptation and adjustment to the environment.

Thus, the mind or consciousness so conceived serves the adaptational function of relating the individual to the environment. Although James (1890) defined psychology as *'the science of mental life'* (p.1), his experimental study of consciousness was however confined to its pragmatic functions. It is exactly here that James seems to have set the future psychological views of the mind firmly within a relational theory or a functional (or instrumental) theory of consciousness: either of the two was to lead to the behaviouristic and materialistic view in psychology. From this angle, the legacy of James' experimental psychology appears to have made the study of the mind no more than a subject of a functional and relational analysis.

However, despite such legacy, it is important to understand James' own view of consciousness and his personal reaction to witnessing psychology's moving towards extreme materialism. His philosophy of pragmatism centres around the key theme that the 'truth' of a concept is determined by its pragmatic consequences (or 'cash value' for the person who holds it). His example of the truth of the concept of God serves to clarify this theme. James argued that the notion that 'God exists' is true for those whose lives have been fostered through holding such a belief. Given that truth is to be determined 'subjectively', James holds that all subjective intrinsic experiences are equally as 'meaningful' as objective experiences that can be empirically observed and ascertained.

Even though James' empiricistic heritage goes back to Hume, he nonetheless rejects the atomistic model of the mental state. With his emphasis on the subjective (or in his own term, 'personified') nature of mental thoughts, James comes to regard consciousness as being the same as the 'subjective life' of the Self. This is evident in James' (1890) description of consciousness: '[It] *does not appear to itself chopped up in bits ... It is nothing jointed; it flows. A "river" or a "stream" are the metaphors by which it is most naturally described. In talking of it hereafter let us call it the stream of thought, of consciousness, or of subjective life*' (p.239). Therefore, while Hume denied the existence of a holistic self (Hume's 'personal identity'), James has not only emphasized the holistic nature of consciousness, but worked out a comprehensive categorization of the constituents of the Self. According to James, the Self is conceptualized either as the *'Empirical Me'* or as the *'Pure Ego'*. The Empirical-Me refers to the known aspects of the Self and further comprises the *material Self, the social Self and the spiritual Self.* From James' writing, it appears that it is the *spiritual Self* with which the notion of qualia most closely identifies. As James writes: *'By the Spiritual Self, ... I mean a man's inner or subjective being, his psychic faculties or dispositions, taken concretely; ... the most enduring and intimate part of the self, that which we most verily seem to be'* (James, 1890, p.296). James referred to this spiritual Self as *'the self of all the other selves'* (p.297) and further described it as being the very 'core' of all aspects of conscious experiences including the qualitative experiences (qualia). In James' own description of the spiritual Self:

> whatever qualities a man's feelings may possesses, or whatever content his thought may include, there is a spiritual something in him which seems to 'go out' to meet these qualities and contents, whilst they seem to 'come in' to be received by it ... It is the home of interest, ... effort and attention, and the place from which appear to emanate the fiats of the will. (p.297)

This spiritual self is also 'permanent', in James' words again, *'being more incessantly there than any other single element of the mental life, the other elements end by seeming to accrete round it and to belong to it'*. These passages seem to suggest that what is now referred to as qualia and related notions of debate around it such as intention and will, are all existing as James' spiritual Self.

As already mentioned, James' philosophical position on Reality, *neutral monism*, is idealistic rather than materialistic.

Given Wundt's Leibnizian (*dual-aspect theory*) heritage, both Wundt and James subscribed to the view of panpsychism. Consistent with this, James believes that consciousness (or stream of thoughts, or subjective life) is all-embracing and includes the vast realm of the nonconscious, yet another view which sets him apart from his empiricistic predecessor Hume. James believed that there are different forms of consciousness, of which the waking consciousness is but one. These other forms of consciousness include hypnotic state, trance, and dreaming. The normal waking consciousness is only a small portion of our entire potential consciousness. Based on his well-known scientific investigations of the psychic phenomenon of mediumship, James rejected the 'spirit hypothesis' which suggested that the mediums are controlled by external disembodied spirits or beings. Instead, James (1902) proposed the 'unconscious fraud theory' which contends that the messages coming through mediums are not of an external source, but are from the medium's own 'unconscious mind'. This psychological explanation thus carries the presumption of the existence of a vast unconsciousness beyond an individual's normal consciousness. Furthermore, James argued that no account of the universe in its totality can be final if these other forms of consciousness are disregarded.

In addition to the spiritual Self discussed earlier, James also identified the *material Self* and the *social Self.* James further argued that the three Empirical Me's (material, social and spiritual) are often in rivalry and conflict with one another, and that one is frequently confronted by the necessity of standing by one of these selves. James (1890) talks about the resolution of such a conflict: '*But to make any one of them actual, the rest must more or less be suppressed. So the seeker of his truest, strongest, deepest self must review the list carefully, and pick out the one on which to stake his salvation. All other selves thereupon become unreal*' (p.310).

As mentioned, even though James' monumental scholarly contribution is to have made psychology an experimental and scientific discipline, his personal views of reality and humanity reflect many features of the metaphysical philosophy of Romanticism (e.g., his emphasis of the Self with feelings and free will, the *pure Ego* or the unconscious). As a prominent psychologist, James found himself weary over the conflict between *'the heart's feeling of freedom and the intellect's scientific declaration of determinism'* (Leahey, 1992, p.262). And this conflict finally led to his quitting psychology and returning to philosophy in 1892. It has also been said (e.g., Reese, 1980) that James' philosophy itself emerged from the tension between a commitment to empirical science and an attraction to metaphysical philosophy. While his authoritative textbooks on psychology advocate that the study of psychology should be a natural science, his two books published after quitting psychology, *The will to believe* (1897) and *Varieties of religious experiences* (1902), are both on the subject of religious faith. Based on his careful study of psychic phenomena, which revealed a convergent consistency in religious testimony, James came to the conclusion that the religious perspective is beyond science and reason and that the consistency of observations points to its 'validity'. And for the remaining years after returning to philosophy, James seemed to be seeking a philosophical position, which can respectably join the two perspectives; this was evident in his later publications such as *A pluralistic universe* (1909).

Freud's psychology of the unconscious: self as constituting the conscious and the unconscious mind

Sigmund Freud's (1856–1940) psychology of the unconscious was a result of his clinical work on 'deviant' rather than 'normal' human behaviour. Much as Wundt's psychology was influenced greatly by German Romanticism, Freudian psychology also received significant input from Romantic philosophy: his idea of the unconscious mind comprising instinctive and untamed forces (the *id*) reflects Schopenhauer's unconscious 'primitive forces' in one's subjective self. In addition to the Romanticism heritage, Freud's concept of the 'pleasure principle' of the *id* closely resembles the Modern philosopher Thomas Hobbes' utilitarian notion of hedonism (cf. Leahey, 1992).

According to Freud, the human mind (i.e., the psyche) is divided into a conscious and an unconscious part and each is further divided into three components: id, ego and superego. The id pertains to the human instincts and desires and is concerned with their gratification. The id therefore follows the 'pleasure principle' which aims to find immediate gratification of these desires. The superego consists of the internalized rules and morals of society; hence it represents the conscience of the individual. Its function is to ensure that one's actions follow strictly the moral rules agreed-upon by members in society. Whenever there is a conflict between the id's desires and the superego's moral ideals, the ego, where possible, tries to find a compromised solution. The functioning of the ego thus follows the 'reality principle' which ensures that one's desires are gratified through rational and practical means or actions.

At times, the ego inevitably fails to find realistic solutions to the conflict between the id and the superego and consequently many of the individual's desires remain unfulfilled. According to Freud, these unfulfilled desires together with the memories of past traumatic experiences are all repressed into the unconscious mind. While repressed and pushed out of conscious awareness, the unconscious mind nonetheless continues to exert an influence on the way the individual processes the information received from the external world. The main premise of psychoanalysis is that all psychosocial problems are the manifested symptoms of the unconscious mind and hence these problems can be relieved only by bringing to consciousness the repressed and undesirable contents of the unconscious mind. This can be done through hypnosis and other means of altering the state of consciousness.

Freud's conception of the self is closely linked with the resolution of the id–superego conflicts in early life experiences as well as the function of the unconscious mind. On the subject of creativity and self-expression, it was Freud who most clearly posited the idea that the unconscious mind may be the driving force behind highly creative activities. Based on his clinical observations of the relationship between mental illness and creativity, Freud (1957) came to regard the unconscious mind as the part of the self that is closer to the 'divine' than the conscious mind. While Freud placed a major emphasis on early conflicts in the development of the self, neo-Freudians (e.g., Adler, Fromm) emphasized the role of social-cultural and interpersonal factors in the development of the self.

All three founding psychologies were concerned with consciousness, even though each had a different focus. It is important to note that regardless of the identical intention of all three to make the study of consciousness a science, Wundt, James and Freud had a similarly 'synthetic' model of the mind which embraces both the known (the conscious mind) and the unknown (the non-conscious mind). As such, the psychology of consciousness for all three rests on the implicit understanding that consciousness is intimately associated with, if not 'identifies with', the holistic Self. For Wundt, self was simultaneously a cognitive agent and a sentient experiencer, and hence is capable of transcending itself. As such, consciousness was to be studied by placing experimental (or physiological) psychology alongside *Volkerpsychologie*. For James, while he saw the self as the all-encompassing 'stream of consciousness', the study of either the self or consciousness was confined solely within the experimental paradigm he himself had created. In this context, the self was primarily defined as an adaptational agent in James' experimental psychology. This approach was later to have proven too restricted and inadequate for James, so he quit psychology and returned to philosophy to continue the pursuit of consciousness. For Freud, the existence of a holistic *psyche* was explicit in his theories of personality and the 'topographic' model of the mind. His study of the unconscious was aimed mainly at a full understanding of the underlying mechanisms of the holistic self. In the context of Freudian psychoanalysis, the self is complete with both its agentic and sentient aspects.

SELF AFTER THE FOUNDING PSYCHOLOGIES

In contemporary psychology, the study of selfhood in general is totally abolished from the areas of behaviourism, cognition and neuroscience; it is a subject of concern to three other domains of psychology: social and personality psychology; psychodynamics; as well as humanistic and phenomenological psychology. Given that social and personality psychologies are also under the heavy influence of the information processing and connectionist paradigms, self theories that have been advanced there typically emphasize the aspect of the self as cognitive-agent. Although theories and research conceptualizing the self as a humanistic guide are found in some neo-Freudian schools of psychoanalysis (e.g., Jung, Erikson), they are advanced primarily under the rubric of phenomenological and humanistic psychology. The following sections survey the major self theories that conceptualize the self as a cognitive agent, separately from those treating the self primarily as a sentient experiencer and humanistic guide.

Self as cognitive agent

In the history of social and personality psychology, theories of self can be divided into three broad categories by virtue of their underlying assumptions as to (1) whether the 'core self' is static and fixed or dynamic and changing, and (2) whether it 'resides' within or outside the individual. At one extreme, some earlier self theories (e.g., Allport, 1961) assume that the core self is relatively fixed and resides primarily within the person. At the other extreme are the postmodern social constructionist theories of the self such as that of Gergen (1994). Such theories view the self as the result of an ongoing dynamic process taking place in the interpersonal realm outside the individual. Self in this context resides completely outside the person and it ceases to be meaningful when taken out of the social environment or the relationship web.

However, most self theories lie between these two extremes and view the core self as resulting from a dialectical process involving the inner core self and the social web. As such, they are typically theories of constructivism: the individual continually constructs and reconstructs notions about him-/herself in light of relevant inputs from the social and cultural surroundings. Instead of 'emptying out' the core self from the person and casting it totally in the interpersonal web, as is the case with the social constructionists, these dialectical or constructivistic theories view the self as the product of an ongoing interplay between an inner-directed core self and its social/cultural surroundings. Therefore, for social Constructionism, it is the social web that constructs the self; for social constructivism, it is the individual person that constructs the self (see Gergen, 1994 for a review of the differences between the two).

Fixed self
For the early personality and trait theorist Gordon Allport (1961), an individual's personality constitutes 'traits' both unique to the person (personal dispositions) and those shared with all persons (common traits). However, an individual's distinct individuality is primarily determined by the characteristics of his/her personal dispositions. Allport defined the core self or personality in terms of a person's internal organization of these 'psychophysical systems' which underlie the typical behaviour and thought of the person. His research focused almost exclusively on identifying such traits and their variations among people, rather than on explaining the core self. Further, traits are assumed to be relatively stable and fixed behavioural

tendencies that are largely biologically-based. This emphasis on the biological origin has been maintained by some later trait theorists in the study of personality. However, more recent trait theorists such as McCrae and Costa (1997), while acknowledging the biological basis of traits, also emphasize the role of 'human meaning systems' (e.g., language, external situations, culture) in their interaction with traits in determining behaviour. In their own words, 'people enter the human world with particular dispositions which are given local color and meaning by the prevailing culture' (p.241). These trait theories therefore reject the fixed-self assumption of their predecessors by moving towards an interactional approach to personality and self.

Dialectical or social constructivist self theories
The term dialectic was first used by Plato to mean a logical process in verbal argumentation and the evolution of thought. The process starts with a 'thesis' about the argument, followed by finding an 'antithesis' (an opposing argument), then a 'synthesis' (or combinatory and reconciliatory argument) of the two. The new synthesis then becomes the 'thesis' for the next thesis–antithesis–synthesis cycle which eventually leads to a more complete understanding or a fuller account of the argumentation or thought.

Hegel expanded on the applicability of the notion far beyond the verbal and conceptual domain and considered the dialectic process as a fundamental and 'necessary law of nature' (Popkin and Stroll, 1993, p.85). Hegel believed that the evolution of political ideologies and the course of human history itself also follow this dialectic process. According to Hegel, it is a necessary and logical law that as every nation adopts a certain ideology it will lead to the emergence of its opposing ideology. The course of history is marked by such dialectic cycles of events.

Hegel's notion of the dialectic has had obvious impacts on not only political and economic philosophy, but also on contemporary sociological and psychological theories. For instance, it is well known that Karl Marx's political ideology was originally inspired by Hegel's work. Kenneth Boulding's (1968) accounts of organizational revolution and of the progression of subsystems within society reflect this dialectic process. Within psychology, the dialectic notion has exerted a great deal of influence over the conceptualization of human thoughts and action.

Most contemporary self theories carry an implicit assumption that self or personal identity involves a dialectic progression. Central to such a dialectic process is the notion of an 'agentic person': the individual actively constructs new theses or 'meaning' out of information received. Therefore, the key elements of this dialectic approach to self are (a) an intrapsychic element: the individual agentic person as a social constructivist, (b) an interpersonal element: the interdependence of the social (cultural, or external) and the individual (intrapsychic or internal) processes, and (c) the emergence of new and synthesized 'theses' or 'meanings' about aspects of the self. Dialectic or social constructivist self theories vary in terms of the relative weight they place upon each of these three elements of the dialectic process. Compared with the early social theorists such as Levin or Mead, the early cognitive schematic theorists (e.g., Piaget) placed a greater weight on the interpsychic than the interpersonal element. However, more recent self theories (e.g., Markus, Deci and Ryan) tend to place a relatively similar weight to the social system and the intrapersonal schematic aspects of the dialectic process.

The cognitive tradition
(1) The cognitive schematic approach
Central to Piaget's seminal work on cognitive development are the notions of 'interiorization', 'accommodation' and 'assimilation' that underlie the construction of mental representations or schemas of knowledge. The dialectic process involved in the creation and updating of these schemas takes place primarily within the individual. As such, the Piagetian notion of a constructivist has been referred to as 'solitary self-constructivist'

(Gergen, 1994); Piaget placed the driving force behind the dialectic process in the social and interpersonal arena. His sociocognitive conflict theory asserts that cognitive conflicts resulting from social interactions would cause feelings of psychological disequilibrium, and it is these feelings that initiate and drive the dialectic process towards a possible resolution. Through accommodating and/or assimilating the inconsistent thought, information or thesis, a new and synthesized meaning emerges.

While Piaget concluded the typical developmental stages with formal operations, some neo-Piagetian theorists (e.g., Kramer, 1990) have argued that the formal operational stage is followed by an even higher stage of 'postformal thinking', which features the ability to mentally manipulate thoughts and ideas in a dialectical manner. Therefore, within the Piagetian framework, not only the longitudinal development of the individual is dialectic (in the Hegelian sense), but the highest level of mental operations that development finally leads to is itself characterized by a dialectic process (in the Platonic sense).

While Piaget's work on cognitive schema has inspired later research in conceptualizing self and personhood in schematic terms (e.g., Markus, Cantor), his main concern was primarily with the cognitive agency aspect of the self rather than with selfhood or self identity. Another social constructivist, George Kelly, also works within the cognitive tradition of charting mental representations. However, Kelly's self theory is more concerned with personal identity than with agentic behaviour or cognitive functioning.

(2) The personal construct approach
George Kelly's personal construct theory assumes that individuals actively create mental representational systems ('constructs') about diverse aspects of the reality they perceive. These constructs are arranged as bipolar dimensions of descriptors like 'relaxed–intense', or 'good me–bad me'. The self construct system constitutes all aspects of the self as perceived

by the person through his/her entire past experiences of interacting with the social environment. According to Kelly, all past experiences concerning the self present themselves as the database from which the self construct system can be constructed. Although the same database allows for many different ways of construction, it is up to the individual to freely select the 'building blocks' for the self constructs. The individual's free will thus leads to what Kelly referred to as 'constructive alternativism': there are alternative ways of constructing one's own realities (e.g., one's own beliefs about one's self identity) pending one's own free choice.

While both these cognitive schematic and personal construct approaches to the self place a primary focus on its representational and intrapersonal aspect, other early self psychologists (e.g., Lewin, Mead) emphasize more the interpersonal aspect of the dialectic process.

The social and system tradition
(1) Gestalt and Field approach
Inspired by Gestalt psychology, Kurt Lewin's (1935) notion of 'life space' is central to his field theory of personality and self. According to Lewin, personality can only be understood through a system or field analysis of all the 'forces' or stimuli, internal and external, that are exerting an influence on the person at any given time. The internal and external forces are interdependent and coexist as inseparable parts of a holistic life field. Lewin applied various physical and mathematical notions (e.g., field, forces and topology) to the analyses of group dynamics in social and interpersonal interactions. The self exists as an individual's perception of, and reaction to, his/her social environment. His system dynamic approach to personality and self identity has paved the way for the development of later cognitive and systemic theories of the self.

(2) Symbolic interaction approach
The thesis of the early social constructivists of the Chicago

School, led by Charles Cooley and George Mead, focuses on the social construction of meaning through interpersonal interactions. Meaning is created from an individual's subjective interpretations of verbal or non-verbal social interactions. Cooley (1902) argued that a person's sense of self is essentially a mirror reflection of his/her interpretations of others' perceptions of him-/herself. In this context, the self is simultaneously the object of others' perceptions as well as the internalized symbolic representation of such mirror images. The primacy of the social in Cooley's view of the self is captured by the phrase: 'the looking-glass self'.

Although Mead emphasized the role of language as well as 'inner speech' in conceptualizing the self as an object of thought (Mead, 1934), he nonetheless placed a greater emphasis on the social environment in the study of the individual within it. Mead argued specifically that the social system (society) is 'prior', rather than secondary, to the individual person and that the latter can only be understood in the context of the dynamic whole (cf. Smith, 1997, pp.767–8).

Combining cognitive schematic and social systemic traditions
(1) Information processing and system approaches

In the schematic tradition, Hazel Markus (1977) also views self-schemas as a mental framework around which all information about the self is constructed, evaluated and organized. Her personality and self theory focuses on the effects of self schemas on the individual's dynamic interactions with the environment, in particular, the ways information gets processed. In other words, the focus is on the self schemas' information-processing consequences such as attention orientation, memory organization or future expectancies.

Markus made several assumptions concerning the self schema. (1) The working self-concept (Markus and Kitayama, 1991): notwithstanding the dynamic and ongoing restructuring feature, there appears to be a core self (the working self-concept) which forms the basis for the dynamic process at any given time. The core working self-concept also provides a sense of unity and identity over time. (2) 'Possible selves' (Markus and Nurius, 1986): these represent the selves that a person would like to, or are afraid to, become. Possible selves serve as motivating forces in directing and shaping the person's perception, emotion and behaviour. (3) An 'ecological' approach to the self schema: an ecological analysis embracing the sociocultural, historical, economic and sociopolitical factors is necessary for the study of the meaning of self and personhood. For Markus, there are no boundaries between the 'individual and the sociocultural, the self and the collective, or the person and the situation', as they represent interdependent realities.

Cantor and Kilstrom's (1987) theory of self has many similar features to that of Markus. The self-concept is seen as one of the many conceptual categories (e.g., furniture, animal) an individual possesses. As such, they applied many notions of the prototypicality theory of category to the self-concept. Essentially, they argue that (1) there is a 'family of selves', with its members arranged in a hierarchical order like the exemplars in any other semantic categories; (2) the 'family resemblance' among the subselves and the 'autobiographical records' together give rise to a sense of unity among them; and (3) the 'prototypic' self may function as the core self, similar to Markus' working self-concept. Furthermore, Cantor and Kilstrom view problem-solving skills as underlying all social and interpersonal interactions. In this context, they propose the notion of social intelligence: an individual's ability to discriminate subtle differences in social cues. People high in social intelligence are better adapted in interpersonal interactions.

Instead of conceptualizing self–social interactions in terms of a problem-solving process, Barclay stresses the roles of language and thought. The self is seen as an 'autobiographical remembering' and 'sociocultural interacting' process. At any point in this process, the person's 'remembered self' comprises the totality of past 'personal and generic memories' (Barclay and Smith, 1993). Because language and thought are both culture-dependent, the remembered selves are therefore heavily influenced by cultural practices.

Although these processing and system theories have placed a greater emphasis on social-cultural factors in the self-system dialectic process, their fundamental assumptions about the self are still primarily couched in cognitive agentic terms. The theme of the self as a sentient being directed by intrinsically motivating forces is however taken up by other dialectic theories with a focus on human motivational processes.

(2) Motivating and regulatory approaches
Deci and Ryan (1991) characterize their self theory as 'organismic and dialectic' in the sense that it places a much greater emphasis on the intrinsic motivational and regulatory functions of the self. According to this view, there exists an innate and inherent core 'self' which consists of intrinsic interests and motivating forces such as the tendency to explore, to relate or to integrate. In their theory of self-determination, Deci and Ryan argue that there are three innate motivating forces. The basic core self has the intrinsic needs for 'competence', 'autonomy' and 'relatedness'. Self develops as it interacts with external forces in a continuous dialectic progression. As external new experiences get assimilated and integrated with the intrinsic core self, a 'restructured' core self emerges. For the theorists, behaviours that are motivated by the core self at any given time are 'self-determined' behaviour; those that do not stem from the core self are 'non-self-determined'. Self-determined behaviours are consistent with the goals and values of the self; they are carried out for intrinsically satisfying reasons, hence are ends in themselves.

The three inherent needs deserve further discussion. The motivation for competence emphasizes the idea of an agentic self that strives for having control over its environment and for being instrumental in achieving desired outcomes. The motivation for autonomy refers to the self's striving for authenticity and self-determination. The need for relatedness emphasizes the strivings of the self towards relating to its social surroundings in a meaningful and harmonious manner.

Fundamental to the three basic needs is the self's strivings towards a harmonious existence both within and without. Deci and Ryan (1991) refer to this as a dialectic dual-level process taking place within the self and outside the self in the social environment. The self's strivings within concern the process leading to the emergence of a competent and fully autonomous being; the self's endeavours in integrating with forces in the social environment lead to a harmonious coexistence with the outside world. This dual-level process characterizing the development of the self thus reflects closely the Aristotelian notion of 'justice' and a 'happy life' (defined as a harmonious balance both within and without *the psyche*).

Many other motivation and self-regulatory theorists also emphasize the regulatory and agentic role of the self; they also view such regulatory process in dialectic terms. While Deci and Ryan speak of general innate needs as intrinsic motivating forces in normative terms, these other theories focus on individual differences in self-regulation and motivation. For instance, Bandura focuses on a situation-specific regulatory force called self-efficacy. Akin to the notion of multitude of selves (e.g., Markus' possible selves and Cantor's family of selves), Bandura's theory implies that there exists a multitude of self-efficacies, each with respect to a specific situation or task (self-efficacies with respect to one's music ability, quantitative ability, or social competence, etc.). According to the social cognitive theory of action (Bandura, 1986), the development of specific self-efficacy follows the same dialectic progression as the emergence of the self. Past relevant experiences of socialization as perceived and interpreted by the individual (the constructivist) help in creating and recreating a global subjective perception about own efficacy in specific tasks or social situations. In that specific task or social situation, self-efficacy perception at any given time has significant consequences for one's action and performance, which then becomes an integral part of one's 'past relevant experience' in the dialectic loop of the progressive restructuring of self-efficacy.

Other self-regulatory models that take an individual differences approach include the self-guides model (Higgins, 1989; Strauman, 1992), the self-monitoring model (Snyder, 1987) and the control model of self-consciousness (Carver and Scheier, 1992; 1998). Higgins' theory of self-guides is reminiscent of the humanistic model of Carl Rogers in that they both place a core focus on such notions as the actual-self, ideal-self and ought-self. In the distinctive social cognitive tradition, Higgins conceptualizes these selves in terms of chronically accessible schematic mental constructs that exert control over the processing of information relevant to the selves. Both Rogers and Higgins maintain that the basic motivating force pertains to closing the gaps between the actual self and the ideal or ought selves. They however postulate different gap-closing processes. Rogers views the process as being intimately related to both the conscious and the nonconscious mind and hence it is a process of natural unfolding in a benign social environment. Higgins deals with only the conscious mind and sees the process in terms of the self's agentic role in the extrinsically-oriented life adaptation.

Snyder's self-monitoring and Carver and Scheier's control models appear to share one common feature in that they both carry the implication of an internal versus external orientation in the self-regulatory process. The self's agentic functioning is primarily directed towards extrinsic goals among those individuals that are high in self-monitoring in Snyder's model and those that are high on 'public' self-consciousness in the control model. In contrast, 'low-self-monitoring' and 'high-private-self-consciousness' individuals appear to be more intrinsically-oriented in their self-regulatory processes.

(3) Social constructionism: social-cultural forces as the constructor of self
The assumption that self is an internal or intrinsic state is

implicit in all the self theories reviewed above in the cognitive and social tradition and most of those (reviewed later in this chapter) in the humanistic and phenomenological tradition. Regardless of whether the self is viewed as a fixed core or a dialectic process, or whether its primary nature is social or cognitive, the self 'resides' within the individual. A hypothetical construct notwithstanding, the notion self in psychology has always been associated with inner-directedness and internalization (or interiorization) of self-related events that are external in origin. However, within the framework of social constructionism (e.g., Gergen, 1994; Gergen and Gergen, 1988), this long-held tradition of an inner self is being deconstructed and replaced by a 'group self' residing outside the individual in the social network.

In line with the general postmodern theme of deconstructionism, Gergen (1994) argues that 'relationship takes priority over the individual self: Selves are only realized as a byproduct of relatedness' (p.249). As such, Gergen locates the 'sources' of human action in relationships, and argues that individual functioning can only be understood in terms of social and 'communal interchange' (p.68). The self is no longer considered as an intrinsic process taking place within the individual's 'mental world'; it emerges and is manifested only in the relationship webs of the external social world (p.243).

Consistent with the key postmodern theme of pluralism, Gergen further posits the notion of 'multiple realities' as the individual's socially constructed realities. Each individual is embraced by, and hence has simultaneous membership claim to, multiple 'relationship nuclei'. From this perspective, multiple selves with reference to the multiple relationship nuclei are distinct possibilities for each individual person.

One of the major implications of casting the self in relationship webs concerns the pivotal emphasis it has given to the social, cultural, and historical factors in the social construction of the self (group self). In other dialectical self theories, the social-cultural environment and the collective historical heritage are either seen as exerting an influence over the construction of, or as co-constructors of, the self. In social constructionism, these external forces *are* the actual builders of the self.

Gergen's self theory shares with other contemporary self theories three important features. First, self is conceptualized in process terms. Second, social and historical factors are given a significant status in the construction–reconstruction process of the self. Third, self, as a manifestation of social relationships, takes the form of a narrative sequence. The self-narratives are the products of, and hence carry the properties of, social accounts or discourse (Gergen and Gergen, 1988). Self in this context is also a set of symbolic representational systems. However, the main distinguishing feature of the social constructionism view of the self concerns its 'exteriorization' of the self. Self in Gergen's theory is completely shifted 'out of the experiencing and sentient person': from the intrinsic mental to the external social realm. This shift carries with it a similar set of implications for human agency as did the early behaviourism of Watson and Skinner. Against the traditional beliefs about individualism and related notions of human agency (individual self-determination and freedom in choice), behaviourism saw external reinforcements of behaviour as the sole controlling agent of human functioning in general (e.g., Skinner, 1971). In the history of psychology, many criticisms have been levelled against behaviourists' stance in ignoring the person and 'situationalizing' human actions (e.g., Bowers, 1973; Harre and Secord, 1972). The relationship between social constructionism's view of the self and behaviourism's notion of human agency will be discussed further later in the chapter.

Self as sentient experiencer and humanistic guide

Self in contemporary psychoanalytic theories
Freud's classical psychoanalytic approach to the self was fo-

cused primarily on the relationship among the components within the human psyche. Little emphasis was given to the interpersonal, sociocultural or historical environment within which the individual is embedded. The neo-Freudian theorists have expanded on the classical theory by acknowledging the significance of various environmental factors for the development of the self. For instance, Carl Jung stresses the influence of the collective human cultural heritage over the individual self. Erik Erikson conceptualizes the self as the result of a life-time ongoing 'unfolding' process of the 'ego'. Sullivan and the object-relations theorists emphasize the importance of interpersonal interactions, actual or symbolic, in shaping the self.

(1) Self as 'collective cultural heritage': Carl Jung
Carl Jung's (1961) idea of the unconscious mind encompasses the Freudian notion of the unconsciousness, which has its origin in the individual's past experiences. Jung referred to this aspect of the unconscious mind as the 'shadow' of the person. But the largest part of the unconscious mind constitutes the 'collective unconscious'. Jung's notion of the collective unconscious, or the 'objective psyche', is founded on a conception of the mind which goes beyond the individual self hence is unbounded by time or space. Jung believed that all minds are part of one 'Collective Mind' which stores the shared memories of all races and the accumulated wisdom of humanity through the ages since the beginning of time. Jung's collective unconscious is thus the product of the collective human evolutionary history. These collective memories are 'stored' in the collective unconscious in the forms of archetypes (i.e., themes of past legends and myths about the essence of all existence) and archetypal images (i.e., symbols and images representing the archetypes). Jung suggested that the collective psyche has an entire history of millions of years, just as that of all existences since the ages past. As a result, there is a vast quantity of archetypal themes and images imbued in the collective unconscious. The most pivotal of these includes the archetype of spiritual heritage, of

growth and transition, and of the Self. The archetype of the Self, or its corresponding image (the 'mandala'), represents the fundamental unity underlying all existence. Self in this sense thus resembles the Heraclitean unbound *psyche* in its entirety. The ultimate aim of individual growth is the attainment of selfhood (Jung, 1961, 1971). Because these archetypes are deeply embedded within the vast unconscious mind, Jung's psychoanalysis is referred to by many as depth psychology. The Jungian self thus goes beyond the individual him-/herself to embrace the entire depth of a collective human heritage.

(2) Self as the lifespan unfoldment of the 'ego'
Erik Erikson's psychoanalysis placed a major emphasis on the role of the following in the development of the self or personhood: (1) the 'ego', (2) psychosocial factors, and (3) a life-long and ongoing unfolding process. The dynamics of the ego, rather than those of the id or superego, are central to Erikson's thesis of lifespan psychosocial development. According to Erikson, there exist rather fixed life-phases, with each phase being associated with a specific type of conflict or 'crisis' confronting the individual. The outcome of the ego's resolution of the crisis of each phase forms a foundation for the psychosocial developments in subsequent life phases.

(3) Self as ' interpersonal interactions'
Many neo-Freudians (e.g., Sullivan, Fairbairn) were influenced by the early social constructivists' (Cooley and Mead) views of the person and self. This influence is twofold. First, social constructivism inspired the interpersonal school of psychiatry (Sullivan, 1953). Second, social constructivism could also be seen as the precursor of object-relations theories (e.g., Fairbairn, 1952). Although both Sullivan's interpersonal psychoanalysis and the object-relations theories placed a key emphasis on interpersonal factors in the formation of the self, they differ in the extent to which such factors are considered to shape up the self. For Sullivan, the self is formed or 'originates' in the

external interpersonal environment and hence, outside this external context, the term self or personhood has no meaning. Instead of 'residing' within the individual, self in Sullivan's theory exists in the social and interpersonal realm. Therefore, although Sullivan was inspired by social constructivism, he essentially turned that tradition (within psychoanalysis) to what is now known as social constructionism (Gergen, 1994).

Like the symbolic interactionists, the object-relations theorists also view the self as the internalization of early interactions with others in the social environment. 'Objects' are the mental representations of people, which include both the person him-/herself and others significant to the person. The mental representations of the self, of the significant others, and of the self–other relations are structured into a multidimensional 'self system'. It is generally assumed (e.g., Kohut, 1977) that the state of a person's psychological well-being would reflect the degree of equilibrium and coherence among various components of this self system.

Self in phenomenological, existential and humanistic theories

Much as Romanticism was a reaction to Enlightenment philosophy, humanistic psychology was against both the biological determinism of classical Freudian psychoanalysis and the situational determinism of behaviourism. Humanistic psychology has its intellectual roots in phenomenological and existential philosophy. The focus of humanistic psychology is on 'being human': on exercising one's own free will and responsibility, on experiencing one's being and existence, and on unfolding one's innate goodness and potentials. Within this general framework, the study of consciousness in psychology during the 1960s also had a new focus on the nature of human conditions and potentials. As mentioned earlier, even though aspects of these humanistic views of the self are held by many neo-Freudians (e.g., Jung, Adler, Erikson), the key figures of humanistic psychology are Carl Rogers, Abraham Maslow and Ronald D. Laing. More recently, there have been further developments within humanistic and phenomenological psychology. These developments are featured in the works of Mihalyi Csikszentmihalyi, Anthony Sutich and Ken Wilber's transpersonal psychology.

(1) Carl Rogers

Rogers' self theory was directly influenced by Gestalt psychology. According to Rogers, the self can be understood through an analysis of an individual's 'phenomenology': the way individuals perceive themselves and their surrounding environment. These perceptions constitute a person's 'phenomenal field' (Rogers, 1951). Like the figure–ground notion in Gestalt psychology, an individual's phenomenal field represents the 'totality of dialectically interdependent relations' (Rychlak, 1981, p.13) among conscious (the figure) and unconscious (the ground) elements. However, Rogers' self theory places a main emphasis on conscious perceptions as determinant of behaviour. An individual's sense of self develops first as a result of his/her early perceptions of the interactions with the parents. Further developments of this rudimentary self-concept not only reflect ongoing experiences, but at the same time, exert influence over such experiences. Three central themes in the humanistic approach to the self or personhood feature prominently in Rogers' theory: (1) the self or personhood can only be understood through the person's own subjective and private experiences, (2) individuals have a basic need for developing and actualizing their innate potentials, and (3) the process of actualizing one's potentials is essentially one of natural unfoldment, provided that the environment is supportive in a genuine, caring and empathic manner (Rogers, 1959).

In Rogers' theory, the notion ideal self is equally important as the notion self. The ideal self constitutes a set of perceptions relevant to self-concept that the person values most. The person's psychological well-being depends on the congruency or incongruency between the self and the ideal self. Roger argues that the need for maintaining the self–ideal congruency and more importantly, the overwhelming need for preserving an overall positive self-regard are at the core of various psychopathological symptoms including the distortion of perceptions of reality. Grounded in this assumption about psychopathology and the humanistic assumptions about the unfoldment of personhood, the Rogerian client-centred therapy thus aims at restoring a self–ideal congruency through the therapist providing a nurturing therapeutic environment which allows for the realignment of the perceptions of the self and of the ideal self.

(2) Abraham Maslow
Abraham Maslow, the father of humanistic psychology, proposed the need-hierarchy theory (Maslow, 1970, 1971) in accounting for man's natural development. The theory contends that the fundamental human needs are arranged in a hierarchical order, beginning with the most basic physiological needs of seeking gratification of hunger and sex, and moving upwards to the highest evolutionary level: the need for self-actualization. Maslow argued that it is man's nature to seek the realization of one's own innate potentials. Such a self-actualization includes doing meaningful and worthwhile work, and for being a 'fair and just' person.

Unlike most other psychologists, Maslow's research focused on psychologically well-developed and highly creative and 'self-actualized' people. Based on his close observations of the experiences of these people, Maslow (1971) identified the human 'peak experience' or the experience of 'transcendence'. Maslow divided the self-actualized people into two types: 'the healthy non-peakers' and 'the transcenders'. The former consists of those people who have achieved the fulfilment not only of one's 'specieshood' (meaning basic physiological and social needs), but also of one's own 'idiosyncratic potentialities'. The latter type of the transcenders are those self-actualizers who have had 'peak experiences' or the transcendental state of being, similar to that experienced in the state of deep meditation. Maslow described the experience as being of different forms including a state of self-forgetfulness, a loss of self- or ego-consciousness, a feeling of timelessness or being 'above it all'. In terms of levels of human consciousness, Maslow regarded the transcendental state of consciousness as the 'highest, and most inclusive and holistic level' of consciousness. In this state, people experience a sense of unity and integration between the self and all other existences including 'the significant others', 'human beings in general', 'other species', 'nature', and also 'the cosmos' (Maslow, 1971). Therefore, Maslow's notion of the peak or transcendental consciousness is identical to the universal consciousness and the essence of existence.

(3) Developments of humanistic psychology
Maslow's propositions of need hierarchy and self-actualization have stimulated a great deal of research in various areas of mainstream psychology including the psychology of personality, individual differences, creativity, and the psychology of work motivation. However, those aspects of his work on conscious experience and in particular, transcendental consciousness, have been met with less enthusiasm in mainstream psychology. Despite the lack of recognition of its merits, research inspired by Maslow on human experience has rapidly gained currency. In recent phenomenological and humanistic literatures of the self, the focus is on the explorations of the self's experience with existence itself. Csikszentmihalyi's work represents such an approach. The notion of moment-to-moment flow in conscious experience (e.g., Csikszentmihalyi, 1997; Csikszentmihalyi and Csikszentmihalyi, 1988) refers to the subjective optimal experience when an individual is completely absorbed in a task at hand. The person appears to have lost him-/herself in this form of extreme concentration. A self absorbed in such moment-to-moment flow thus brings to the fore the self's sentient-experiencer aspect.

Maslow's work on transcendental consciousness and peak experience has inspired the development of transpersonal psychology. The main task of transpersonal psychology therefore deals with human higher consciousness and its attainment through self-transcendence. The most pivotal presumption of transpersonal psychology thus concerns the existence of a universal consciousness. The subjective reality of the universal consciousness is characterized by an awareness of the fundamental undifferentiated unity of all existence.

The definition of transpersonal psychology was given by Anthony Suitch in the inaugural issue of the *Journal of Transpersonal Psychology* in 1969. The focus of transpersonal psychology is on issues pertaining to ultimate human capacities and potentialities. Such issues include

> becoming, individual and species-wide meta-needs, ultimate values, unitive consciousness, peak experiences, B-values, ecstasy, mystical experience, awe, being, self-actualization, essence, bliss, wonder, ultimate meaning, transcendence of the self, spirit, oneness, cosmic awareness, individual and species-wide synergy, maximal sensory awareness, responsiveness and expression, and related concepts, experiences and activities.

The goal of transpersonal psychology is to carry out empirical and scientific research into these issues and to responsibly implement such findings.

Suitch argued that these issues and goals that transpersonal psychology is concerned with had not found 'systematic place' in mainstream psychology up till that time. Suitch identified three main areas or main 'forces' in psychology up till 1970: positivistic or behaviouristic psychology ('first force'), classical psychoanalytic psychology ('second force'), and humanistic psychology ('third force'). Psychology, as an academic discipline, has however undergone a tremendous growth since then. Several paradigm shifts have taken place within the discipline (e.g., the cognitive revolution–cognitive science–connectionism shift), together with the emergence of many new fields in the applied arenas. However, even though psychology has expanded greatly its domain and accommodated new content areas, the discipline as a whole is still sceptical about the issues dealt with by transpersonal psychology. This is partly due to the fact that, while transpersonal psychology deals with the topic of consciousness, it is not concerned with what Chalmers (1996) calls 'psychological consciousness' (objective and functional aspects of the mind), rather, it focuses on 'phenomenal consciousness' (subjective experiential and sensational aspects of the mind). As such, it naturally extends to and may overlap with spirituality, a topic still considered 'unscientific' by most contemporary psychologists. So again, this sense of doubt is grounded in the entrenched mentality of the separation of the intellectual mind from the fundamental spirit.

Notwithstanding the unsympathetic academic environment, transpersonal psychology has made a groundbreaking progress towards the understanding of ultimate human potentialities. Its research into human consciousness has illuminated greatly the nature of the interconnectedness of the individual and the universal mind. For instance, Ken Wilber's (1982, 1996) developmental framework of human consciousness integrates notions of Eastern spirituality and Western existential humanistic psychology. Wilber first identified ten different levels of consciousness and then specified the mechanisms of transcending to higher levels of awareness. According to Wilber, there are three lower levels of consciousness: *matter, raptile* and *mammal (body)*. These levels are within the 'subconscious sphere' which entails the upward development of consciousness from matter to body.

The next three levels up are within the 'self-conscious sphere': *persona, ego* and *centaur*. Following the Jungian tradition, Wilber's *ego* (i.e., one's accurate and healthy self-image) combines both the *persona* (i.e., the public or 'fraudulent' self-image) and the *shadow* (i.e., the repressed unconscious mind). However, a healthy ego is not quite the whole individual self. Here, Wilber introduced the notion *centaur*, which unites the '*ego* mind' and the 'body-*soma*' (i.e., the life force or energy field surrounding the living). It is only when the ego (mind) and the vitality and energizing life force are united that the real identity of the individual as an integrated self is realized. Wilber expressed the ideas in these two equations: (1) *persona* + *shadow* = *ego*, and (2) *ego* + *body soma* = *centaur*. Thus the highest level of development within the self-conscious sphere would require a total unity of the human mind and the animal body in order to actualize the centauric self.

The last four levels are the superconsciousness within the 'transpersonal or the universal sphere': *psychic, subtle, causal* and *ultimate*. While the *psychic* consciousness is within the realm of the transpersonal psychic powers, the *subtle* consciousness moves into the realm of the archetypes and the individual's 'personal deity'. The *causal* consciousness encompasses the 'unmanifest void', and finally, the highest level of the *ultimate* consciousness unites the individual *centaur* with the ultimate spirit to reveal a 'Supreme Identity', which Wilber likens to Bucke's notion of the 'cosmic consciousness' (Wilber, 1982). Both terms are also similar to Maslow's transcendental consciousness discussed earlier. All these terms denote the highest level of human awareness: the profound cognizance of the essence of all existence and an enlightened sense of fundamental unity. The development of consciousness at the transpersonal level thus involves the transition from the 'soul' towards the 'spirit', finally reaching the realization that the individual self and the entire nature are but one ultimate and unified entity.

SELF IN CONTEMPORARY SOCIO-POLITICAL AND CULTURAL-HISTORICAL ANALYSES

Outside psychology, the notion self is also a subject of enquiry in other fields of human sciences. The works of the social critics including Carl Marx, Max Weber, Emile Durkheim and Christopher Lasch, have concerned the impacts of the changing society and its political-economic ideologies on individual existence and the self. While the philosophical and psychological analyses focus primarily on the individual and the immediate social surroundings, the frame of reference for these analyses is the larger society and the cultural and political systems within which individuals are embedded. According to these critics, human nature and behaviour can only be understood from a grand system perspective that goes beyond the social psychological definitions of the 'social' as immediate and identifiable relationships or interrelated networks. Individuals are seen not only as a product of the immediate social forces, but more so of the larger sociopolitical and cultural-historical forces.

Marx's political and economic philosophy centres around the idea of 'class' struggles within a prevailing political or economic system. Given that the free-market ideology is prevalent in today's societies, his analysis of the effects of capitalism on the person is relevant here. Essentially, Marx argued that the tension between the controlling class of the capitalists and the controlled class of the workers results from the inequitable distribution of the profits which the production of the workers has generated. According to Marx, capitalism forces those without the capital (workers) to sell their labour as a 'commodity', for which the employer pays. Social relations in this context constitute in essence an economic exchange relationship with a focus on the final outcome or the goal of the exchange.

In the climate of quickly accelerating economic activities (both industrial and technological), Weber aimed to understand human actions and their underlying rationalization. He distinguished amongst others, two different types of actions and the governing rationality: goal-directed action governed by instrumental rationality and value-oriented action governed by value rationality. Weber argued that modern times are characterized by the ethos of, and the commitment to, goal-directed action. Human actions are centred around 'commodity' production and profit exchange. The consequences of this macro-social system of capitalism for the individual self are devastating. According to

Weber, the instrumental pursuit of wealth in a modern capitalistic society has not only enslaved individuals in an 'iron cage', but more importantly, resulted in a disenchanted world. In this modern world, the ultimate and supreme human values in terms of intrinsic meaning and purpose of life have disappeared from public institutional and working life (Smith, 1997; Taylor, 1989).

In these macro analyses of the influence of capitalism over the individual self, a picture of the self emerges as primarily one of economic agent with a clear goal found in economic exchanges. The 'instrumentalized' self identifies with the collective materialistic values of the commercialized system.

Instead of focusing on the 'production' aspect of the societal influence on the self, as did Marx and Weber, Durkheim's sociological analysis placed a greater emphasis on the well-being of the individual self. Durkheim (1952) used suicide as a social phenomenon to analyse the societal influence on the self. Durkheim took the view that human nature is intrinsically 'social' and hence the society plays a prominent role in the development and well-being of the self. The deficiency of society's influence can be seen in two types of suicide: the egoistic and the anomic. Egoistic suicide results from a society's failure to include the individual in its collective activity and hence deprives him/her of a sense of purpose or meaning. Anomic suicide results from a society's failure in having clear norms or regulations and hence leaving the individual without a 'check-rein' (Durkheim, 1952).

Other social critics have also presented a pessimistic analysis of the influence of modern society on the self. For instance, Wheelis (1958) argued that the modern society with its focus on group rather than individual values, has resulted in a weakening of the superego and a concomitant expansion of the ego. This shift also characterizes Turner's (1976) discussion of a self from one that is 'institutional' (emphasizing self-control and social commitment and values) to an 'impulsive' self (rejecting institutional norms that constrain individual expression of impulses). In a similar vein, other sociological analyses have focused on the influence of large modern corporations on the self. They have spoken of the 'corporatization' or 'colonization' of the self by these post-industrial organizations (e.g., Casey, 1995; Lasch, 1978, 1984). The traditional self with a sense of inner-directedness and inner judgement is now replaced by an outer-directed self governed by the authority of the utility-driven bureaucratic corporations.

KEY ISSUES IN RECENT SELF RESEARCH

Two major trends in recent psychological research into the self are of significance to the understanding of human consciousness. These trends are: (1) a conceptual shift from a self that has a dual internal and external focus to one with solely an external focus, (2) a broadened research agenda that embraces micro neurobiological and macro systemic approaches. Possible consequences of these trends for consciousness research are noted briefly.

Self with an internal versus external focus

The issue of whether the self has an internal or external focus is essential in understanding human nature and consciousness. In Classical philosophy, the self being the intrapsychic core that contains potentials for human good was never questioned. It was through the agentic and guiding operation of this inner-focused self that an individual may attain a state of harmony both within and without. However, the intrinsic self's guiding function was largely taken over by religious institutes during Scholasticism. In modernity, the Enlightenment philosophers formally reduced *psyche* to its agentic aspects. And along with the reduction, *psyche's* role as a sentient humanistic guide was also ousted from the inner core. The guiding role was now played by socially-contracted rules explicit in the Kantian categorical imperatives of moral duties or the Rawlsian contractarian principles of justice. As a result of the agency–sentience separation, the entire void of the inner *psyche* was filled by an externally-guided self whose agentic function involves solely the exercise of 'disengaged ration'. Against this background, the Romantic philosophers still saw the self as being inner-focused and constituting 'nature as source within' (Taylor, 1989). However, with the postmodern deconstructionism movement, there is a 'disappearance' of the core self (e.g., Smith, 1997).

In psychology, the 'dialectic' self is typically seen as having both an internal and external focus. The self is at the same time self-regulatory and externally-regulated. However, this tradition seems to have also been challenged by the postmodern movement. Self in this context has a totally extrinsic focus; it is formed and maintained solely with reference to external social environments. The self has disappeared from within the individual person and now resides outside in the social networks of relationship. For instance, the recent conceptualization of the self as a set of 'relational narratives' represents such a challenge (e.g., Gergen and Gergen, 1988; Gergen, 1994). Influenced by the 'linguistic turn' (Smith, 1997) in the contemporary intellectual climate, Gergen's view is similar to that of Wittgenstein in the sense that the selves are socially-constructed symbols in the form of relationship narratives. Also in that broader intellectual context, Gergen's view further reflects the image of the self portrayed in recent socio-political and cultural-historical theories.

The possible consequences of this conceptual shift for consciousness research are worth noting. There appear to be both positive and negative consequences. On the negative side, the consequence of this postmodern shift in the notion self may parallel that of radical behaviourism or situationism in the history of psychology. The deconstruction of the notion self as an intrinsic source of nature and its recasting into the social arena is reminiscent of the radical behaviourists' stance on intrinsic mental states. Recall that although consciousness was the core subject of all the three founding psychologies, the rise of behaviourism virtually put an end to the study of intrinsic mental states. However, the dialectic progression of intellectual history has shown repeatedly that the extreme form of any thesis, or its antithesis, by itself can at best reveal a partial truth.

There are at least two positive consequences for consciousness research. First, as a result of this conceptual shift, the importance of the larger socio-political and cultural-historical factors in shaping the individual self has been brought to the fore. The operations of such factors in affecting the self are often beyond conscious awareness. This theme is well reflected in both the Freudian and Jungian unconscious. Cast in this context, this postmodern shift has provided, albeit indirectly and unintentionally, a justification for the role of the nonconscious in the shaping of the individual self. The second positive consequence concerns postmodernism's emphasis on pluralism. The postmodern notion of the self also carries the assumption that for each individual, the self is a set of relational narratives (Gergen and Gergen, 1988) and hence there can be as many selves as the number of socially-defined 'relationship nuclei' (Gergen, 1994). This idea of multiple selves is central to a system-dynamic approach to consciousness (hence mind and self), as discussed briefly in the following section and later in Chapter 7.

Self research: neurophysiological correlates and system-dynamic features

The idea of multiple selves is a common assumption shared by the traditional social constructivist theories of the self and the postmodern deconstructionist models. Ever since the early social constructivists such as Mead argued for multiple selves in terms of the varied social roles (cf. Casey, 1995, p.57), the view has been upheld in later social psychological and personality theories on the self. The existence of multiple possible selves and their interacting dynamics suggest that the notion self can best be approached from a system-dynamic perspective (this point will be returned to later in Chapter 7). Several researchers have already taken this line by applying theories of dynamic systems to the notion self and personality (e.g., Carver and Scheier, 1998; Zohar, 1991).

Consistently with such a system-dynamic approach to the notion self, recent research in personality has applied the connectionist notion of modularity to the conceptualization of subself or sub-personality systems. For instance, Cloninger's (1998) psychobiological model of personality draws the distinction between two subsystems of the self: temperament and character. The former refers to inherent predispositions and includes further subsystems for the activation, inhibition, dependence and persistence of behaviour. The latter constitutes learned adaptations and further includes three subsystems of self-directedness, cooperativeness and self-transcendence. These hierarchically-organized subsystems of the self are causally independent but functionally interactive. Each of the subsystems has a distinct set of neural networks in the cortical or subcortical brain as its neurobiological correlate. All these functional neuralnets are at once dissociable from, and yet interconnected with, one another.

Therefore, viewing the self from a connectionist or system-dynamic perspective can account for the organization of multiple subselves in terms of modularity, at both functional and neurobiological levels. Such an interactive and hierarchical conceptualization of the self further allows for theoretical speculation over the emergence of higher mental states or cognitive capabilities, at both ontogenetic and phylogenetic levels (see Cloninger, 1998 for a review). From a lifespan developmental perspective, the psychobiological model of personality has included the humanistic or existential notion of self-transcendence as a legitimate subsystem of the self. And by having further identified its possible neurobiological correlates in the cortical regions, the model can serve as a ground framework for further interdisciplinary and integrative research into the dynamics of the self.

6
Qualitative Consciousness: Its Existence and Function

A holistic model of consciousness needs to be grounded in the notion of a holistic self, or the *psyche*. As previously reviewed, the *psyche* was considered as having no bounds by the early Greek philosophers. Going further back in time, the misty-time image of the *psyche* was immersed in nature itself, undifferentiated and inseparable. As such, the vastness of the *psyche* or the holistic self is readily seen. Therefore, a model of consciousness that places any boundary around the holistic *psyche* is not able to capture the phenomenon in its fullness.

Philosophers and poets have marvelled at the vastness of the mind or consciousness. With reference to remembering, which is but one of the numerous activities of the mind, St Augustine (1939) commented:

> ... Great is this force of memory, excessive great ... a large and boundless chamber! who ever sounded the bottom thereof? ...Yet not these alone does the unmeasurable capacity of my memory retain. Here also is all, learnt of the liberal sciences and as yet unforgotten; removed as it were to some inner place, which is yet no place ... (p.213)

The Romantic writer Shakespeare spoke of the vastness of the inner states through Hamlet: *'I could be bounded in a nutshell and count myself the king of infinite space ...'* Thus the holistic mind with its 'unmeasurable capacity' seems to be occupying the same infinite space as the boundless physical reality itself.

From early philosophy through to contemporary psychology, the study of the mind and consciousness has been constrained by the dominant paradigm of the time, yet paradigms wax and wane in the fashion captured by Kuhn's (1970) description of the evolution of scientific paradigms. Within philosophy, the influential paradigms since the Classical period have been predominantly positive philosophies, and they were marked by Aristotle's rationalistic naturalism, Locke and Hume's empiricism, Comte's positivism, Peirce and James' pragmatism, Dewey's instrumentalism, Wittgenstein and the Vienna logical positivism, and more recently, Quine's scientific naturalism and Ryle's logical behaviourism. The dominance of such positivistic and analytic approaches to philosophy ensures that the study of consciousness pertains only to the functional and relational aspects of consciousness (i.e., the quantitative aspect of the mind). As for psychology, given that it was founded in the spirit of empirical science and hence as a discipline, it is totally committed to scientific naturalism and reductionistic materialism. As a result, the study of the mind or consciousness in psychology is also similarly restricted to its quantitative aspect.

An empirical and scientific approach to the mind is only capable of dealing with its quantitative aspect which is, as pointed out earlier, the first issue of the mind–body problem. To understand the mind as a whole requires that the second mind–body problem, or the qualia issue, be addressed and fully accounted for. The qualia problem however does not reside in the 'vastness' of the mind nor the richness of experience, it lies in the contemporary sole emphasis on scientific empiricism or naturalism in the acquisition of any kind of knowledge. Knowledge about the non-qualitative aspects of the mind is directly obtainable within the scientific paradigm and hence it is considered legitimate. Knowledge about the qualitative aspects of the mind cannot be so attained; and so long as the enquiry into the mind is restricted in its method, there can be no solution apart from denying its existence totally or reducing it entirely to physical or cellular activities. As a result, the study of qualitative experience has been completely shifted out of the main branches of philosophy (positivistic and analytic philosophy) and contemporary mainstream psychology. Outside these main intellectual paradigms, qualitative experience has become the focus of 'peripheral areas' of psychology including phenomenological, humanistic and transpersonal psychology. It is in these areas, peripheral to the intellectual *Zeitgeist* that the terms 'self' or 'consciousness' are consistently used to denote being and becoming in its entirety, a usage more closely reflecting the meaning of the early terms *psyche* or *spirit*.

It is argued that this forced separation of qualitative from non-qualitative experiences is the primary cause of the qualia problem. To rectify this problem, it is argued that the right directions to take are fundamentally twofold: (1) to dissolve such a conceptual separation and to see both qualitative and non-qualitative experience as integral to and part and parcel of human consciousness in its entirety, and (2) to identify the unique specialization and function of qualitative experience (given that non-qualitative experience is well understood as 'adaptation to one's environment'). The rest of this chapter deals with these two themes in that order.

DISSOLVING THE CONCEPTUAL SEPARATION BETWEEN QUALIA AND NONQUALIA

Regarding the task of dissolving the conceptual boundary, several approaches have been suggested by theorists working from two different perspectives: Shannon's information-state perspective (Chalmers, 1996) or Schrodinger's quantum wave function (superposition) perspective (e.g., Penrose, 1997; Zohar, 1991; Zohar & Marshall, 1994; Marshall, 1989). These two approaches share one fundamental assumption concerning the very nature of an underlying reality, or the universe. Both are consistent with the position of neutral monism (e.g., Leibniz, James, Russell): reality exists in a superpositioned neutral state, which can be realized as being either physical or phenomenological.

In the following section, existing theories which aim at dissolving the separation between qualia and non-qualitative experiences are reviewed first. Following the review, some suggestions are made for future directions of research along the lines of these theories.

Chalmers' information-state model of consciousness

Most models of consciousness in cognitive neuroscience have been proposed in order to account for non-qualitative consciousness and awareness (e.g., Shallace, Johnson-Laird, Baars; see review in Chapter 4). These models were not aiming in the first place at dissolving the boundary between qualitative and non-qualitative experience. Rather, they were still built upon, and operated within, the separation premise. Chalmers' (1996) model is consistent with the main argument of the present book, since it aims at the dissolution of the conceptual separation between qualitative and non-qualitative experience. Couched within the naturalistic tradition, Chalmers' model represents the most comprehensive account of the structure, content and ontology (albeit speculative) of qualitative experience.

The model makes an assumption that the most fundamental property of the actual physical world is information (as many physicists do). This concept of information is adopted from Shannon's (1948) mathematical theory of communication, which deals with the amount of information carried by an information state. While Shannon was primarily concerned with the amount or the quantity of information (bits) carried in a specified information state, Chalmers was concerned with the qualitative structure of the information space and the various related information states within it. The main contribution of

Chalmers' model lies in its postulate pertaining to the coherence principle, that governs the relationship between qualia and non-qualitative aspects of conscious experiences. The principle implies a concomitant and dual-aspected coexistence of the 'two kinds' of conscious experiences. Proceeding from there, Chalmers further speculates that this dual-aspected coexisting state also characterizes the entire information space: one single neutral reality exists which has a dual (physical as well as mental) property.

As direct quotes will be taken from Chalmers in describing his model, it needs to be noted that some confusion may arise with the terms used in Chalmers and this book. Chalmers used the terms 'phenomenal consciousness' or 'experience' to mean 'qualia'. In contrast, he used the terms 'psychological consciousness' or 'awareness' to mean 'non-qualitative consciousness'. And for most of his book, he further simplified the usage by using 'consciousness' to mean just qualia, and 'awareness' to mean non-qualitative consciousness (p.31). With these semantic differences in mind, the following are the key points of Chalmers' model.

Relationship between qualia and nonqualia consciousness: coherence principle

His chapter on 'the coherence between consciousness and awareness' addresses the relationship between qualia (in this book's terms) and non-qualitative consciousness. There he argues that because *'the phenomenology and the psychology of the mind do not float free of each other; they are systematically related'*, so it seems to him that *'the most promising way to get started in developing a theory of consciousness is to focus on the remarkable coherence'* between the two (p.218). His coherence principle reflects the psychophysical laws and refers to the coexistence between consciousness and awareness (qualia and non-qualitative consciousness in this book). Put in information terms, the principle contends that both a 'psychological' (i.e., non-qualitative conscious experience) and a 'phenomenal' (i.e., qualitative) aspect of consciousness are actualized or realized concomitantly once a set of the 'information state' (i.e., reality) is brought under the 'global control' of an information-processing system.

In Chalmers' fundamental theory, an information-processing system can be anything, so long as it is able to realize (make manifest) a set of the information state. This would include not only the brain, the visual or other perceptual systems within a living organism, but also any dynamic systems, capable of processing or 'affording' information, such as a thermostat. For all information-processing systems, this coexisting coherence principle applies to both the structural and the functional levels of consciousness. The structural coherence principle (p.225) stipulates that the cognitive structural representations of non-qualitative experiences (e.g., visual perception) correspond and mirror those implicit representations of their qualia counterparts.

In terms of function, the organizational invariance principle (pp.248–9) states that so long as different information-processing systems share the same 'fine-grained functional organization', the systems will have 'qualitatively identical experiences' (i.e., identical qualia). In other words, conscious experience carries the property of 'organizational invariance'. As Chalmers shows in a series of thought experiments, this functional coherence rule logically leads to the conclusion that so long as functional organization is preserved, the 'physical material' that makes up a dynamic processing system can be widely different (e.g., brain neurons replaced one by one by silicon chips) and yet the same qualia are preserved.

Relationship between physical and mental properties: one single information reality with dual properties

Generating from his fundamental propositions of the coherence principle, Chalmers further speculates on the nature of an information state. He argues that the coexistence of qualitative and non-qualitative experience, as the one single realization of the same set of information states, already 'puts a strong constraint' on the basic structure of the universe (as information space). To be manifested concomitantly as two properties would carry a strong implication for the nature of the unmanifested information state: it exists as a neutral stuff, but has both an intrinsic phenomenological property and a non-intrinsic physical property; upon realization by the processing system, it reveals both the phenomenological and the physical properties.

The dual-aspected view of the world is consistent with Russell's (and James') neutral monism. Chalmers describes the nature of information states this way: '*We might say that internal aspects of these states are phenomenal, and the external aspects are physical. Or as a slogan: Experience is information from the inside; physics is information from the outside*' (p.305). In this context, whenever a set of the 'neutral but dual-aspected' information state is realized, both its qualitative and physical properties are concomitantly realized. In terms of the categorization of his theory, Chalmers commented that while the theory is clearly one of a dual-property type and hence belongs to the dualism tradition, the theory can also be classified as a monistic (dual-aspected) theory.

Consciousness and brain

Consciousness, according to the information-state model, is the result of the concomitant realization of qualitative and non-qualitative properties of a set of information states. Realizations of the originally neutral information are the works of any processing system such as the eye or the brain. In the physical brain (or its perceptual cortices), the physical properties of information state are '*realized in the experience's physical substrate*' (Chalmers, 1996, p.284). This means that the realized non-qualitative or physical properties take the 'form' of neurally coded representations. Such neuronal codes can then be measured. However, given its non-reductivistic stance concerning qualia, the theory assumes that the concomitantly realized qualitative properties cannot be reduced to a physical or neuronal level, hence there is no similar physical representation in the form of neuronal codes for the qualitative properties of experience.

To summarize, Chalmers' naturalistic model proposes that both qualitative and non-qualitative aspects of consciousness are concomitantly realized properties of the same set of information states. The non-qualitative aspect is manifested physically in the form of cellular activities, whereas the qualitative aspect is realized phenomenologically and is irreducible to physical matter. As Chalmers has pointed out, his information model of consciousness places a constraint on the nature of the information state. For the psychophysical coherence principles to work well, the information state, prior to its being actualized, has to possess the dual physical and phenomenological properties. In other words, the unmanifested information state has to have the potential for a realization of both a physical and a phenomenological state.

Regardless of this further speculation about the nature of the underlying reality, the most significant point of Chalmers' model concerns the (structural) coherence principle that stipulates the concomitant existence of qualitative and non-qualitative experience. It is at this very point that diverse theoretical perspectives on consciousness may converge: these perspectives are grounded in information theory, biology, chaos or dynamic systems, and quantum mechanics.

Superposition of qualia and non-qualitative experience: a convergent view

This concomitant 'both-and' state of existence characterizes quantum reality. As reviewed earlier in Chapter 4, quantum objects possess both properties of being discrete (digital, particle-like) and being continuous (analog, wave-like). This dual-aspected state of existence within the quantum realm is referred to as a superposition (a wave fuction). A superposition can be seen as the unmanifested or unactualized state of potentialities. This superpositioned state of potentialities is neither static nor unchanging; it is in a constant 'flux'. The dynamics of the progression or evolution of quantum objects, when in their unmanifested state, are governed by the Schrodinger equation. This differential equation describes the co-evolutionary path of each quantum object in the superpositioned state. The key point here is the quantum notion of superposition seems to be most suitable to describe the both-and state of qualitative and non-qualitative experience. Several converging perspectives are summarized below.

Information theory perspective: Chalmers

As discussed, the central tenet of Chalmers' fundamental model of the conscious mind is the inseparable coexistence of qualia and non-qualitative experience. Consciousness is thus concomitantly both qualitative and non-qualitative in nature. Therefore, what Chalmers refers to as the dual-aspected information state within the framework of information theory appears parallel to the superpositioned state conceptualized from the perspective of quantum mechanics. Here, even though Chalmers did not rely on the quantum notion of superposition in his model, he did point out in the final chapter of the book that his model, while grounded in information theory, *'implies the superposition principle'* (p.350).

Biological perspective: Searle

Although Chalmers' model was accepted by many, some have cast doubts on its many propositions. Searle (1997) recently reviewed Chalmers' model. Consistent with his view that consciousness is an emergent property of the biological brain and hence must be studied as a natural biological phenomenon (e.g., Searle, 1992), Searle rejected Chalmers' fundamental stance of grounding consciousness in information space.

Further, consistent with his position as an ardent opponent of strong artificial intelligence (e.g., Searle, 1980), Searle argues against Chalmers' functional coherence (organizational invariance) principle. Even though Searle (1997) basically rejects Chalmers' information model as an account of conscious experience, he has nonetheless been advocating the inseparability and oneness of consciousness and qualia from his biological emergence perspective. Indeed, Searle sees the separation of qualitative and non-qualitative experience as the basic barrier to understanding consciousness.

Speaking of his emergence view, Searle acknowledges that it is unclear as to how brain processes which are biological in nature, and publicly and objectively observable, could give rise to the inner qualitative and private states or states of 'sentience'. However, he argues that there should be no such separation in the first place. Searle has argued against the separation between consciousness and qualia and that between qualia and non-qualitative experience. Regarding the consciousness–qualia separation, Searle (1997) writes:

> I myself am hesitant to use the word 'qualia' and ... 'quale,' because they give the impression that there are two separate phenomena, consciousness and qualia. But ... all conscious phenomena are qualitative, subjective experiences, and hence are qualia. There are not two types of phenomena ... There is just consciousness, which is a series of qualitative states. (p.9)

Regarding the separation between non-qualitative and qualitative experience, he writes:

> we must not get sidetracked into thinking that there are really two kinds of consciousness, an information-processing consciousness that is amenable to scientific investigation and a phenomenal, what-it-subjectively-feels-like form of consciousness ... No, the unity of consciousness guarantees that for each of us all the variety of the forms of our conscious life are unified into a single conscious field. (p.200)

In addition to the inseparability of qualia and non-qualitative experience, Searle shares another view with Chalmers: that qualia are irreducible to molecular activities. Searle argues that the biological brain has a 'biological capacity to produce experiences' which only exist when they are 'felt' by specific individual persons in a first-personal sense. Searle's point is that reducing first-personal subjective phenomena to third-personal objective phenomena is going to result in leaving out the subjectivity which defines that experience. This non-reductive emergence view of consciousness and hence of qualia is also shared by other neuroscientists including Roger Sperry and Sir John Eccles.

Chaos and dynamic systemic perspective: Hardcastle

As reviewed in Chapter 4, many neuroscientists (e.g., Basar, Freeman, Hardcastle) have also conceptualized the brain and its various neural nets as dynamic systems whose behaviour is governed by the physical laws of nonlinear complex systems. Although a complete application of chaos and dynamic systemic notions to the brain still awaits further quantitative evidence, existing empirical evidence based on qualitative analyses seems to suggest that this could be a fruitful direction to pursue. Based on existing evidence, Hardcastle (1995) has put forward the proposition that consciousness can be a property corresponding to the brain's higher level (system level) oscillations. As such, she has defined consciousness in terms of coherent 'system-dynamic oscillations'. Although the proposition that qualia and non-qualitative experience coexist in a superposition has not been made explicit in the model, Hardcastle nonetheless has included subjective first-personal experiences (qualia) as an integral part of consciousness. She argued that third-personal neuronal level explanations can help derive what first-personal qualitative experience must be like, although they may not completely explain some features of qualia such as the apparent differences among individuals. As mentioned in

Chapter 4, accounts of consciousness from the chaos perspective often converge with those from the perspective of quantum theory, to which the notion of superposition is foundational.

Quantum mechanics perspective: Penrose
As also reviewed in Chapter 4, researchers have already made an appeal to quantum notions in modelling consciousness. The main premise underlying such an approach lies in the scientific reductionistic conviction that consciousness, as a naturally occurring phenomenon, can only be understood by approaching it as any other 'object' of nature and physical reality. The methods of physical sciences are then the most appropriate ones in unveiling the nature of consciousness. However, recent advances in physics have shown that, although the Newtonian view of the physical reality still holds for the Classical world at the macro level, it is inconsistent with the picture of the micro world of the quantum reality. If conscious experience is to be reductively understood as micro-level cellar atomic activities, then it becomes imperative for those activities to be reconceptualized in the light of the 'new physics' which pertains to the micro-level physical reality.

Several theorists have taken this line, in researching consciousness. As reviewed in Chapter 4, this approach rests on the fundamental assumption of the superposition of the quantum physical reality. Accordingly, atomic activities at the neuronal or microtubular levels are conceptualized as following the wave function law that governs the activities of quantum particles. In this context, consciousness is typically said to correspond with the collapse of the superposition or wave function towards a synchronized coherent oscillating pattern, akin to that in a Bose-Einstein condensate. The quantum-coherent oscillations have been hypothesized to take place at various loci and they give rise to consciousness. According to Penrose, they account for computational consciousness; the quality of consciousness or the non-computational conscious experience (such as mathematical insights and understanding) is accounted for only by objective collapse (OR, no external cause) inside the cytoskeleton microtubes.

What Penrose refers to as the non-computational consciousness is equivalent to qualia. This is made clear in a commentary paper by Abner Shimony (Penrose, 1997), in which Shimony pointed out that Penrose's term 'non-computational conscious experience' includes other aspects of consciousness: '*sensory qualia, ... sensations of pain and pleasure, ... feelings of volition, ... intentionality (which is the experienced reference to objects or concepts or propositions), etc. ...*' (p.145). From Penrose's own writing, it is clear that he considers the non-computational consciousness as an integral part of all conscious experience. Here, he writes: '*non-computability in some aspect of consciousness and specifically, in mathematical understanding, strongly suggests that non-computability should be a feature of* all consciousness. This is my suggestion' (Penrose, 1997, p.117). Therefore, it is reasonable to argue that implicit to Penrose's quantum-coherence model is the assumption that both qualia (i.e., non-computational) and non-qualitative experiences (i.e., computational) exist in a superposition, prior to their actualization. The OR, and SR, quantum-collapse processes are responsible for the actualization of qualia and non-qualitative experiences respectively.

To sum up, these different theoretical perspectives appear to converge directly or indirectly on the inseparable and hence superpositioned existence of qualia and non-qualitative experience. The actualization of one aspect would concomitantly make manifest the other.

The question of 'binding' naturally arises at this point: Given that qualia and non-qualitative experience exist in an indeterminant superpositioned state, there is the obvious difference between this indeterminant state and the 'definite' state of the observable world around us. From an information theoretic perspective, Chalmers attempted several alternative possible solutions including postulating further psychophysical bridging laws. However, he writes: *'In any case, I will leave this question open. It is certainly the hardest problem ... ; but it is not obvious that it cannot be solved'* (p.307).

From the cognitive and information-processing perspective, recent research has shown that attention (awareness) is essential for feature binding in the parietal cortex. However, the underlying binding mechanisms may involve more information that is *'implicitly available than we can consciously access'* (Treisman, 1998, p.1295). As such, Treisman (1998) concluded that *'the binding problem may be intimately bound up with the nature of consciousness, but that is a story that I think no one is yet ready to tell'* (p.1305).

For the other perspectives (biological, chaos and quantum views), the binding issue seems to be nicely resolved by the notion of synchronized or coherent patterns of oscillation at a network or system level, as suggested by Penrose's (1987, 1989) notion of 'globality' of consciousness as well as Hardcastle's (1995) conceptualization of binding as a 'property of the brain's higher-level oscillations' (p.131).

The foregoing analysis has provided justifications for the inseparability between qualia and non-qualitative experience. Various existing theoretical frameworks converge in suggesting that the two aspects of conscious experience can be described as being in a superpositioned state. Prior to actualization, both coexist as unmanifested potentialities; upon actualization, both exist concomitantly. The implications of this proposition will be returned to and discussed more fully in the next chapter. The rest of this chapter turns to the second issue of the function of qualitative experience, or the possible causal role that such raw feels may play in affecting behaviour.

THE FUNCTION OF QUALIA

Within the prevailing functionalism paradigm, any notion is deemed meaningless if it does not have a causal role to play in terms of observable action or behaviour. Consequently, this superposition proposition which formalizes the existence of qualia begs the question of its causal function. However, the superposition proposition has also provided an answer to this question. As mentioned before, the function of non-qualitative experience has been well understood: it serves the causal function of life's adaptation in general, although some theorists have maintained that no credible adaptationist account of consciousness is available (e.g., Flanagan and Polger, 1995). The superposition proposition, by interweaving qualia with non-qualitative experience, suggests that the function of qualia may also be intimately intertwined with that of their non-qualitative counterparts: the two complement each other and work together towards the general goal of life adaptation. In other words, through their intertwined coexistence, there is also a 'functional complementarity' in their correlative causal adaptational role.

Functional complementarity in system terms implies that each aspect of the system has a specialization which supplements that of the other by having ongoing operational dialogues. Because of the intricate dialectic interconnection between the two, each aspect alone is incomplete in terms of the functioning of the system as a whole. The quantum system notion of complementarity has been applied to the functions of the two sides of the brain. The brain's information processing function is only completed when the two hemispheres work together as if in a complex 'package deal' (e.g., Zohar and Marshall, 1994). This presumed dialectic 'cross-talk' between the two hemispheres appears to be consistent with existing evidence of hemispheric functional asymmetry based on clinical patients as well as normal individuals.

Extending the complementarity principle to consciousness means that each of its two superpositioned aspects has a specialization of its own, but is in constant need of the expertise of the other in order for the system to be fully functional. In information processing and computational terms, a prerequisite for a system to be fully functional is to have available to it all relevant information as data for processing at every level of analysis. Within such an information-processing framework, it has been argued that the one single most important function of consciousness is to increase the flow of information between otherwise separate information subsystems. And as such, consciousness serves to create pathways, sometimes novel ones, to less accessible information (Baars, 1997).

Given that consciousness serves this general function, it is argued that its non-qualitative aspects specialize in increasing the flow of information pertaining primarily to the 'conscious mind', and that its qualitative aspects specialize primarily in creating accesses to information pertaining to the 'non-conscious'. Analogous to the systemic functioning of the physical brain, consciousness also possesses the emergent property of constant 'cross-talk' between the two specialized functions. This cross-talk thus allows for the free flow of information between the conscious and the nonconscious. Therefore, increased flow of information from different regions of the mental workspace means (1) enhanced activation of, and hence greater accessibility to, the information contents of these different regions; and (2) enhanced dialectic feedback of information from different regions and subsystems of the workspace.

The purpose of enhancing information flow and activation is for the 'construction of mental conclusions' (e.g., Marcel, 1983; Mandler, 1989, 1997; Oatley, 1988). The conclusion-constructing or synthesizing process is ongoing and takes place at different levels of analysis. At each specific level, the synthesis or the mental conclusion so constructed may constitute the current experience of awareness. This consciousness-as-constructive-process view, first proposed by Marcel (1983), is thus consistent with the complex-system-dynamic view that conceptualizes consciousness in terms of system dynamics.

To sum, the function of consciousness is towards life adaptation. Consciousness serves the ongoing process of creating and increasing accessibility to relevant information in the mental workspace for the continual construction of mental conclusions. To this end, consciousness's two aspects work together in a complementary and dialectic fashion, with qualia specializing in activating the unconscious regions and non-qualia, the conscious domains of the entire mental workspace. In the following section, the two key functions of activation and construction are discussed in greater detail with reference to both the conscious and the nonconscious.

Accessing information within mental workspace: qualia and the activation of the nonconscious

Within the framework of his theatre model of consciousness (see Chapter 4), Baars (1997) lists the following as the functions of consciousness: (i) 'the prioritizing function' – consciousness is needed to prioritize the importance of input stimuli (e.g., cocktail party phenomenon), it is also needed to change behaviour and reorganize priorities; (ii) 'problem-solving functions' – consciousness acts as the 'gateway' to unconscious information and as such it creates access to unconscious knowledge resources; (iii) 'executive control facilitation' – consciousness can facilitate decision-making, detect errors and edit action plans, partly through gaining access to unconscious sources of information; (iv) 'learning and adaptation function' – while the debate over whether learning can occur without conscious awareness is unsettled, it is certain that conscious attention is needed for the acquisition of new knowledge.

In the mental theatre or the workspace of the mind, the spotlight on stage illuminates aspects of the working memory for current experience of awareness. Outside the spotlight, there exist other conscious as well as nonconscious mental elements that are usually separate from one another. Baars argues that, in addition to the specific functions listed above, consciousness serves a 'universal access function'. Baars writes: *'It seems that the single most prominent function of consciousness is to increase access between otherwise separate sources of information*' and that this universal access function seems *'to facilitate the flow of information between different elements of the mental theater'* (pp.162–3).

As discussed, Baars places a great deal of importance on the unconscious, albeit limited to the cognitive unconscious, in his workspace model of the mind. As such, information processing in the mental workspace is to include not only the accessing and activating of both conscious and nonconscious information, but also the continual dialectic interactions between these two kinds of mental elements. The close link between the non-qualitative aspects of consciousness and the activation of the conscious mental elements has been the explicit assumption underlying the research of cognitive neuroscience. That research has clearly shown that nonqualia are primarily associated with information accessing and processing, and hence the overall functioning, pertaining to the conscious mind. Given that both qualia and the nonconscious have been ignored, or remained in the peripheral, of scientific approaches to the mind, the coincidence itself may suggest a link between qualia and the nonconscious. It could be that, parallel to the nonqualia's role in the activation of conscious information, qualia may be involved in nonconscious processing. While coincidence of omission simply suggests such a link, there are reasons to believe that qualia may be primarily related to the accessing and activation of the nonconscious elements in the mental workspace.

Reasons based on lexicon and philosophical speculations
The proposed qualia–nonconscious link is made clearer by both

a lexical and a philosophical analysis. Regarding the lexical analysis, it has been frequently noted that the word consciousness refers to 'co-knowing' or 'knowing with others' (Heaton, 1985; Oatley, 1988; Wilkes, 1988). The nonconscious is thus the 'non-co-knowable'. In the sense that qualia are private, intrinsic and first-personal, by definition then, qualia are not shared or sharable knowledge. Rather, they are experiences of the nonconscious (i.e., non-co-knowable) kind. The lexical analysis thus reveals the original semantic and meaningful link between qualia and the nonconscious.

Two sources of philosophical speculations are also suggestive of a qualia–nonconscious link. In the Pythagoras–Plato–Plotinus tradition of separating *Senses* from *Ideas*, Plato believed that sense experience of physical objects may stimulate memory of the 'innate knowledge' of the *Ideas* which is acquired between 'incarnations' of the soul (e.g., Gulley, 1962; Ross, 1951). Given that the Platonic innate knowledge of the *Ideas* resembles closely the Jungian collective unconscious, Plato thus linked subjective sense experience to information in the nonconscious.

Julian Jaynes' (1976) speculation over the 'bicameral mind' may also be seen as being suggestive of a qualia–nonconscious link. According to Jaynes, consciousness (so is the case with written language) did not come into existence until about 3,000 years ago. Human beings before then were 'unconscious' in the sense that they had a bicameral mind whereby the two brain hemispheres worked rather independently of each other. The 'inner voices' generated from within their 'unconscious' mind (right hemisphere) were heard and sensed by the person as the voices of the gods and hence such subjective sensory experience was associated with feelings of great force and power. Therefore, in the context of the bicameral mind and a lack of conscious awareness, subjective human experiences seemed to be almost entirely tied to the workings of the nonconscious mind. The nonconscious was capable of generating information that gave rise to subjective emotive experiences.

To sum, Plato pointed to the effect of subjective experience (generated from external sense stimulation) in terms of accessing and activating information stored in the nonconscious. Jaynes, on the other hand, noted the role of subjective experience (generated from the nonconscious itself) in guiding behaviour. These two types of philosophical speculation thus relate subjective experience to the nonconscious in opposing directions: externally-generated experience activating nonconscious information (Plato) versus nonconscious-generated experience guiding outer behaviour (Jaynes). They are nonetheless convergent in suggesting a close link between subjective sensory experience and the nonconscious process.

Reasons based on empirical research

Empirical research is also supportive of the proposed qualia–nonconscious link. Given that qualia are intrinsic raw feels or the subjective qualitative experience, they are then inseparable from any processing involving emotion of which raw feels are core elements. Given that qualia are private and first-personal experiences, often of the 'words-fail-to-capture' type, they are closely related to preverbal levels of processing. There is empirical evidence suggesting that both emotional (in particular, negative emotions) and preverbal processing are taking place primarily in the nonconscious. Such evidence comes from research into information processing in the cerebral hemispheres, during dream sleep, hypnosis and synaesthesia.

(1) Hemispheric specialization research: right hemisphere's preverbal, emotional and nonconscious processes

Hemispheric specialization research suggests a close association among preverbal, emotional and unconscious processing in that these kinds of processing take place primarily in the right hemisphere. The evidence for the differential hemispheric specializations in terms of preverbal, emotional processing are discussed in turn.

It is well established that the two hemispheres, while working in tandem with each other, nonetheless specialize in different functions. The left hemisphere is primarily responsible for linguistic processing and the right hemisphere specializes primarily in preverbal processing. However, in normally functioning people, the ongoing dialectic interchange between the two sides via the corpus collosum ensures the obvious unified manifestation which characterizes normal awared experience. The differential specialization of the two hemispheres becomes noticeable only when the interhemispheric neural pathway is severed (e.g., Sperry, 1968). Hemispheric research using split-brain patients has provided evidence of an unconscious information processing system that cannot be brought into awareness and hence cannot be verbalized (e.g., Spriger and Deutsch, 1993). For instance, when a stimulus (e.g., a snow scene, or the word pencil) was presented to the right hemisphere of a split-brain patient, although the patient reacted appropriately (i.e., picking up a shovel when shown the snow scene), the patient's verbal response clearly indicated that he/she did not actually 'see' the stimulus (Gazzaniga, 1983; 1989). In other words, the patient had no actual 'awareness' of the perceptual experience and hence was unable to verbalize that perceptual experience.

In addition to a specialty in preverbal processing, the right hemisphere has also been shown to be more active in processing emotional aspects of stimuli. Among split-brain patients, findings parallel to that reported above were obtained with emotion-provoking stimulus. When a picture of a nude was presented to the right hemisphere, the patient giggled with embarrassment even though the patient was unaware of seeing the picture. These findings thus led Gazzaniga (1983, 1989) to postulate that the various cognitive systems within the brain work in a modular fashion and that there exists a 'narrative interpreter of experience' in the left hemisphere (Gazzaniga,

1995, 1998). When the interhemispheric connection is severed, the right hemisphere is left without the help of a verbal interpreter to incorporate and to articulate its perceptual experience. As such, the right hemisphere's experience remains at its modularized preverbal level.

To sum, preverbal, emotional, and nonconscious (unawared) processing characterizes the right hemisphere's expertise. Given that qualitative sensory experiences can also be best described as being primarily beyond-words and emotion-relevant, it is plausible that qualia are part and parcel of such nonconscious processes. If this was correct, qualia may then play a specialized role in accessing and activating information flow in the unconscious mental domains.

(2) Dream research: nonconscious dynamics
The qualia–nonconscious link in relation to emotional and preverbal processing is also implicated in the psychodynamic literature. The literature suggests that emotions, and in particular negative and traumatic emotions, feature prominently in the unconscious. For Freud, the unconscious mind constitutes repressed memories of early unpleasant experiences. The 'shadow' of the Jungian unconscious is also so constituted. For Goleman (1997), the *'lacuna'* refers to *'an attentional mechanism that creates a defensive gap in awareness'* (p.107). This gap in awareness, a mental product of negative and traumatic experiences, falls as well within the unconscious mental workspace.

The workings of the nonconscious are also revealed by research into dream sleep, as Freud asserted that dreams are 'the royal road to a knowledge of the unconscious activities of the mind' (Freud, 1938). Neurophysiological research into dream sleep has shown that its physiological activities are at a similarly high level as those observed during normal waking states. During dream sleep, while an individual appears to be completely paralysed physically, there are however high levels of involuntary physiological activities including rapid eye movements (hence dream sleep is also referred to as REM sleep), increased heart and respiratory rate and increased arousal level in sexual organs. The electroencephalograph (EEG) recordings of brain waves also show that the brain is more 'active' than it is in the waking state. Hence in the absence of afferent signals from external stimuli during REM sleep, information processing in the brain appears to be rather profound. This is further confirmed in recent experiments using PET scans, which show that brain processes typically resulting from external afferent input are also active during vivid dreams (Posner and Raichle, 1994).

The high level of activation and processing of unconscious information during dream sleep thus raises the question as to the exact function of such profound unconscious processing. Several theories are available in this regard, with some of them arguing for a cognitive type of function while others posit an emotional type of function. Regarding dreams' cognitive functions, two recent computational theories argue that the unconscious processing during dream sleep serves the function of either the prevention of information overload, by eliminating spurious information from the neural network (Crick and Mitchison, 1983), or the updating of memory databanks by reorganizing the experience of the day (Evans, 1984).

Regarding dreams' 'emotional' function, Freud (1900/1975) maintained that dreams are expressions of repressed wishes and hence they serve the function of wish fulfilment in a disguised form. For Freud, the unconscious is the storehouse of repressed memories of early anxiety-provoking experiences. Although its contents are inaccessible through introspection, they nonetheless exert significant motivating and orienting influence over behaviour (e.g., slips of the tongue or dreams). The utility of the unconscious processing during dreams seems to be one of cleansing the emotional 'residuals' of the waking experiences. In other words, dreams act as an unconscious mechanism for psychological restoration. The emotional restorative account appears to be consistent with the content of REM dreams that are typically charged with emotions and are illogical. It is also consistent with the findings that clinical patients with psychological disturbances had higher percentages of REM sleep, and that longer REM sleeping was recorded among women with premenstrual symptoms of irritability and depression (e.g., Hartmann, 1984). However, other studies have shown that in some cases the deprivation of REM sleep could result in relieving depression (e.g., Horne, 1991). In either case, dreams are relevant to emotional processes.

The unconscious processes in dreams serve both a cognitive and an emotional function. This points to the inseparability of the cognitive and emotive processes in the workings of the unconscious. This theme is implicit in the activation-synthesis hypothesis of dreams (Hobson, 1988; Hobson and McCarley, 1977) which relates dreams' functions by tracing them to the neural activation of the subcortical brain stem. According to the hypothesis, the nonconscious processing during REM sleep is a result of the additional activation of the neurons in the pons in the lower brain stem, which is primarily responsible for wakefulness and waking states of consciousness. Thus, during REM sleep, even though the brain receives no external afferent input, it is still activated by neuronal firing originating in the same subcortical pons area that is responsible for wakeful states. Given the disparate and often contradictory signals from the lower brain, dreams then are simply the cortical brain's efforts to synthesize such random signals by accommodating them in higher mental schemas (Hobson and McCarley, 1977; Kiester, 1984). Further, the additional unconscious activating processes accompanying dreams may provide more information for the system to generate creative solutions to latent problems. Dreams' synthesizing processes, by going beyond the cognitive-emotive processing divide, are likely to produce new or creative insights. This shows that the nonconscious processes during dreams are associated with, and may give rise to, a great array of subjective, intrinsic or insightful sense experiences. Therefore, dream research has again illustrated the close link between subjective experience and the underlying nonconscious dynamics.

(3) Hypnosis research
The use of hypnosis as a technique in probing the workings of the nonconscious has been problematic in several research areas including recovered memory of past traumatic events. The controversial debate there, often cast in legal contexts, concerns the validity of the 'memories' so 'recovered' (Andrews et al., 1995; Ceci and Loftus, 1994; Pope and Hudson, 1995). Despite such problems, the limited hypnosis research has provided further clues to the workings of the nonconscious. For instance, under hypnosis, people were able to write automatically without being aware of what they were writing. Hypnotized people were also capable of experiencing pain when instructed to place a hand in icy cold water. Like the cognitive task, these hypnotized people typically were unaware of the pain, as indicated by their direct verbal response. However, when both tasks were required of the hypnotized subjects, their verbal reports gave the indication that they were either unaware of the pain or were only aware of 'a little' pain, while their automatic writings described that a great deal of pain was felt (Hilgard, 1977).

To explain the results, Hilgard proposed that there is a 'dissociation' (an idea akin to modularity) between the cognitive systems in the registering and the reporting of the pain experience. Hilgard further suggested that a 'hidden observer' dissociated from conscious awareness was reporting the pain. While this latter ghost-in-the-machine type of interpretation has been widely disputed (e.g., Baker, 1990; Spanos, 1983), the research finding itself remains significant for consciousness research. In the context of the neuro-cognitive basis of consciousness, Weiskrantz (1997, pp.237–8) recently speculates that the performance–awareness dissociations induced by hypnosis may be linked with syndromes of blindsight or amnesia. Regardless, the findings of hypnosis research show clearly that not only do cognitive and emotional processes take place without conscious awareness, but also that these two processes are closely tied together in the nonconscious mental workspace. Therefore, similar to dream research, Hilgard's studies of hypnosis have also provided evidence on the close interconnectedness of the cognitive and emotional processes in the nonconscious.

(4) Synaesthesia

The recent literature on the phenomenon of synaesthesia (Brown, 1988; Cytowic, 1995) provides further clues to the nature and neural correlates of subjective qualitative experiences. Synaesthesia refers to the 'involuntary' subjective experience of a 'cross-modal association' (Cytowic, 1995). Synaesthesia thus means 'joined sensation': the stimulation of one sensory modality involuntarily causes a subjective 'perceptual experience' in one or more other senses. For instance, for a 'sight and sound' synaesthete, seeing the colour red may trigger off a simultaneous auditory experience like 'shards of glass'. Cytowic (1995) identifies several key features of synaesthesia:

> (i) Synaesthesia is an involuntary, unsupressable and passive experience. Each of the cross-sensory associations (i.e., the conjured-up sensory experience in modalities other than the one corresponding to the external stimulus) is automatically elicited by the external stimulation. These cross-sensory associations are consistent in content and persistent over long periods of time.

> (ii) The cross-sensory associations are projected into the personal space around the synaesthete. For instance, on hearing music, a 'sound-movement' synaesthete may 'see' objects such as gold balls floating on a 'screen' directly in

front of his/her nose.

(iii) The extra-sensory associations often aid memory of the original stimulus. There seems to be a link between synaesthetes and hypermnesis. The memory processes pertaining to the synaesthetic experience appear to be driven by the holistic overall sensation, which then unfolds and reveals the original specific stimulus.

(iv) Synaesthesia is accompanied by raw feels or 'a sense of certitude'. Cytowic (1995) likens such raw feels to 'ecstasy', a word used by William James in describing the feelings typically associated with religious or mystical experiences.

(v) Experimental results from psychophysical sensory matching tasks, drug-induced synaesthetic perceptual responses and brain metabolism research suggest that synaesthetic experiences are accompanied by the activation shifts within the left hemisphere. During synaesthetic experiences, the activities of the left hemisphere show 'large metabolic shifts away from the neocortex that result in relatively enhanced limbic expression' (for a review, see Cytowic, 1995).

Specifically, Cytowic identifies the hippocampus as being necessary for synaesthetic experiences. This is consistent with existing neurophysiological evidence on synaesthesia. It is also consistent with other findings showing that the hippocampus is related to other altered states of consciousness that are qualitatively similar to synaesthesia (e.g., LSD-induced perceptual experience, limbic epilepsy, experiential responses resulted from electrical stimulation of the limbic brain).

Extending from the neurocognitive evidence suggesting the subcortical limbic system's involvement in subjective experiences, Cytowic (1995) concludes that the emotional brain (the limbic subcortex) deals with 'qualitatively' significant information. Given that subjective sensory phenomena such as synaesthesia are largely experiential, Cytowic has in effect linked qualia to the limbic brain's emotional processes.

The foregoing review suggests that the nonconscious processes corresponding to the construction of mental conclusions are best conceptualized in terms of system dynamics. At the neuronal level, nonconscious processes pertaining to subjective qualitative experiences are all traceable to the neural activities of both the right hemisphere and the subcortical brain. Recall that the activation and synthesis hypothesis of dreams (e.g., Hobson, 1988) identifies the lower brain stem as the main centre of activation during dream sleep. The subcortical brain stem is thus primarily involved in nonconscious processes during dream sleep. Dreams' synthesizing processes, by going beyond the cognitive–emotive processing divide, are likely to produce new or creative insights. This shows that the nonconscious processes during dreams are associated with, and may give rise to, a great array of subjective, intrinsic or insightful sense experiences. Therefore, cast in system-dynamic terms, while the nonconscious processes are traceable to micro-level neuronal activities, aspects of dreams' contents (i.e., the products of the synthesizing or creative processes) may then be seen as emergent properties of system dynamics.

Similarly for synaesthetic and related sensory experiences, Cytowic also proposes that the subcortical limbic system is primarily involved in such experiences and that this region of the lower brain deals with all 'qualitatively significant information'. Here, again in system-dynamic terms, synaesthetic and other similar qualitative experiences are not unlike dreams, they may also be seen as emergent properties out of the micro-level neuronal processing and the physical brain's dynamic processes.

Conceptualizing qualia as a core and integral part of the nonconscious dynamics implies that their functions are also explicable in system-dynamic terms. A fuller discussion of the implications of such a conceptualization appears in the next chapter. But in the context of ongoing system dynamics, qualia serve not only to access and activate the unconscious mental representations, they also work together with non-qualia in constructing mental conclusions and in feeding back such conclusions to the system to allow for further information activating and accessing processes. However, before moving on to the discussion of mental conclusions, a summary of the functions of qualia pertaining to the underlying unconscious constructing processes is in order. The previous review suggests qualia's role in accessing and activating relevant information in the nonconscious. Another role of qualia in the unconscious constructing stage has been proposed by Goldman (1993). In this proposal, qualia serve to 'monitor' the construction processes in preparation for awareness. These functions are discussed further below.

(1) Qualia serve to access and activate the nonconscious
The empirical evidence based on research of hemispheric specialization, dream, hypnosis and synaesthesia is convergent in suggesting a close interconnectedness between subjective qualitative experience and preverbal, emotional and nonconscious processes. Subjective experiences may be part and parcel of the nonconscious dynamics and as such, qualia are likely to play a key role in the accessing and activating of information pertaining to the nonconscious.

The qualia's specialized role in nonconscious processing represents a further refinement of existing views of the function of consciousness in general. In discussing the constructive role of consciousness, Mandler (1997) argues that the information relevant to current mental conclusions involves both conscious and unconscious mental structures and schemas. He further points out that all underlying conscious and unconscious representations (i.e., the not-recently-activated unconscious and the Freudian preconscious) are subject to activations, and that it is the unconscious representations and processes that generate all mental processes. As a result, Mandler asserts that, regardless of awareness, *'the unconscious is where the action is'* (p.482). Extending and refining this view, the present book argues that these underlying activating and constructing processes are functionally modularized, with nonqualia being primarily involved in the constructing processes of the conscious (awared) mental elements and qualia, the nonconscious ones.

(2) Qualia serve to monitor and execute the underlying preconscious constructing process
Another specific role of phenomenal states (qualia) in the conclusion constructing process has been suggested by Goldman (1993). Based on Weiskrantz's (1988) work on blindsight, Goldman proposed that phenomenal states (qualia) serve the function of internally monitoring the constructing process. According to Weiskrantz, many blindsight patients could accurately discriminate between distinctly horizontal gratings and vertical ones, just like people with normal vision. However, the difference between the two groups surfaced when they were then asked to indicate whether they were actually 'seeing' or 'guessing'. The blindsight patients typically responded with 'guessing'. Weiskrantz referred to this as a difference in 'monitoring' activities. The blindsight patients' lack of 'awareness' of the visual experience may be linked with the absence of an internal monitoring activity which is responsible for integrating and linking the underlying mental constructing processes.

Goldman (1993) extends Weiskrantz's work and argues that 'phenomenal states' (qualia) may serve such an internal monitoring role. According to Goldman, phenomenal states play a general intrinsic role in a common cognitive task of mentalistic classification. They do so by triggering monitoring activities which then lead to the production of verbal self-attributions. As such, qualia play a significant internal role in the execution of the cognitive task of the classification of one's own mental states. According to Goldman, qualia thus monitor the underlying unconscious constructing process in preparation for later conscious awareness. Without qualia, conscious awareness of mental conclusions is then not possible, as in the case of the blindsight patients.

Mental conclusions: transition between covert parallel construction and overt serial manifestation

As mentioned, Marcel (1983) first proposed the idea that consciousness is a constructing process and that specific 'awared' states are constructed out of a variety of 'preconscious' mental states. As previously discussed, the underlying constructing processes involve the activation of relevant domains of the mental workspace. Although an individual is aware of the manifested mental conclusions, the constructing processes that precede such conclusions remain outside conscious awareness. With the constructing processes being continual and ongoing, mental conclusions are constantly formed in the nonconscious. Once formed, they demand overt expression or manifestation in awareness.

The transition from a covert unawared state to a manifested awared state constitutes what Mandler (1992, 1997) calls a 'bottleneck' problem, which refers to a vast number of underlying potential mental conclusions competing with one another for limited opportunities for the expression in awareness. According to Mandler, the bottleneck problem is created by the differences in nature between unconscious and conscious (awared) dynamics. These differences are in terms of both 'capacity' and 'seriality'. As Mandler (1997) puts it: *'Conscious and unconscious processes are – in major ways – contrasted by their differences in seriality and capacity. Conscious processes are serial and limited in capacity ... whereas unconscious processes operate in parallel and are, for all practical purposes, "unlimited" in capacity'* (p.490).

Before the discussion of qualia's possible functional role during this transitional phase, it becomes necessary to first ascertain the validity of the proposed capacity and seriality differences between the conscious and the nonconscious states.

Evidence on the serial–capacity differences between nonconscious and awared states

A closer examination of the seriality and capacity notions reveals that they are fundamentally linked to the notion of 'time'. It appears that the limited serialized processing mode is the result of the constraint imposed upon the 'awared reality' by the directionality or 'arrow' of time' (Eddington, 1928; Prigogine, 1997). The nonconscious mental reality appears to transcend such a constraint of time in the sense that processes of the nonconscious are simultaneous. Thoughts and images corresponding to past memories, current situations, and future anticipations may be concomitantly conjured up in parallel. There are reasons for postulating the time-transcending nature of the nonconscious. In the humanistic and transpersonal literatures (see Chapter 5), this transcendental state is associated with the highest level of consciousness, which has been variously referred to as 'peak experience', 'unity or cosmic consciousness'. In this state, the most profound sense for the individual experiencer is one of complete unity with 'all there is': a sense of expansion that dissolves all boundaries including those imposed by time or space. In the context of creative insights, both the humanistic philosophers Nietzsche and Heidegger have noted a 'moment of vision' which describes the time during which *'the past, present and future are all united in one creative instant'* (Zohar, 1991, p.105). In the psychodynamics literature, a similar notion is found in Jung's 'collective unconscious' wherein lies the archetype of the unity of humanity (the mandala). In the cognitive science literature, this altered state of consciousness observable among advanced meditators has been referred to by Mandler (1997) as a 'frame-freezing' or 'consciousness stopping' experience. Similar time-transcending experiences have been observed in relation to extreme cases of memory functioning. At the end of 'perfect memory', one of Luria's mnemonics (Mr S) often failed to distinguish the past from the present (Gregory, 1996, citing Luria, 1968). At the other end of memory loss, a patient with dense amnesias reported living in a 'permanent present' without any conscious awareness of the future (Mandler, 1997, citing Tulving, 1985). These cases combined seem to suggest that 'normal' memory functioning, and hence normal conscious awareness in daily reality, requires 'seriality'; time-transcending is then incompatible with normal moment-to-moment and day-to-day functional adaptations.

In sum, there seem to be valid reasons for supporting Mandler's proposal that the awared and the nonconscious states differ in seriality and capacity. These differences have obvious implications for the function of consciousness and hence qualia.

Function of qualia pertaining to mental-conclusion transition
Qualia also may play a functional role in the transitional phase. Due to the limited capacity of awareness, the transition from a parallel state of pluralistic potentialities to a serial state of 'sequential' awareness' leaves a great deal of constructed conclusions unawared. This naturally raises the question, 'Which mental conclusion(s) out of all those currently formed in the potential pool get the special privilege for expression?' Put differently, 'What factors determine the manifestation of a specific mental conclusion as the current state of awareness?' The question concerns the criteria of 'choice'. These choices from moment to moment are affected by all conscious and nonconscious forces operating both intrapsychically (e.g., immediate mental state; past memories; future anticipations)

and extrapsychically (interpersonal and cultural-historical factors). The final manifested or awared mental conclusions therefore represent the collective influence of all these forces over the choice process.

The final choice, however, seems to orient towards the overriding goal of functional adaptation to immediate and current problems (e.g., Marcel, 1983; Mandler, 1997). According to Marcel, the mental conclusions that a person is aware of are those that are constructed out of as much data as possible and are at the *'most functionally useful'* level possible (Marcel, 1983). Mandler puts forward a similar argument:

> One will experience (be conscious of) whatever is consistent with one's immediate preceding history as well as with currently impinging events. The most important schemas that determine current conscious contents are those that represent the demands and requirements of the current situation. (Mandler, 1997, p.484)

Possible functional roles of consciousness in relation to the transition of mental conclusions have been postulated. For instance, Mandler (1997) himself, having identified the capacity–seriality differences in the transition, further argues that consciousness (the mind) serves the function of *'the conversion from a parallel and vast unconscious to a serial and limited conscious representation'* (p.491). Similarly, Bargh (1997) argues that consciousness serves the function of 'fitting a parallel mind to a serial world' (p.53). In addition, Oatley (1988) emphasizes the importance of socio-cultural factors in the expression of particular mental conclusions. He places the Meadian notion of a socially constructed model of self at the centre of conscious adaptations. As such, the main function of consciousness is then to *'draw mental conclusions from a socially constructed model of self'* (p.387).

In all three contexts of Mandler, Bargh and Oatley, consciousness serves the conclusion–transition function in a systemic fashion with two-way feedback processes. More specifically, consciousness at once is involved in choosing the most functionally effective mental conclusions for expression, and in feeding back the awared conclusions for activation of relevant information for the continual construction of additional mental conclusions. Mandler (1997) describes this feedback phase as *'the selective activation (priming) by conscious representations that changes the unconscious landscape by producing new privileged structures*' (p.491).

However, while all three speak of the transitional tasks as being the function of 'consciousness' in general, none refers to the role of qualitative experience per se. It is Richard Gregory (1996) who first singles out the qualitative aspects of consciousness (qualia) as being the 'agent' in dealing with the seriality problem. According to Gregory, qualia serve the function of 'flagging the present' so as to make salient the past, present and future directions of time. By having 'the present moment' made salient in current awareness, possible confusions between mental conclusions manifested as current awared reality and those that remain unexpressed in the nonconscious can then be avoided. As already seen, the avoidance of such confusion is necessary for a functional adaptation to the current lived reality.

To sum up qualia's possible functions, they are likely to share the adaptational role with nonqualia in a complementary fashion. In the ongoing dynamics of schematic activation, conclusion construction and information feedback within the entire mental workspace, nonqualia may specialize in these functions pertaining primarily to the conscious mental domains, whereas qualia may perform a similar function with the vast nonconscious. However, given their inseparable superpositioned relationship, the continual dialectic dialogue between the modularized conscious and nonconscious processing would render it both inadequate and misleading to study 'consciousness' by excluding its qualitative aspects.

The proposed role of qualia in dealing with the seriality

problem during mental-conclusion transitions (Gregory, 1996) has a significant implication for consciousness research in general. The seriality–capacity difference between the nonconscious and awared states may be the very feature that underlies the seemingly uncompromisable divide between the cognitive neuroscience perspective and the humanistic transpersonal perspective on consciousness. For the former, consciousness is approached with a 'snapshot' and 'third-personal' methodology and a conceptual focus on the 'awared' mental states. For the latter, the same subject is studied with a longitudinal and 'first-personal' methodology and a conceptual focus predominantly on the nonconscious. Given the riches of the nonconscious dynamics and their pivotal role in human action and behviour, many have questioned the utility of the prevailing snapshot approach to a fuller understanding of human conditions and systems (e.g., Carver and Scheier, 1998). This point will be returned to in the next chapter.

7
An Unbound Mental Workspace

The key themes so far are that (a) both qualitative and non-qualitative aspects of human experience coexist in a superposition, and that (b) the superpositioned coexistence of these two aspects of consciousness constrains their functioning. It is likely that qualia and nonqualia share complementarily the processing functions in the nonconscious and conscious mental domains. As such, their functions are also integrally bound together in constant dialectical interaction.

However, in addition to the superposition proposition, several related issues that are central to the study of consciousness deserve careful consideration. These pertain to (a) a complete notion of consciousness, (b) the multiplicity and emergence features of the mind and self, and (c) appropriate methods of enquiry into consciousness.

A COMPLETE NOTION OF CONSCIOUSNESS

A 'complete' model of consciousness is one that is capable of capturing human experience in its entirety. Such a model requires that the notion 'consciousness' embrace the entire range of the conscious mind and the unconscious mind. In this complete sense, the assumed superpositioned state of qualia and non-qualitative experience then characterizes the entire spectrum of consciousness. The first step towards such a complete notion of consciousness involves transcending the current conscious–unconscious conceptual divide.

Undoing the mind bondage: returning to the unbounded *psyche*

Based on the review, there have been significant shifts in the usage of the terms, consciousness, mind and self. However, none of these modern terms denotes the complete meaning of the original Greek word *psyche* or its Latin equivalent *spiritus*: breathing or being alive. A living human being is at the same time a cognitive agent and a sentient self: a cognitive agent capable of adapting to the demands of both outer and inner environments; a sentient self complete with private and intrinsic feelings accompanying every step of the adaptational process.

However, as the review shows, these two supposedly dialectically intertwined aspects of the *psyche* have been separated and studied as two independent human phenomena. The *psyche*'s cognitive agency aspect forms the focus of contemporary studies of the 'mind' in positive philosophy and in mainstream psychology. The mind's incessant partner, sentience and the sentient self has become peripheral to the study of human science and relegated to the domain of phenomenological philosophy and humanistic psychology. As Wilkes pointed out, the term *psyche* was replaced by 'mind' (Wilkes, 1988), and this change in the lexicon and common discourse has *'subtly changed the meaning of what was held to be essential to human beings'* (Smith, 1997, p.121).

The study of consciousness is really about being alive and hence about the *psyche* in its entirety. To confine the study to either its cognitive-agency or its sentient-self aspect would risk the neglect of all consequences of the agency–sentience dialectical process, a neglect exactly as implied by the motto of gestalt psychology: the whole is more than the sum of the parts. As pointed out before, the qualia debate comes into being precisely because of the separation of the agency (non-qualitative) and sentience (qualitative) aspects of human experience. Conceptualizing the superpositioned coexistence of the two aspects would be the first step towards bringing the study of human experience closer to its entirety, as this new conceptualization explicitly acknowledges the inseparability and the never-ceasing dialectical dynamics and entanglements between the cognitive and the sentient.

But the superpositioning assumption needs to be anchored with reference to the entire *psyche*, not just with respect to a bounded range within it. Chalmers' model is consistent with the coexistence assumption, but it only pertains to a specific domain of the *psyche:* the 'conscious mind' or the domain within awareness. A conceptual extension as suggested would mean including the 'unconscious' which incorporates both the two main kinds of known unconscious processes: the Freudian intrapersonal dynamics within an individual lifespan and the extended Jungian transpersonal dynamics pertaining to the collective human cultural and historical heritage. In either the Freudian or the Jungian sense, the dynamics of the unconscious is a function of time: the former corresponds to each individual's longitudinal progression within a lifetime; and the latter embraces the collective marks etched on the individual by the collective human progression with the arrow of time.

It is in this very context of the dynamics of time that the unconscious adds a unique and differential dimension to human existence, to being alive, and hence to the *psyche*. The dynamics of the awared mind are intricately interwoven with those of the unconscious. *Psyche* so defined is then the totality of the awared and the unconscious.

Therefore, the suggestion that a study of consciousness be grounded in the entire *psyche* points to the need to undo the bondage of the mind. The modern 'mind' is in bondage and is separated from the unconscious, and all this is traceable back to the pre-Socratic philosophers' (Heraclitus and Parmenides) contemplation over the 'wakeful and thinking states'. Undoing the bondage of the 'mind' as suggested is to take seriously the vast varieties of the non-wakeful and the non-awared (non-thought-of) human experiences as part of living and being alive.

Embracing the unconscious: transcending the conscious–unconscious divide

A conceptual return to *psyche* through embracing both the Freudian and the Jungian unconscious means transcending the big conscious–unconscious divide. The main contribution of the Freudian theory of the mind lies in its acknowledging the multi-facetedness of the intrapsychic structure as well as the dialectical and intertwined interactions between the conscious and the unconscious mind. While the Freudian unconscious constitutes the repressed memories of an individual's past experiences with the immediate social environment, the Jungian unconscious embraces the more distal and remote social environments via collective memories (in the form of archetypes) of human evolutionary history. The contribution of the Jungian unconscious thus lies in its postulating an intrinsic mechanism through which culture and history directly exert influence over the conscious mind. To incorporate both types of the unconscious within *psyche* would carry the clear implication that the transmission process of the 'social-cultural' influence (in the Jungian sense) is almost as fundamental as that at the biological level.

The suggestion of including the unconscious, in particular, the Jungian collective unconscious, would certainly meet opposition from mainstream philosophers and psychologists. However, it is clear from the previous review of recent models of consciousness that the research trend is in the direction consistent with the suggestion. The trend of bringing back various notions of the unconscious is evident in cognitive neuroscience. Many theorists (e.g., Shallice, Johnson-Laird, Umilta) are starting to include certain 'cognitive unconscious' experiences as the *explanada* of consciousness.

Recently, Searle (1997) has argued that that the 'unconscious' should be the starting point for approaching the 'mystery of consciousness' (p.199). Citing the 'blindsight'

(Weiskrantz, 1986) cases as examples of 'unawared sighting' of external stimuli, Searle argues that these cases provide a promising starting point in the analysis of the differences between the conscious and the unconscious. Weiskrantz (1997) himself has voiced the same view. According to Weiskrantz, new advances in imaging technologies and neuroscientific methods can illuminate questions of consciousness only when these questions are 'posed appropriately'. He writes: *'among the phenomena that allow appropriate formulation ... are those that arise out of the neuropsychological syndromes which demonstrate the difference between performance with and without awareness'* (Weiskrantz, 1997, p.242). In a similar vein, Baars (1997) also argues for the virtue of conducting 'contrastive analysis' in consciousness research. Contrastive analysis refers to the comparison *of 'two active brain processes that are similar in most ways but differ in respect to consciousness'* (p.21). However, Baars further argues that although this kind of analysis may not be the last step in answering questions about consciousness, *'it could be the first'* (p.21).

As discussed, neurocognitive scientists have already taken on board the suggestion of starting consciousness research with an analysis of the 'unconscious' (e.g., Bogen, 1995; Farah, 1994; Koch and Braun, 1996; Squire and Kosslyn, 1998; Weiskrantz, 1997). The exploration has covered some intriguing 'wakeful' (e.g., blindsight, visual agnosia and neglect, and subliminal perception) as well as 'non-wakeful' (e.g., dreaming) phenomena. These intriguing phenomena are compared and contrasted with typical or normal conscious states in an effort to identify the kinds of incongruences and discontinuities between them in terms of neuronal record of processing, subjective awareness of the experience (indexed by verbal reporting), and the processing outcome at behavioural level (indexed by behavioural consequences of processing).

The suggested 'difference' or 'contrasting' approach could be applied to investigate the varieties of 'unconscious' processes which have been reported extensively in the psychodynamic literature, but have so far been excluded from current cognitive neuroscience literature. In the psychodynamics literature, there is by now robust evidence suggesting that even though the unconscious (both intrapsychical and interpsychical) lies beyond intentional awareness, its vast content could be brought into 'awareness' when the individual is under deep relaxation (e.g., Brown, 1991). However, such 'subjective awareness' discontinues when the person resumes normal wakeful states. The apparent dissociation between subjective awareness of experience and biological awareness (or memory) of experience makes these unconscious phenomena a similarly suitable candidate as blindsight or subliminal perception for neurocognitive research into human consciousness. While casting doubt on the validity of 'putative dissociations that occur in the psychiatric domain', Weiskrantz (1997) nonetheless acknowledges that hypnosis-induced dissociations may make *'an interesting link to forge with the syndromes'* of blindsight and amnesia (p.238).

With respect to the Jungian unconscious, phenomena that are suitable for the suggested contrasting approach to consciousness abound in the literatures of transpersonal psychology and parapsychology. For instance, information processing and verbal reporting during trance states by 'mediums' also involve a similar subjective–biological dissociation in awareness. As reviewed in Chapter 5, William James held the view that the non-conscious constitutes a large portion of human consciousness. His research into the psychic phenomenon of mediumship led him to the conclusion that relevant information processing underlying mediumship takes place in the medium's own 'unconscious mind' (James, 1902). At the 1993 International Symposium on Science and Consciousness, Tart (1993) presented a comprehensive review of scientifically gathered data pertaining to transpersonal and parapsychological conscious phenomena. Based on the convergence of data, Tart argues for a combined psychological, transpersonal and parapsychological approach to consciousness.

By dissolving the interpsychical boundaries at the collective unconscious level, the Jungian unconscious may be associated with the processing mechanisms underlying most interpersonal psychical phenomena. However, from a longitudinal and evolutionary perspective, the Jungian notion is also relevant to the progression along the developmental stages of consciousness. The highest stage of development to be reached ('transcendental' or 'global' consciousness) features the subjective experience of total unity with all that is and the dissolution of any boundaries that separate one's own self and others (e.g., Wilber, 1996). Research into the psychological and neurobiological correlates associated with different stages of consciousness can also make profound contributions towards a fuller understanding of human consciousness. For instance, research has already explored the neurocognitive processing underlying the states of 'self-transcendence' or the total-unity level of consciousness (e.g., Cloninger, 1998; Goleman and Thurman, 1991; Hinrichs and Machleidt, 1992; Persinger and Makarec, 1992).

The complete notion of consciousness, that constitutes the conscious mind and the nonconscious, thus means an unbounded consciousness. The theoretical implications of grounding research of human experience firmly in this complete notion of unbounded consciousness are many, and some of these have been briefly noted. However, this raises many questions at the methodological and practical levels. The questions are to do with first, the scientific validation of the existence of the unconscious, and second, the exact nature of the complex and thoroughly intertwined dynamics that may govern the relationship between the conscious and the nonconscious. These questions are of serious practical and legal concern, such as in the case of the debate over recovered memory (e.g., Andrews et al., 1995) as well as the debate over multiple personality disorders. Although these questions are tied primarily with the

Freudian unconscious, within the framework of the unbounded consciousness, they are also intimately related to the Jungian unconscious. However, even though there exist ample accounts of case histories in the literature of transpersonal psychoanalysis and clinical psychiatry, their validation by standard scientific experimental methods remains an open and unanswered question.

Recent advances in metacognitive research may be of relevance here. In the context of metacognitive self-monitoring behaviour including 'knowing-of-knowing', 'feeling-of-knowing', or 'subjective judgement-of-learning', recent research has shown that such metacognitive processes may be dissociable from cognitive processes. The dissociation is both in terms of cognitive functioning (e.g., Metcalfe and Shimamura, 1994; Nelson, 1992) and their neuronal basis (e.g., Nelson, 1996). Recent work on metacognitive memory and text comprehension has also cast doubt on earlier findings on the 'illusion of knowing' (e.g., Garner, 1987; Nelson, 1994). Further metacognitive research in memory monitoring and 'distortions' may contribute to the validation of what people really know and what they feel that they know. In this sense, this research may help to clarify the debate over recovered memory.

And in a wider context, metacognitive research is of significance for human consciousness in general, as it pertains to the relationship between an individual's awared nonqualitative states and his/her subjective, and possibly nonawared, qualitative states. As such, the research is needed for a fuller understanding of other mental phenomena of dissociated states as discussed in the previous chapter. Exploring blindsight and visual agnosia from a metacognitive perspective, Shimamura (1994) argues: *'One remarkable observation from studies of the neuropsychology of metacognition is that certain cognitive functions can operate without conscious knowledge ... Based on these investigations ... it is possible ... to speculate about the biology of conscious awareness'* (p.276).

MULTIPLICITY AND SELF-ORGANIZATION CHARACTERIZE CONSCIOUSNESS

The notion of unbounded consciousness, as consisting of both the conscious and the unconscious thus refers to the entirety of *psyche*. In its original usage, the term *psyche* signifies two essential ideas: that it is part and parcel of the natural world or nature itself; and that it is the totality of life itself. Given the current knowledge about the dynamics of nature and life, it appears possible to speculate over the key feature of *psyche* and hence human consciousness itself.

As reviewed in Chapter 4, current neurocognitive research suggests that the human brain exhibits features akin to those of a nonlinear dynamic system as well as those of a quantum system. Based on the convergence of findings from chaos theory and quantum mechanics perspectives, it seems plausible to suggest that the human brain can be conceived of as a dynamic system at both the macro-classical level and the micro-neuronal level. Human consciousness in this context is then seen as a higher-level property of system dynamics. This line of research has been followed up independently from the chaos (e.g., Freeman, Hardcastle) and the quantum (e.g., Penrose, Hameroff) perspectives. Research from either perspective has shown that highly coherent and synchronized oscillatory patterns 'arise' from lower-level neuronal computations which simply obey deterministic algorithmic rules.

The implications of conceptualizing consciousness in chaos and quantum terms are twofold: (1) covert multiplicity – its covert structure can best be described as multifaceted and as constituting multiple possibilities at any point in time; (2) self-organization – its dynamics are characterized by the ongoing formation and emergence of coherent states out of the underlying multiple possibilities. Such overt coherent states may not always be predicted from lower-level computational rules. The self-organizing process of consciousness thus is capable of bringing about both an 'integrated' coherent state and an 'emergent' coherent state. In the following sections, these features of consciousness are discussed in turn.

Multiplicity as a covert property of consciousness

Evidence of covert multiplicity
While the application of two contemporary theories of physical systems (chaos and quantum) results in the covergent prediction that consciousness possesses the feature of covert multiplicity, this feature is also explicit in computational and neural network mind models that do not postulate a top-level central executive processor. An example is Dennett's (1991) information-processing model which excludes the central control module present in his earlier network models. This version of the network model views the mind as being organized (self-organization) into various mental modules, with each having a specialized function in the individual's adaptation to the environment. This notion of the mind's modularity is a *'special case of modula, hierarchical design in "all" complex systems'* (Simon cited in Pinker, 1997, p.92). Varela (1996) has also identified the commonality of the modularity concept among many research domains (e.g., cellular automata, artificial life, the biological immune and nervous systems). In all these complex systems, modularized operations can bring about the emergence of new system properties. Given that these complex systems share many common features with chaotic systems (e.g., Horgan, 1996), the application of chaos theory to the study of consciousness could be seen as an extended step in applying the neural network framework.

All three perspectives of the neuralnet models, chaos theory and quantum mechanics point to the same proposition that covert multiplicity is a key feature of human consciousness. Given that consciousness has been explored separately under the subject titles of 'the mind' and 'the self', evidence of covert multiplicity exists separately for the mind and for the self. Under the subject title of the mind which focuses on the cognitive agency notion, all self-organizing neural network models carry the assumption that the mind consists of multiple modules, each performing a different and specialized function. Multiplicity then is associated with the mind's modularity. It is in this context that Minsky (1985) speaks of 'societies of mind' as consisting of multiples of 'functional agents and agencies'. Hofstadter and Dennett (1981) posit the idea of multiples of homunculi in the mind's 'I'. Mind as either society or homunculi has the features of 'insulated' multiplicity: at any chosen level of analysis, each society or homunculus is functionally insulated from the others so that each does its own job independent of all others.

Quite independently in the personality literature, the prevailing view has been that there exists a multiplicity of subselves rather than one single unified core self. In addition to those mentioned in Chapter 5 such as Markus's 'possible selves' and Cantor's 'family of selves', a variety of other terms have been used to denote the multiplicity view of the self. These include the 'multicentred self', the 'many-dimensional man', 'mental compartmentalization', 'the multifaceted individual decision-maker', 'community of selves', 'states or composite of mind', 'subpersonality', or 'subselves as small group synergy' (for a review, see Lester, 1993–94). The notion of multiplicity is also explicit in the postmodern view of the self. For instance, in line with the pivotal postmodern theme of pluralism, Gergen (1994) argues for the self's 'multiple realities'. These multiple selves are now cast in the external interpersonal domain and are conceptualized in the forms of 'relational nuclei'.

Therefore, the idea of multiple selves is core to contemporary social and personality self theories. It has been present in the social constructivist theories ever since Mead conceptualized the self in terms of multiple social roles. It is also present in the recent social constructionist self theories such as Gergen's. Furthermore, the idea of multiplicity is also central to the debate over issues of personality disorder. There have been extensive discussions of the dissociative personality disorders (e.g., Humphrey and Dennett, 1991; Piper, 1994); however, these issues have remained inconclusive.

Implications of covert multiplicity

If consciousness, as both mind and self, is characterized by covert multiplicity, what would be its implication for human adaptation and functioning? The immediate functional implication would be that covert multiplicity demands further postulations that would allow for the coherence seen in its actualized overt state. This relates to the 'binding' issue. The binding together of the covert multi-states into a coherent whole is a self-organization process. In the literature of the self, the principle of integration has been proposed (e.g., Lester, 1993–94) which can serve the function of 'binding' the multiple subselves. In the mind literature, binding is typically considered an emergent property of the computational system (the brain). These binding mechanisms as self-organization of subselves and subminds are returned to later in the discussion.

But consciousness's covert multiplicity appears to have a deeper conceptual implication for human adaptation and function: the existence of vast non-actualized potentialities. To see this more clearly, it helps to recall the notion of the superpositioned state of consciousness: that all qualitative and non-qualitative experiences coexist in a 'both-and' state. Superposition itself thus implies multiplicity of underlying possibilities. In Shimony's (1997) words: *'The idea of potentiality is implicit in the superposition principle'* (p.150). Zohar and Marshall (1994) develop this idea further and argue that the superpositioned reality constitutes *'a vast sea of potential'* (p.24) and that the 'expressed' or actualized potentiality is but one tiny bit that is plucked out of the *'pool of deeper, underlying and multi-faceted potentiality'* (p.121).

Thus, consciousness' covert multiplicity carries the important implication of a vast hidden and unactualized underlying set of human potentialities. This implication has been made explicitly clear only within the framework of conceptualizing consciousness in terms of quantum notions. If this implication turns out to be the case, then it is likely that the so-far mysterious noncomputable emergent properties of consciousness could still be accounted for by simple underlying algorithms that operate over the 'entire sea of underlying possibilities'. In other words, all actualized consciousness (thoughts, actions, language, creativity, etc.) can then be accounted for if the underlying 'domain' available for computations is extended to embrace the entire sea of possibilities. Again, what is suggested here is simply the dissolution of mind bondage, and the embracing of both the conscious and the vast known unconscious as the 'workspace' (in Baars' term) of this unbounded mind. This remains speculative. The discussion to follow returns to the self-organization of consciousness.

Self-organization as a dynamic process of consciousness

To recap, both mind and self have been conceptualized in terms of multiplicity (as consisting of multiples of subminds or subselves). However, as discussed before, dynamic-system theories stipulate that while such systems follow the entropy principle (i.e., the systems tend to evolve over time towards entropic or chaotic states), their dynamics are also governed by the self-organization principle (order emerges out of chaos through self-organization). Therefore, conceptualizing consciousness as system dynamics would allow the self-organization principle to operate. Thus, the covert heterogeneity of consciousness is balanced off with a self-organized harmonizing principle which ensures the 'binding' together of the underlying multi-states into a manifested apparent 'whole'. Such self-organizing mechanisms are discussed separately for the self and the mind.

Self-organization of subselves: self-integration

In the literature of the self, it has been suggested that the principle of integration (Lester, 1993–94) governs a normal and healthy development of the person by integrating *'various subselves into one unified whole or to mutual coexistence between the subselves'* (p.322). However, it seems that such a harmonizing integration of the subselves does not come about 'peacefully'; the psychodynamics literature is replete with notions of the intrapsychic conflicts and struggle towards integration. Such notions include 'libidinal ego attacking and persecuting the internal saboteur' (Fairbairn, 1954), or 'do battle with ourselves' (Mair, 1977). And according to Berne's (1961) transactional analysis, when one subself wins the battle and gets to be 'self-expressed' for a moment of glory as the person's 'unified self', the other subself states are said to be 'decommissioned'.

Such competitions and battles are ongoing and are an integral part of the integration dynamics of the intrapersonal selves. However, it needs to be noted that in the context of lifespan development, the transpersonal literature has further suggested that there exists an ideal developmental state whereby all of an individual's subminds or subselves are integrated within a unified higher mind or self that transcends each individual person. This ideal state of the unified mind or self is alternatively referred to as group mind or self, cosmic mind or self, and universal mind or self. This ideal unified state thus characterizes Wilber's highest stage of consciousness development: cosmic consciousness. Recent neurophysiological research has shown that such self-transcendent mental states are evident in episodes of creative insights that are reflected in an EEG pattern showing a coherence of neural activities in related cortical areas (e.g., Hinrichs, and Machleidt, 1992). Therefore, there exists neurophysiological support for the subjective experience being part of a larger unity.

From a psychological perspective, it seems that the dissolution of boundaries that exist around either intrapersonal subselves (subminds) or interpersonal individual selves (or individual minds) can be seen as a continuing integration process from an intrapersonal to an interpersonal level. Given that both theories of the mind and of the self have likened the individual-level subselves to 'little autonomous beings', there seem to be sound reasons to further undo the mind bondage by transcending the interpersonal boundaries.

Self-organization of subminds: emergent properties of mind
In the literature of the mind, the neuralnet and connectionist frameworks allow for the emergence of new properties that are different from those of the individual parts of the network, but that can be accounted for from a complete knowledge of (a) the nature and behaviour of the parts, (b) the patterns of the connections among the parts, and (c) the roles for adjusting the relative 'weight' given to individual parts (Crick, 1994, p.185). This is essentially the definition of emergence in all dynamic or chaotic systems capable of self-organization.

By definition then, this kind of emergence is still theoretically 'computable'; it is not considered computable at the present time, because advances in science are yet to be made in order to discover the precise underlying algorithm for the interconnections and relative weightings of component parts. Still, by this definition, many hypothetical constructs about the mind that have been proposed can be seen as examples of emergent properties of the mind; some of them can serve the function of binding together the underlying multifaceted states. Examples of the emergent mechanisms capable of the binding function include 'the director self' (Baars, 1997), 'the narrative interpreter of experience' or 'the interpreter device' (Gazzaniga, 1995; 1998), 'the generative assembly device' (Corballis, 1991), '40 Hz coherent neuronal oscillation' (Crick and Koch, 1990), or 'superpositioned

Bose-Einstein-Condensate coherence' (Zohar and Marshall, 1994). These are examined further below.

(1) The 'self'
Cognitive neuroscience has been ambivalent about the notion self. On the one hand, it denies the existence of one holistic self-entity or a fixed-core-self that exerts executive top–down control. Each one of the coexisting 'multiple selves' seems to be capable of independently representing the individual person and acting on behalf of all the other selves for some of the time. For each such self to get the chance of total expression, however temporarily, it has to compete fiercely with the others. This notion of competing for a chance of self-expression seems to be identical to the psychoanalytic views of the conflicting, battling, attacking and persecuting selves. These cognitive selves (homunculi) compete for emergence by having 'shouting matches'; the one that shouts the loudest gets the glory to emerge as the temporary 'head of mind' (Humphrey and Dennett, 1991) and to get to control the whole system's processing.

Cognizant of the fact that models of consciousness are 'groundless' without a notion of a unifying self, many theorists have recently argued for the indispensability of the construct self (and subjectivity) in modelling consciousness, even though the self is only confined to its cognitive agency aspect (e.g., Johnson-Laird, Baars). It is in this context that the notion self has been posited as higher-order emergent properties of the mind. The function of this 'emergent self' is the pooling together of the distributed 'bits' of experience into a coherent whole. And in this capacity, the self serves the general synthesizing function of guiding, directing and interpreting the individual's role as a cognitive agent. The self is seen as either the deep background context of consciousness (Baars, 1997) or the inevitable 'by-product' of the 'interpreter device' located in the left hemisphere (Gazzaniga, 1998).

(2) The generative assembly device
At the system level, the linguistic-based generative mode of representations, which was hypothesized to be the function of the generative assembly device, or GAD (Corballis, 1991), can also be seen as an emergent property of the mind's lower-level rule-following computations. As a mechanism, the GAD assembles 'products' of lower-level mental computations and creates higher-order representations. As such, it is said to profoundly enrich the overall functioning of the entire dynamic system. According to Corballis, it endows human beings with a general adaptive power greater than the demands of the natural environment, it expands the thought processes for allowing for recursive self-introspections and meta-cognitive thoughts. Further, as a tool of creativity, it may also *'greatly raise the stakes of creative effort'* (p.313).

(3) Oscillatory coherence
At the micro-neuronal level, the various constructs pertaining to oscillatory coherence and synchronization can also be seen as emergent properties of the neuronal networks. Through either the collapse of the wave function and the formation of BEC coherence, or the synchronization of 40 Hz neuronal oscillations, or the combination of both, a coherent state emerges. This kind of emergence can occur at different levels of the hierarchy in the system. Such an emergent property (a coherent state) serves primarily the 'binding' function (e.g., Crick, 1994; Hardcastle, 1995; Penrose, 1997; Zohar and Marshall, 1994). Several authors have further speculated that the quantum-based coherence may be the neuronal basis for mathematical understanding and insights (Penrose, 1997) or for creativity in general (e.g., Shimony, 1997; Zohar and Marshall, 1994).

Integrating the cognitive-neuroscientific and the quantum-chaos systemic approaches

To sum, the mind's emergent self-organizing feature is evident in both the computational and cognitive neuroscience literature, as well as the more recent works taking either a chaos-system-dynamic or quantum-mechanic approach. Given that these approaches combined are likely to contribute to a greater overall understanding of human experience, the suggestions for such joint efforts in consciousness research have been voiced. For instance, at the early stage of the development of system-dynamics and complexity theories in physical and biological sciences, Varela, Thompson and Rosch (1992) wrote about 'the embodied mind' and argued for taking a combined 'emergent system' and cognitive neuroscience approach to the mind. They wrote that: *'The emergence view ... both in its early phase of the study of self-organizing systems and in its present connectionist form, is open to encompassing a greater variety of cognitive domains. An inclusive or mixed mode seems ... a natural strategy to pursue'* (p.103). More recently, Trefil (1998) advocates a similar complex system approach to consciousness. In particular, Trefil notes the relevance of the complexity theoretic notion of emergence to human conscious experience. He argues that any of the current neurocognitive theories of consciousness including those of Craik and Edleman, *'could develop into a theory that embodied the notions of emergent properties'* (p.206).

Among those advocating the application of quantum notions to consciousness research (e.g., Eccles, 1989; Hameroff and Penrose, 1996; Lockwood, 1989; Shimony, 1997; Zoltan, 1999), Zohar and Marshall (1994) have argued for a two-tier theory of consciousness. The theory combines the features of the neuronet connectionist approach and the quantum-system approach. In this two-tier complex, the role of self-organization and emergence is a fundamental feature: *'Consciousness is a pattern-forming process. It is one kind of self-organizing system. So through its physics, a quantum-based consciousness would constantly be forming new, ordered, coherent wholes – that is, new patterns draw chaos into order, or that draw simpler patterns into more complex ones*' (pp.140–1). In addition to quantum processes, the two-tier model gives equal credence to the information processing and computational processes postulated in cognitive neuroscience. However, they argue that the computer models of the mind by itself *'is only telling us half the story'* by focusing on the output axon end of the neuron while ignoring the input dendrites end, as it is the dendrites that 'give rise to' the oscillations in ion channels (p.59). Accordingly, the authors argue for a combined two-tier approach to consciousness whereby the brain's computational system (including both its sequential and parallel processing) and its quantum system work with each other 'in tandem'.

METHOD OF ENQUIRY INTO THE UNBOUND CONSCIOUSNESS

As defined, the unbound consciousness constitutes the conscious mind and all the known nonconscious (both Freudian and Jungian unconscious). This unbound consciousness can be viewed as a superposition of the conscious and the nonconscious. Pending the angle of analysis, the same superposition can be seen as that of the mind and the (sentient) self, or of qualia and nonqualia. Such a conceptualization thus poses problems for measurement and method of enquiry. Superposition by definition implies 'entanglement' (Penrose, 1997; Shimony, 1997) and the resultant emergence. As such, to explore individual elements separately from the entire system would risk the neglect of all interacting dynamics as well as the emergent properties that may arise out of these dynamics. However, because conscious and nonconscious processes differ in both processing style (i.e., 'seriality–capacity' difference: Mandler, 1997) and underlying neurophysiological correlates (e.g., Cloninger, 1998), different enquiring methods are then needed in making sense of consciousness in its entirety.

Experimentation and hermeneutics: sense-making in tandem

It appears that the two sense-making processes of scientific experimentation and hermeneutic interpretation are both required for a fuller understanding of the unbound consciousness. Scientific experimentation yields explanations that are directly verifiable across individuals; sense-making through hermeneutics yields interpretations that may be intrinsic and first-personal in nature and hence may not lend themselves readily to third-person scientific verification.

Of the unbound consciousness, its 'nonqualia', 'the conscious', and 'the mind' aspects are suitable objects for scientific experimentation, as has been the practice in empirical psychology. However, its 'qualia', 'the nonconscious' and 'the sentient self' aspects appear to be first-personal and private. The experimental normative approach involves cross-sectional sampling of a 'snapshot' of an ongoing and ever-changing reality; as such it is able to deal with the commonalities of human experiences. The individual longitudinal approach, on the other hand, focuses on the continual ongoing dynamics of individual experience as experienced by each individual experiencer. The significance of the latter approach for consciousness research lies in its casting human experience in a 'historical' context.

As such, each method alone would leave unexplored essential aspects of the unbound consciousness. The normative experimental method alone leaves out the unique depth and quality human culture and history have 'preferentially' etched on each individual experiencer. The individual longitudinal approach alone cannot reveal the width of the common marks that culture and history have 'equitably' left for all. Therefore, not only are human beings at once cognitive agents and sentient selves, we are also at once a gene-governed biological entity and a meme-spreading cultural agent. To leave any aspect unattended is to risk leaving the full potentiality of humanity quite unrealized.

In recent years, much has been written about the imbalanced weighting placed upon these two supposedly complementary methods of enquiry into consciousness and human experience. As repeatedly argued, the problem pertaining to qualia, hence to consciousness, is causally linked to the prevailing intellectual *Zeitgeist* of 'scientism'. In this regard, many have expressed the idea that this *Zeitgeist* since the days of Descartes to the present is not entirely positive in terms of its purported overriding goal of the betterment of humanity. The most significant failing, as has been voiced in Romanticism, phenomenological, humanistic and existential paradigms, is that the scientific experimental approach to issues of humanity largely leaves out any considerations of humanness or the subjectivity and uniqueness of human experience as experienced by the individual self. Science has therefore tried to gain an understanding of humanity through the analysis of a 'shrunken soul' or a 'contracted mind' (Sheldrake and Fox, 1996). As such, the pre-Cartesian notion of the *psyche* or the unbound consciousness has been 'contracted into' the physical brain. Given this bounded focus on humanity, while science has indeed fostered a greater understanding of human cognitive agency, it has perhaps hindered the understanding of humanity in a fuller sense.

It seems that within the prevailing *Zeitgeist*, physicalism and scientific experimentation have indeed become a 'dogma' and have led 'to violent intolerance' of alternative viewpoints, exactly as Helmholtz forewarned (see Chapter 2) nearly 120 years ago when psychology was about to become a fully experimental discipline. In an effort to redress the imbalance, many have argued for placing history and hermeneutic interpretation at the core of human and psychological sciences (e.g., Dilthey, 1977). This position was taken most obviously by Dilthey who argued that *'the totality of human nature is only to be found in history; the individual can only become conscious of it and enjoy it when he assembles the minds of the past within himself'* (Smith, 1997, p.870). Accordingly, Dilthey placed pivotal importance on interpretation over scientific explanation, as a method for human sciences.

Hermeneutics refers to a method of interpretation, as opposed to scientific experimentation. Casting human experience in historical terms would also require that it be understood through interpretation rather than experimentation. Hermeneutics is thus the best tool in making sense of human actions and potentials by piecing together their deeper subjective 'meaning'. And it is in this context that the terms 'interpretive psychotherapy' or 'hermeneutic psychoanalysis' have come to denote the individual and longitudinal sense-making approach to human experiences, as opposed to the normative and cross-sectional approach of scientific experimentation.

The experimentation–hermeneutic imbalance is at the core of the perennial debate over the status of human sciences. Roger Smith (1997) has reviewed the literature on the uniqueness of human sciences as distinguished from physical sciences. While leaving open the solution to the debate over the status of history and scientific truth in human sciences, Smith argues for keeping open the debate and notes that *'the debate about the identity of the human sciences should be a live issue at the end of the twentieth century'* (p.861).

While keeping the debate going is necessary for research in human sciences in general, it is not sufficient for research into consciousness and human experience. One of the key themes of the present book is that consciousness research needs to be grounded in the complete conception of an unbound *psyche*. But the readmission of the nonconscious into consciousness research would require hermeneutics. Accordingly, it is argued that a fuller understanding of humanity (and hence the unbound consciousness) requires the inclusion of hermeneutics as an equal partner, with scientific experimentation, in its enquiry. The importance of hermeneutics for psychology as a discipline has been expressed repeatedly.

Oatley (1988) has expressed a similar view. As discussed in the last chapter, in his effort to integrate the cognitive-agentic mind (i.e., the Helmotzian and Wolfian consciousness) and the socially-constructed self (Vygotskyan and Meadean consciousness), Oatley (1988) also argued for the need to include hermeneutics as a second tool in studying consciousness. Oatley thus speaks of a combined method of enquiry:

> The Vygotskyan and Meadean consciousness is the self, its doings, its intentions, its presence as an object of thought. This needs to be understood interpretively rather than as mechanism. The implication is that, in understanding consciousness, a rapprochement is needed between natural science with its concern for mechanism, and human or social science ... with its concern for interpretation. (p.377)

In a larger context for psychology as a whole, the contemporary philosopher Edward Spranger first asserted that the main aim of psychology is a hermeneutic (an interpretation) of the human spirit (Reese, 1980). More recently, Leahey (1992) expressed a similar sentiment and argued for the possibility of taking hermeneutics as a model for psychology and the social sciences, which aim at understanding humanity. Leahey writes: '*hermeneutics concerns itself with human life: with right and wrong, with love and hate, with what it means to be human rather than animal, and this is not obviously inferior to science*' (p.476). And a joint paradigm embracing scientific experimentation and hermeneutic interpretation seems to be the 'middle way' in the celebration of both the commonness and the uniqueness of human experience.

Epilogue

One central theme of this book concerns the necessity of closing the agency–sentience divide that features prominently in contemporary intellectual *Zeitgeist*. It is this intellectual divide that is at the core of the mind–mind problem of qualia. To close this divide requires the vastly daunting task of synergistic syntheses between the conscious and the nonconscious. Chalmers (1996) acknowledged that the differences among the various views of qualia (e.g., eliminativism, reductivism or non-reductivism) may be too wide to overcome. He concedes that no argument can resolve such differences. There is an important point he made while commenting on the arguments between two people holding different views:

> then I can only conclude that when it comes to experience we are on different planes. Perhaps our inner lives differ dramatically. Perhaps one of us is 'cognitively closed' to the insights of the other. More likely, one of us is confused or is in the grip of a dogma. In any case, once the dialectic reaches this point, it is a bridge that argument cannot cross. (p.167)

There are three points worth pursuing; one concerns possible individual differences in 'inner lives', second, the 'dogma' that closes one's mind, and third, the 'bridge that argument cannot cross'.

With reference to individual differences in inner lives, there seems to be little doubt that individuals differ, sometimes enormously, as to the 'level of consciousness' that one has attained or experienced. The literature on humanistic psychology and in particular, transpersonal psychology, has provided ample evidence of such differences cast in longitudinal lifespan terms. These subjective experiences of the inner life range from the more commonly known altered states to the less frequently attained 'cosmic consciousness', which is characterized by the feeling of oneness with all. Moreover, these inner experiences appear to have paramount significance for the individual experiencer in that they often mark the turning point in his/her outlook towards life and existence.

John Horgan, a science writer with the *Scientific American* recently gave a good example. In his bestselling book, *The End of Science*, Horgan (1997) recounts a cosmic experience that he had earlier and remarked: *'the mystical episode ... is the most important experience of my life. It had been burning a hole in my pocket, as it were, for more than 10 years, and I was determined to make use of it, even if it meant damaging what little credibility I may have as a journalist'* (p.281). The comments appear to affirm the personal significance of such intrinsic subjective experience for the experiencer. While others may be compelled to search for the immediate reason or the deeper meaning of such experiences, Horgan was 'determined to make use of' the experience. Perhaps as a result of his determination, Horgan went on to write specifically about the 'undiscovered mind' (1999), where he asserts that *'Inner space may be science's final – and eternal – frontier'* (p.14). Although individual reactions may vary, the point is that subjective experiences do have pragmatic consequences. Cast in the philosophical framework of Charles Peirce and William James, as long as any 'subjective' belief or experience has 'cash value' for the person, it is then a 'truth' to that person. The book's argument against the agency–sentience separation is congruent with the pragmatic philosophy's notion of multiple forms of truth.

The fear of 'damaging one's credibility' which Horgan refers to is closely linked with Chalmers' second point concerning the mind-closing effect of dogma. Given that it is simply a human condition for each of the debating parties to see the other as being blinded by a dogma, the stalemate can only be ended by refraining from any 'cognitive closure'. Cognitive closure can no doubt be indicative of a deep conviction to a set of well-educated beliefs, and yet given that wide individual differences in inner conscious experience exist, there is a need for each to thoughtfully consider the other's points of view. It is our mind bondage that prevents such considerations without prejudice. To undo the mind bondage and hence to loosen the grip of any dogma, requires tolerance, courage and hard work: tolerance in keeping an open mind; courage in risking going against the tide; and hard work in educating oneself with all relevant literatures.

Once the mind bondage is undone, there will naturally be no 'bridge that argument cannot cross'. As once the agency–sentience divide is closed, a higher level of synthesis is reached in the thesis–antithesis dialectic. The sentiment of an agency–sentience synthesis has been framed in different terms. In *Sources of the self*, Charles Taylor (1991) portrays the making of the modern identity in terms of a dialectic of the instrumental value of our 'disengaged reason' and the intrinsic purpose of our 'inner source'. Taylor argues for *'the need to recognize a plurality of goods ... which other views tend to mask by delegitimizing one of the goods in contest'* (p.518). In *The passion of the Western mind*, Richard Tarnas (1991) also calls for such a synthesis in terms of an 'archetypal marriage' of man's differentiating intellectual mind and its participatory spiritual nature. And in this integration,

> Each perspective ... is here both affirmed and transcended, recognized as part of a larger whole; for each polarity requires the other for its fulfillment. And their synthesis leads to something beyond itself: It brings an unexpected opening to a larger reality that cannot be grasped before it arrives, because this new reality is itself a creative act. (p.445)

In this larger context, consciousness, mind or self betokens the same reality: it is the greatest and most glorious gift of nature. And it has no bounds.

Bibliography

Adrian, E.D. (1942). Olfactory reactions in the brain of the hedgehog. *Journal of Physiology, 100,* 459–73.

Allen, R. (1966). *Greek philosophy from Thales to Aristotle.* New York: Free Press.

Allison, H. (1986). *Kant's transcendental idealism.* New Haven: Yale University Press.

Allport, G. (1961). *Patterns and growth in personality.* New York: Holt, Rinehart & Winston.

Andrews, B., Morton, J., Bekerian, D.A., Brewin, C.R., Davies, G.M., & Mollon, P. (1995). The recovery of memories in clinical practice: Experience and beliefs of British Psychological Society practitioners. *Psychologist, 8,* 209–14.

Andrews, M.R., Townsend, C.G., Miesner, H.-J., Durfee, D.S., Kurn, D.M., & Ketterle, W. (1997). Observation of interference between two Bose condensates. *Science, 275,* 637–41.

Augustine, St (1939). *Confessions* (translated by E.B. Pusey: Everyman's Library). London: Dent.

Ayers, S. (1997). The application of chaos theory to psychology. *Theory and Psychology, 7,* 373–98.

Baars, B. (1988). *A cognitive theory of consciousness.* Cambridge: Cambridge University Press.

Baars, B. (1996). Understanding subjectivity: Global workspace theory and the resurrection of the observing self. *Journal of Consciousness Studies, 3,* 211–16.

Baars, B. (1997). *In the theater of consciousness: The workspace of the mind.* Oxford: Oxford University Press.

Baars, B., & Newman, J. (1994). A neurobiological interpretation of the global workspace theory of consciousness. In A. Revonsuo & M. Kamppinen (eds), *Consciousness in philosophy and cognitive neuroscience.* Hillsdale, NJ: Erlbaum.

Bak, P., & Chen, K. (1991). Self-organized criticality. *Scientific American,* (January), 46–53.

Baker, R.A. (1990). *They call it hypnosis.* New York: Prometheus Books.
Bandura, A. (1986). *Social foundations of thought and action: A social cognitive theory.* Englewood Cliffs: NJ: Prentice-Hall.
Barclay, C., & Smith, T. (1993). Autobiographical remembering and self-composing. *International Journal of Personal Construct Psychology, 6,* 1–25.
Bargh, J.A. (1997). The automaticity of everyday life. In R.S. Wyer, Jr. (ed.), *Advances in social cognition* (Vol. 10). Mahwah, NJ: Lawrence Erlbaum.
Barnes, H.J. (1998). Concurrent processing during sequential finger tapping. In D.A. Rosenbaum, & C.E. Collyer (eds), *Timing of behavior: Neural, psychological, and computational perspectives.* Cambridge, MA: MIT Press.
Barton, S. (1994). Chaos, self-organization and psychology. *American Psychologist, 49,* 5–14.
Basar, E. (ed.) (1990). *Chaos in brain function.* New York: Springer.
Basar, E., Rosen, B., Baser-Eroglu, C., & Greitshus, F. (1987). The associations between 40 Hz-EEG and the middle latency response of the auditory evoked potential. *International Journal of Neuroscience, 33,* 103–17.
Bell, J.S. (1988). *Speakable and unspeakable in quantum mechanics.* Cambridge: Cambridge University Press.
Berlekamp, E., Conway, J., & Guy, R. (1982). *Winning ways* (Vol. 2). New York: Academic Press.
Berne, E. (1961). *Transactional analysis in psychotherapy.* New York: Grove.
Bisiach, E. (1988). The brain and consciousness. In A. Marcel & E. Bisiach (eds), *Consciousness in contemporary science.* Oxford: Oxford University Press.
Block, N. (1995). On a confusion about a function of consciousness. *Behavioral and Brain Sciences, 18,* 227–47.
Bogen, J.E. (1995). On the neurophysiology of consciousness. An overview. *Consciousness and Cognition, 4,* 52–62.
Bohm, D. (1951). *Quantum theory.* New York: Prentice-Hall.
Bohm, D. (1980). *Wholeness and the implicate order.* London: Routledge & Kegan Paul.
Bohm, D. (1986). A new theory of the relationship of mind and matter. *Journal of the American Society for Psychical Research, 80 (2).*

Bohr, N. (1934). *Atomic theory and the description of nature.* Cambridge: Cambridge University Press.
Boulding, K. (1968). *The organizational revolution.* Chicago: Quadrangle.
Bowers, K.S. (1973). Situationism in psychology: An analysis and critique. *Psychological Review, 80,* 307–36.
Bowie, M. (1991). *Lacan.* London: Fontana.
Brennan, B. (1992). *Dictionary of scientific literacy.* New York: Wiley.
Brockman, J. (1996). *The third culture.* New York: Touchstone.
Broekstra, G. (1998). An organization is a conversation. In D. Grant, T. Keenoy & C. Oswick (eds), *Discourse and organization.* London: Sage.
Brown, J.W. (1988). *The life of the mind.* Hillsdale, NJ: Lawrence Erlbaum.
Brown, P. (1991). *The hypnotic brain.* New York: Yale University Press.
Cantor, N., & Kihlstrom, J.F. (1987). *Personality and social intelligence.* Englewood Cliffs, NJ: Prentice-Hall.
Carver, C.S., & Scheier, M.F. (1992). *Perspectives on personality* (second edn). Boston: Allyn & Bacon.
Carver, C.S., & Scheier, M.F. (1998). *On the self-regulation of behavior.* Cambridge, MA: Cambridge University Press.
Casey, C. (1995). *Work, self and society: After Industrialism.* New York: Routledge.
Casti, J. (1990). *Paradigms lost.* New York: Avon Books.
Casti, J. (1995). *Complexification: Explaining a paradoxical world through the science of surprise.* London: Abacus.
Cavanaugh, J.C., & McGuire, L. (1994). Chaos theory as a framework for understanding adult lifespan learning. In J.D. Sinnott (ed.), *Interdisciplinary handbook of adult lifespan learning.* Westport, CT: Greenwood.
Ceci, S.J., & Loftus, E.F. (1994). Memory work: A royal road to false memories. *Applied Cognitive Psychology, 8,* 351–64.
Chalmers, D. (1996). *The conscious mind: In search of a fundamental theory.* Oxford: Oxford University Press.
Churchland, P.M. (1984). *Matter and consciousness.* Cambridge, MA: MIT Press.
Churchland, P.M. (1989). *A neurocomputational perspective: The*

nature of mind and the structure of science. Cambridge, MA: MIT Press.
Churchland, P.M. (1995). *The engine of reason, the seat of the soul: A philosophical journey into the brain.* Cambridge, MA: MIT Press.
Churchland, P.S. (1986). *Neurophilosophy: Towards a unified science of mind-brain.* Cambridge, MA: MIT Press.
Cloninger, C.R. (1998). Temperament and personality. In L.R. Squire & S.M. Kosslyn (eds), *Findings and current opinion in cognitive neuroscience.* Cambridge, MA: MIT Press.
Combs, A., Winkler, M., & Daley, C. (1994). A chaotic systems analysis of rhythms in feeling states. *Psychological Record, 44,* 359–68.
Cooley, C.H. (1902). *Human nature and the social order.* New York: Scribner.
Copleston, F. (1993). *A history of philosophy.* New York: Doubleday.
Corballis, M.C. (1991). *The lopsided ape: Evolution of the generative mind.* Oxford: Oxford University Press.
Coveny, P., & Highfield, R. (1995). *Frontiers of complexity: The search for order in a chaotic world.* New York: Fawcett Columbine.
Crick, F. (1994). *The astonishing hypothesis: The scientific search for the soul.* New York: Touchstone.
Crick, F., & Koch, C. (1990). Towards a neurobiological theory of consciousness. *Seminars in the Neurosciences, 2,* 263–75.
Crick, F., & Mitchison, G. (1983). The function of dream sleep. *Nature, 304,* 111–14.
Csikszentmihalyi, M. (1997). *Finding flow: The psychology of engagement with everyday life.* New York: Basic Books.
Csikszentmihalyi, M., & Csikszentmihalyi, I.S. (eds) (1988). *Optimal experience: Psychological studies of flow in consciousness.* New York: Cambridge University Press.
Cytowic, R.E. (1995). Synesthesia: Phenomenology and neuropsychology: A review of current knowledge. *Psyche: An Interdisciplinary Journal of Research on Consciousness, 2.*
D'Espagnat, B. (1989). *Reality and the physicist: Knowledge, duration and the quantum world.* Cambridge: Cambridge University Press.
Dahlbom, B. (1993). Mind is artificial. In B. Dahlbom (ed.), *Dennett and his critics.* Oxford: Blackwell.
Davidson, D. (1989). The myth of the subjective. In M. Krausz (ed.),

Relativism, interpretation and confrontation. Notre Dame, IN: Notre Dame University Press.

De Broglie, (1930). *An introduction to the study of wave mechanics.* New York: Dutton.

De Riencourt, A. (1980). *The eye of Shiva.* New York: William Morrow.

Deci, E.L., & Ryan, R.M. (1991). A motivational approach to self: Integration in personality. In R. Diensbier (ed.), *Nebraska Symposium of Motivation* (Vol. 38). Nebraska: University of Nebraska Press.

Dennett, D. (1978). *Brainstorms: Philosophical essays on mind and psychology.* Montgomery, VT: Bradford.

Dennett, D. (1983). Artificial intelligence and the strategies of psychological investigation. In J. Miller (ed.), States of mind. New York: Pantheon.

Dennett, D. (1988). Quining qualia. In A.J. Marcel & E. Bisiach (eds), *Consciousness in contemporary science.* Oxford: Clarendon.

Dennett, D. C. (1991). Consciousness explained. Boston: Little, Brown.

Dennett, D., & Kinsbourne, M. (1992). Time and the observer: The where and when of consciousness in the brain. *Brain and Behavioral Sciences, 15,* 183–200.

Derrida, J. (1978). *Writing and difference.* Chicago: Chicago University Press.

Descartes, R. (1980). *Meditations on First Philosophy* (translated by D. Cress). Indianapolis: Hackett.

Dilthey, W. (1977). *Descriptive psychology and historical understanding.* The Hague: Martinus Nijhoff.

Dreske, F.I. (1995). *Naturalizing the mind.* Cambridge, MA: MIT Press.

Durkheim, E. (1952). *Suicide: A study in sociology.* London: Routledge & Kegan Paul.

Eccles, J.C. (1989). *Evolution of the brain: Creation of the self.* London: Routledge.

Eckhorn, R., Reitbock, M., Arndt, M., & Dicke, P. (1989). A neural network for feature linking via synchronous activity: Results from cat visual cortex and from simulations. In R.M.J. Cotteril (ed.), *Models of brain function.* Cambridge: Cambridge University Press.

Eddington, A. (1928). *The nature of the physical world*. Cambridge: Cambridge University Press.

Edelman, G.M. (1989). *The remembered present: A biological theory of consciousness*. New York: Basic Books.

Edelman, G.M. (1992). *Bright air, brilliant fire*. New York: Basic Books.

Elbert, T., & Rockstroh, B. (1987). Threshold regulation: A key to the understanding of the combined dynamics of EEG and event-related potentials. *Journal of Psychophysiology, 1*, 317–33.

Engel, A.K., Roelfsema, P.R., Fries, P. Brecht, M., & Singer, W. (1997). Role of the temporal domain for response selection and perceptual binding. *Cerebral Cortex, 7*, 571–82.

Evans, C. (1984). *Landscapes of the night: How and why we dream*. New York: Viking.

Everett, H. (1973). The theory of the universal wave function. In B.S. deWitt & N. Graham (eds), The many-worlds interpretation of quantum mechanics. Princeton: Princeton University Press.

Fairbairn, W.R.D. (1952). *Psychoanalytic studies of the personality*. London: Tavistock.

Fairbairn, W.R.D. (1954). *An object-relations theory of the personality*. New York: Basic Books.

Farah, M. (1994). Perception and awareness after brain damage. *Current Opinion in Neurobiology, 4*, 252–5.

Feigenbaum, M.J. (1978). Quantitative universality for a class of non-linear transformations. *Journal of Statistical Physics, 19*, 669–706.

Feustal, T.C., Shriffrin, R.M., & Salasoo, A. (1983). Episodic and lexical contributions to the repetition effect in word identification. *Journal of Experimental Psychology: General, 112*, 309–46.

Finke, R.A., & Bettle, J. (1996). *Chaotic cognition: Principles and applications*. Mahwah, NJ: Lawrence Erlbaum.

Flanagan, O. (1992). *Consciousness reconsidered*. Cambridge, MA: MIT Press.

Flanagan, O., & Polger, T. (1995). Zombies and the function of consciousness. *Journal of Consciousness Studies, 2*, 313–21.

Fodor, J. A. (1983). *The modularity of mind*. Cambridge, MA: MIT Press.

Freeman, W.J. (1987). Simulation of chaotic EEG patterns with a dynamical model of the olfactory system. *Biological Cybernetics, 56*, 139.

Freeman, W.J. (1994). Neural networks and chaos. *Journal of Theoretical Biology, 171*, 13–18.
Freeman, W.J., & Baird, B. (1987). Relation of olfactory EEG to behavior: A spatial analysis. *Behavioral Neuroscience, 101*, 393.
Freeman, W.J., & Barrie, J. (1994). Chaotic oscillations and the genesis of meaning in cerebral cortex. In G. Buzaki (ed.), *Temporal coding in the brain*. Berlin: Springer-Verlag.
Freeman, W.J., Yao, Y., & Burke, B. (1988). Central pattern generating and recognizing in olfactory bulb: A correlation learning rule. *Neural Networks, 1*, 277.
Freud, S. (1900/1975). *The interpretation of dreams*. London: Hogarth.
Freud, S. (1938). *The basic writings of Sigmund Freud*. New York: Modern Library.
Freud, S. (1957). The unconscious. In *The Standard edition of the complete psychological works of Sigmund Freud* (Vol. XIV). London: Hogarth.
Frohlich, H. (1986). Coherent excitations in active biological systems. In F. Gutman & H. Keyzer (eds), *Modern biochemistry*. London: Plenum.
Frohlich, H., & Kremer, F. (eds) (1983). *Coherent excitations in biological systems*. Berlin: Springer-Verlag.
Frost, S.E. Jr (1962). *Basic teaching of the great philosophers*. New York: Doubleday (1989: Anchor Books).
Gardner, M. (1971). On cellular automata, self-reproduction, the Garden of Eden and the Game of Life. *Scientific American, 224*, 112–17.
Garner, R. (1987). *Metacognition and reading comprehension*. Norwood, NJ: Ablex.
Gazzaniga, M.S. (1983). Right hemisphere language following bisection: A 20-year perspective. *American Psychologist, 38*, 525–37.
Gazzaniga, M.S. (1989). Organization of the human brain. *Science, 245*, 947–52.
Gazzaniga, M.S. (1995). Consciousness and the cerebral hemispheres. In M.S. Gazzaniga (ed.), *The cognitive neurosciences*. Cambridge, MA: MIT Press.
Gazzaniga, M.S. (1998). *The mind's past*. Berkeley, CA: University of California Press.
Genberg, L., Richard, L., McLendon, G., & Dwayne-Miller, R. (1991). Direct observation of global protein motion in hemo-

globin and myoglobin on picosecond time scales. *Science, 251*, 1051–4.
Gergen, K. (1994). *Realities and relationships: Soundings in social construction.* Cambridge, MA: Harvard University Press.
Gergen, K., & Gergen, M. (1988). Narrative and the self as relationship. *Advances in Experimental Social Psychology, 21*, 17–56.
Glass, L., & Mackey, M. (1988). *From clocks to chaos: The rhythms of life.* Princeton, NJ: Princeton University Press.
Gleick, J. (1987). *Chaos: Making a new science.* London: Abacus.
Goldin-Meadow, S., & Alibali, M.W. (1995). Mechanisms of transition: Learning with a helping hand. In D. Medin (ed.), *The psychology of learning and motivation* (Vol. 33). San Diego, CA: Academic Press.
Goldman, A.I. (1993). Consciousness, folk psychology and cognitive science. *Consciousness and Cognition, 2*, 364–82.
Goldstein, J. (1997). Social psychology and nonlinear dynamical systems theory. *Psychological Inquiry, 8*, 125–8.
Goleman, D. (1997). *Vital lies, simple truth: The psychology of self-deception.* London: Bloomsbury.
Goleman, D., & Thurman, R.A.F. (eds) (1991). *Mind science* (The Harvard Mind Science Symposium, MIT). Boston: Wisdom Publications.
Golledge, H.D.R., Hilgetag, C., & Tovee, M.J. (1996). Information processing: A solution to the binding problem? *Current Biology, 6*, 1092–5.
Gould, S.J. (1991). Exaptation: A crucial tool for an evolutionary psychology. *Journal of Social Issues, 47*, 43–65.
Gray, C.M., Konig, P., Engel, A.K., & Singer, W. (1989). Oscillatory responses in cat visual cortex exhibit inter-columnar synchronization which reflects global stimulus properties. *Nature, 338*, 334–7.
Gregory, R. (1996). What do qualia do? *Perception, 25* (4), Editorial.
Gulley, N. (1962). *Plato's theory of knowledge.* London: Methuen.
Guthrie, W.K. (1977). *A history of Greek philosophy.* Cambridge: Cambridge University Press.
Hameroff, S. (1994). Quantum coherence in microtubules: A neural basis for an emergent consciousness? *Journal of Consciousness Studies, 1*, 91–118.
Hameroff, S. (1998). Did consciousness cause the Cambrian evolutionary explosion? In S. Hameroff, A. Kaszniak, & A. Scott (eds),

Toward a science of consciousness II: The 1996 Tucson discussions and debates. Cambridge, MA: MIT Press.

Hameroff, S., & Penrose, R. (1996). Orchestrated objective reduction of quantum coherence in brain microtubules: The 'Orch OR' model for consciousness. In S. Hameroff, A. Kaszniak, & A. Scott (eds), *Towards a science of consciousness.* Cambridge, MA: MIT Press.

Hampshire, S. (1962). *Spinoza.* Harmondsworth: Pelican.

Hardcastle, V. (1995). *Locating consciousness.* Amsterdam: John Benjamins.

Harre, R., & Secord, P.F. (1972). *The explanation of social behavior.* Oxford: Blackwell.

Harrington, D.L., & Haaland, K.Y. (1998). Sequencing and timing operations of the basal ganglia. In D.A. Rosenbaum, & C.E. Collyer (eds), *Timing of behavior: Neural, psychological, and computational perspectives.* Cambridge, MA: MIT Press.

Hartmann, E. (1984). *The nightmare.* New York: Basic Books.

Hatab, L.J. (1992). *Myth and philosophy: A contest of truths.* La Salle, IL: Open Court Publishing.

Heaton, J. (1985). Knowledge and consciousness. *Bulletin of the British Psychological Society, 38*, A36.

Heisenberg, W. (1989). *Physics and philosophy.* New York: Penguin.

Hey, T., & Walters, P. (1987). *The quantum universe.* Cambridge: Cambridge University Press.

Higgins, E.T. (1989). Knowledge accessibility and activation: Subjectivity and suffering from unconscious sources. In J.S. Uleman & J.A. Bargh (eds), *Unintended thought: The limits of awareness, intention and control.* New York: Guilford.

Hilgard, E.R. (1977). *Divided consciousness: Multiple controls in human thought and action.* New York: Wiley-Interscience.

Hinrichs, H., & Machleidt, W. (1992). Basic emotions reflected in EEG coherences. *International Journal of Psychophysiology, 13*, 225–32.

Hobson, J.A. (1988). *The dreaming brain.* New York: Basic Books.

Hobson, J.A., & McCarley, R.W. (1977). The brain as a dream state generator: An activation-synthesis hypothesis of the dream process. *American Journal of Psychiatry, 134*, 1335–48.

Hodgson, D. (1988*). The mind matters: Consciousness and choice in a quantum world.* Oxford: Oxford University Press.

Hodgson, D. (1991). *The mind matters.* Oxford: Oxford University Press.
Hofstadter, D.R., & Dennett, D.C. (eds), (1981*). The mind's I.* New York: Basic Books.
Horgan, J. (1997*). The end of science.* New York: Broadway Books.
Horgan, J. (1999). *The undiscovered mind.* New York: Free Press.
Horne, J.A. (1991). Dimensions to sleepiness. In T.H. Monk (ed.), Sleep, sleepiness and performance. New York: Wiley.
Hume, D. (1975). *A treatise of human nature.* Oxford: Oxford University Press.
Humphrey, N., & Dennett, D. (1991). Speaking for ourselves. In D. Kolak & R. Martin (eds), *Self and identity: Contemporary philosophical issues.* New York: Macmillan.
Issacs, K.S. (1998). *Uses of emotion: Nature's vital gift.* Westport, CT: Praeger.
Jackendoff, R. (1987). *Consciousness and the computational mind.* Cambridge, MA: MIT Press.
James, W. (1890). *Principles of psychology.* New York: Dover.
James, W. (1902). *Varieties of religious experience: A study in human nature.* London: Longmans Green.
Jaynes, J. (1976). *The origins of consciousness in the breakdown of the bicameral mind.* Boston: Houghton Mifflin.
Johnson-Laird, P. (1983). *Mental models.* Cambridge: Cambridge University Press.
Johnson-Laird, P. (1988). A computational analysis of consciousness. In A. Marcel & E. Bisiach (eds), *Consciousness in contemporary science.* Oxford: Clarendon Press.
Jung, C. (1961). *Memories, dreams, reflections.* New York: Pantheon.
Jung, C. (1971). *The portable Jung.* New York: Viking.
Kauffman, S. (1993). *Origins of order: Self-organisation and selection in evolution.* New York: Oxford University Press.
Kauffman, S. (1995). *At home in the universe.* New York: Oxford University Press.
Kelso, J.A.S. (1995). *Dynamic patterns: The self-organization of brain and behavior.* Cambridge, MA: MIT Press.
Kenny, A. (1973). *Wittgenstein.* Cambridge: Harvard University Press.
Kiester, E. (1984). Images of the night. In M. Waraven & H.E. Fitzgerald (eds), *Psychology.* Guilford, CT: Dushkin.

Kihlstrom, J. (1987). The cognitive unconscious. *Science, 237*, 1445–52.
Koch, C., & Braun, J. (1996). Towards the neuronal correlate of visual awareness. *Current Opinion in Neurobiology, 6*, 158–64.
Kohut, H. (1977). *The restoration of the self.* Madison, CT: International Universities Press.
Korner, S. (1955). *Kant.* Harmondsworth: Pelican.
Kramer, D.A. (1990). Conceptualizing wisdom: The primacy of affect-cognition relations. In R.J. Sternberg (ed.), *Wisdom: Its nature, origins, and development.* New York: Cambridge University Press.
Kuhn, T. (1970). *The structure of scientific revolutions.* Chicago: University of Chicago Press.
Lacan, J. (1968). *The language of the self.* Baltimore: Johns Hopkins University Press.
Lacan, W.G. (1996). *Consciousness and experience.* Cambridge, MA: MIT Press.
Langton, C. (ed.) (1989). *Artificial life.* Reading, MA: Addison-Wesley.
Langton, C., Taylor, C., Farmer, D., & Rasmussen, S. (eds) (1992*). Artificial life II.* Reading, MA: Addison-Wesley.
Lash, C. (1978). *The culture of narcissis*m. New York: Warner.
Lash, C. (1984). *The minimal self: Psychic survival in troubled times.* New York: Norton.
Latane, B., Nowak, A., & Lie, J. (1994). Measuring emergent social phenomena: Dynamism, polarization and clustering as order parameters of social systems. *Behavioral Science, 39*, 1–24.
Leahey, T.H. (1992). *A history of psychology: Main currents in psychological thought* (3rd edn). Englewood Cliffs, NJ: Prentice-Hall.
Lester, D. (1993/1994). On the disunity of the self: A systems theory of personality. *Current Psychology: Developmental, Learning, Personality, Social, 12*, 312–25.
Levy, D. (1994). Chaos theory and strategy: Theory, application and managerial implications. *Strategic Management Journal, 15*, 167–78.
Lewin, K. (1935). *A dynamic theory of personality.* New York: McGraw-Hill.
Lewin, R. (1992). *Complexity.* New York: Macmillan.
Llinas, R., & Ribary, U. (1992). Rostrocaudal scan in human brain: A global characteristic of the 40-Hz response during sensory input.

In E. Basar & T. Bullock (eds), Induced rhythms in the brain. Boston: Birkhauser.
Locke, J. (1975). *An essay concerning human understanding.* (P. Nidditch, ed.) Oxford: Clarendon.
Lockwood, M. (1989). *Mind, brain and the quantum.* Oxford: Blackwell.
Loudon, R. (1983). *The quantum theory of light.* Oxford: Clarendon Press.
MacIntyre, A. (1985). How psychology makes itself true-or false. In S. Koch & D. Leary (eds), *A century of psychology as science.* New York: McGraw-Hill.
McCrae, R., & Costa, P. (1977). Personality trait structure as a human universal. *American Scientist, 52,* 509–16.
McGinn, C. (1991). *The problem with consciousness.* Cambridge, MA: Blackwell.
McGinn, C. (1997). *Minds and bodies.* Cambridge: Cambridge University Press.
McKeon, R. (1941). *The basic works of Aristotle.* New York: Random House.
Mair, J.M. (1977). The community of self. In D. Bannister (ed.), New perspectives in personal construct theory. New York: Academic.
Mandelbrot, B. (1982). *The fractal geometry of nature.* San Francisco: Freeman.
Mandell, A. (1985). From molecular biological simplification to more realistic central nervous system dynamics: An opinion. In J.O. Cavenar (ed.), Psychiatry: Psychobiological foundations of clinical psychiatry. New York: Lippincott.
Mandler, G. (1989). Memory: Conscious and unconscious. In P.R. Solomon, G.R. Goethals, C.M. Kelley & B.R. Stephens (eds), *Memory: Interdisciplinary approaches.* New York: Springer-Verlag.
Mandler, G. (1992). Toward a theory of consciousness. In H.-G. Geissler; S.W. Link & J.T. Townsend (eds), *Cognition, information processing and psychophysics: Basic Issues.* Hillsdale, NJ: Lawrence Erlbaum.
Mandler, G. (1997). Consciousness redux. In J.D. Cohen & J.W. Schooler (eds), *Scientific approaches to consciousness.* Mahwah, NJ: Lawrence Erlbaum.
Marcel, A.J. (1983). Conscious and unconscious perception: An

approach to the relations between phenomenal experience and perceptual processes. *Cognitive Psychology, 15*, 238–300.

Marcel, A.J., & Bisiach, E. (eds), *Consciousness in contemporary science*. Oxford: Clarendon.

Margenau, H. (1984). *The miracle of existence*. Woodbridge, Connecticut: Ox Bow Press.

Margulis, L. (1993). *Symbiosis in cell evolution* (2nd ed.). New York: Freeman.

Margulis, L., & Sagan, D. (1995). *What is life?* New York: Simon & Schuster.

Markus, H. (1977). Self-schemata and processing information about the self. *Journal of Personality and Social Psychology, 35*, 63–78.

Markus, H., & Kitayama, S. (1991). Culture and the self: Implications for cognition, emotion and motivation. *Psychological Review, 98*, 224–53.

Markus, H., & Nurius, P. (1986). Possible selves. *American Psychologist, 41*, 954–69.

Marshall, I. (1989). Consciousness and Bose-Einstein Condensates. *New Ideas in Psychology. 7*, 73–83.

Maslow, A. (1970). *Motivation and personality* (2nd ed.). New York: Harper & Row.

Maslow, A. (1971). *The farther reaches of human nature*. New York: Viking.

Mead, G.H. (1934). *Mind, self and society*. Chicago: University of Chicago Press.

Messick, D.M., & Liebrand, V.B.G. (1995). Individual heuristics and the dynamics of cooperation in large groups. *Psychological Review, 102*, 131–45.

Metcalfe, J., & Shimamura, A. (1994). *Metacognition: Knowing about knowing*. Cambridge, MA: Bradford Books.

Minsky, M. (1985). *The society of mind*. New York: Simon & Schuster.

Nagel, S. (1992). Instabilities in a sandpile. *Reviews of Modern Physics, 84*, 321–5.

Nagel, T. (1974). What is it like to be a bat? *Philosophical Review, 83*, 435–56.

Nagel, T. (1979). *Mortal questions*. Cambridge: Cambridge University Press.

Nelson, T.O. (1992). *Metacognition: Core readings*. Boston: Allyn & Bacon.

Nelson, T.O. (1996). Consciousness and metacognition. *American Psychologist, 51,* 102–16.

Nelson, T.O., & Narens, L. (1994). Why investigate metacognition? In J. Metcalfe & A.P. Shimaura (eds), *Metacognition: Knowing about knowing*. Cambridge, MA: Bradford Books.

Newell, A. (1992). SOAR as a unified theory of cognition: Issues and explanations. *Behavioral and Brain Sciences, 15,* 464–92.

Newston, D. (1994). The perception and coupling of behavior waves. In R.R. Vallacher & A. Nowak (eds), *Dynamic systems in social psychology*. San Diego, CA: Academic.

Nietzsche, F. (1968). *Basic writings of Nietzsche* (W. Kaufman, Ed.). New York: Modern Library.

Norman, D.A., & Shallice, T. (1988). Attention to action: Willed and automatic control of behavior. In R.J. Davidson, G.E. Schwartz & D. Shapiro (eds), Consciousness and self-regulation: Advances in research and theory (Vol. 4). New York: Plenum.

Nowak, A., Szamrej, J., & Latane, B. (1990). From private attitude to public opinion: A dynamic theory of social impact. *Psychological Review, 97,* 362–76.

Oatley, K. (1988). On changing one's mind: A possible function of consciousness. In A. Marcel & E. Bisiach (eds), *Consciousness in contemporary science*. Oxford: Oxford University Press.

Ozanne, J. (1999). Hermeneutics. In P.E. Earl & S. Kemp (eds), *The Elgar companion to consumer research and economic psychology*. Cheltenham: Edward Elgar.

Peat, D. (1996). *Blackfoot physics: A journey into the native American universe*. London: Fourth Estate.

Peitgen, H., Jurgens, D., & Saupe, D. (1992). *Fractals for the classroom*, parts 1 & 2. New York: Springer.

Penrose, R. (1987). Minds, machines and mathematics. In C. Blakemore & S. Greenfield (eds), *Mindwaves*. Oxford: Blackwell.

Penrose, R. (1989). *The emperor's new mind*. Oxford: Oxford University Press.

Penrose, R. (1994). *Shadows of the mind: A search for the missing science of consciousness*. Oxford: Oxford University Press.

Penrose, R. (1997). *The large, the small and the human mind*. Cambridge: Cambridge University Press.

Persinger, M.A., & Makarec, K. (1992). The feeling of a presence and verbal meaningfulness in context of temporal lobe function: Factor analytic verification of the muses? *Brain and Cognition, 20,* 217–26.

Pinker, S. (1997). *How the mind works.* Victoria: Penguin Press.

Piper, A. (1994). Multiple personality disorder. *British Journal of Psychiatry, 164,* 600–12.

Pope, H., & Hudson, J. (1995). Can memories of childhood sexual abuse be repressed? *Psychological Medicine, 25,* 121–6.

Popkin, R.H., & Stroll, A. (1993). *Philosophy made simple.* New York: Doubleday.

Posner, M.I., & Raichle, M.E. (1994). *Images of mind.* New York: Freeman.

Poundstone, W. (1985). *The recursive universe.* New York: Morrow.

Prigogine, I. (1997). *End of certainty: Time, chaos and the new law of nature.* New York: Free Press.

Prigogine, I., & Stengers, I. (1984). *Order out of chaos.* New York: Bantam.

Putnam, H. (1987). *The many faces of realism: The Paul Carus lectures.* LaSalle, IL: Open Court Publishing.

Quine, W.V.O. (1960). *Word and object.* Cambridge, MA: MIT Press.

Redhead, M. (1987). *Incompleteness, nonlocality and realism.* Oxford: Clarendon.

Reese, W.L. (1980). *Dictionary of philosophy and religion.* Atlantic Highlands, NJ: Humanities Press.

Reidbord, S., & Redington, D. (1992). Psychophysiological process during insight oriented therapy: Further investigations into nonlinear psychodynamics. *Journal of Nervous and Mental Disease, 180,* 649–57.

Riser, J. (1997). *Hermeneutics and the voice of the other.* New York: SUNY Press.

Rogers, C. (1951). *Client-centered therapy.* Boston: Houghton Mifflin.

Rogers, C. (1959). A theory of therapy, personality, and interpersonal relationships, as developed in the client-centered framework. In S. Koch (ed.), *Psychology: A study of a science* (Vol. 3). New York: McGraw-Hill.

Roschke, J., & Aldenhoff, J. (1992). A nonlinear approach to brain function: Deterministic chaos and sleep EEG. *Sleep, 15,* 95–101.

Rosenbaum, D.A., & Collyer, C.E. (eds), (1998). *Timing of behavior:*

neural, psychological, and computational perspectives. Cambridge, MA: MIT Press.
Rosenthal, D.M. (1996). A theory of consciousness. In N. Block, O. Flanagan, & G. Guzeldere (eds), *The nature of consciousness.* Cambridge, MA: MIT Press.
Ross, D. (1951). *Plato's theory of ideas.* Oxford: Oxford University Press.
Rumelhart, D., McClelland, & the PDP Research Group (1986). *Parallel distributed processing: Explorations in the microstructure of cognition.* Cambridge, MA: MIT Press.
Russell, B. (1967). *The basic writings of Bertrand Russell* (R.E. Egner & L.E. Dennon, eds) New York: Simon & Schuster.
Russell, B. (1968*). A history of western philosophy.* London: Allen & Unwin.
Rychlak, J.F. (1981). Philosophical basis of personality theories. In F. Fransella (ed.), *Personality: Theory, measurement and research.* New York: Methuen.
Ryle, G. (1949). *The concept of mind.* London: Hutchinson.
Sartre, J.-P. (1956). *Being and nothingness: A phenomenological essay on ontology* (translated by H.E. Barnes). New York: Citadel.
Sartre, J.-P. (1959). *Nausea* (translated by L. Alexander). New York: Directions.
Schrodinger, E. (1958). *Mind and matter.* Cambridge: Cambridge University Press.
Schroeder, M. (1991). *Fractals, chaos, power laws.* New York: Freeman.
Searle, J. (1980). Minds, brains and programs. *Behavioral and Brain Sciences, 3*, 417–24.
Searle, J. (1992). *The rediscovery of the mind.* Cambridge: Cambridge University Press.
Searle, J. (1997). *The mystery of consciousness.* New York: The New York Review of Books.
Shallice, T. (1988). Informational-processing models of consciousness: Possibilities and problems. In A. Marcel & E. Bisiach (eds), *Consciousness in contemporary science.* Oxford: Clarendon Press.
Sheldrake, R., & Fox, M. (1996). *Natural grace.* London: Bloomsbury.
Shimamura, A.P. (1994). The neuropsychology of metacognition. In J.

Metcalfe & A.P. Shimaura (eds), *Metacognition: Knowing about knowing*. Cambridge, MA: Bradford Books.

Shimony, A. (1997). On mentality, quantum mechanics and the actualization of potentialities. In R. Penrose, *The large, the small and the human mind*. Cambridge: Cambridge University Press.

Siegler, R.S. (1994). Cognitive variability: A key to understanding cognitive development. *Current Directions in Psychological Science, 3*, 1–5.

Singer, M.S. (1997). *Ethics and justice in organisations: A normative-empirical dialogue*. Aldershot: Avebury.

Skinner, B.F. (1971). *Beyond freedom and dignity*. New York: Knopf.

Smith, R. (1997). *The Fontana History of the Human Sciences*. London: Fontana Press.

Snyder, M. (1987). *Public appearances, private realities: The psychology of self-monitoring*. New York: Freeman.

Spanos, N.P. (1983). The hidden observer as an experimental creation. *Journal of Personality and Social Psychology, 44*, 170–6.

Sperry, R. (1977). Fore-brain commissurotomy and conscious awareness. *Journal of Medicine and Philosophy, 2*, 101–26.

Sperry, R. (1992). Turnabout on consciousness: A mentalist view. *Journal of Mind and Behavior, 13*, 259–80.

Sperry, R.W. (1968). Hemisphere deconnection and the unity of conscious experience. *American Psychologist, 23*, 723–33.

Springer, S.P., & Deutsch, G. (1993). *Left brain, right brain* (4th edn). New York: Freeman.

Squire, L.R., & Kosslyn, S.M. (eds), (1998*). Findings and current opinion in cognitive neuroscience*. Cambridge, MA: MIT Press.

Squire, L.R., & Zola-Morgan, S. (1991). The medial temporal lobe memory system. *Science 253*, 1380–6.

Stacey, R. (1991). *The chaos frontier: Creative strategic boundaries between order and chaos*. San Francisco: Jossey-Bass.

Stacey, R. (1995) The science of complexity: An alternative perspective for strategic change processes. *Strategic Management Journal, 16*, 477–95.

Stadler, M., & Kruse, P. (1994). Gestalt theory and synergetics: From psychophysical isomorphism to holistic emergentism. *Philosophical Psychology, 7*, 211–26.

Stapp, H.P. (1993). *Mind, matter and quantum mechanics*. Berlin: Springer-Verlag.

Stenger, V.J. (1988). *Not by design: The origin of the universe.* New York: Prometheus Books.

Stenger, V.J. (1990). *Physics and psychics: The search for a world beyond the senses.* New York: Prometheus Books.

Strauman, T. (1992). Self-guides, autobiographical memory, and anxiety and dysphoria: Toward a cognitive model of vulnerability to emotional distress. *Journal of Abnormal Psychology, 101*, 87–95.

Stroud, B. (1981). *Hume.* London: Routledge & Kegan Paul.

Stryker, M. (1989). Is grandmother an oscillation? *Nature, 338*, 297–8.

Sullivan, H.S. (1953). *The interpersonal theory of psychiatry.* New York: Norton.

Swinney, H. (1983). Observations of order and chaos in nonlinear systems. *Physica, 7*, 3–15.

Tarnas, R. (1991). *The passion of the Western mind: Understanding the ideas that have shaped our world view.* New York: Ballantine.

Tart, C. & Institute of Noetic Sciences (1993). Consciousness: A psychological, transpersonal and parapsychological approach. Paper presented at the Third International Symposium on Science and Consciousness, Ancient Olympia.

Taylor, C. (1989). *Sources of the self: The making of the modern identity.* Cambridge, MA: Harvard University Press.

Thelen, E. (1995). Motor development: A new synthesis. *American Psychologist, 50*, 79–95.

Tinsley, D.J. (1993). Responses to steps toward a science of free will: Determinism, nondeterminism and the distinction between uncaused and unpredictable behaviour. *Counselling and Values, 38*, 67–71.

Tovee, M.J. (1998). *The speed of thought: Information processing in the cerebral cortex.* Berlin: Springer-Verlag.

Trefil, J. (1998). *Are we unique? A scientist explores the unparalleled intelligence of the human mind.* New York: Wiley.

Treisman, A. (1998). Feature binding, attention and object perception. *Philosophical Transactions of the Royal Society of London, 353*, 1295–306.

Turner, R. (1976). The real self: From institution to impulse. *American Journal of Sociology, 81*, 989–1016.

Tye, M. (1995). *Ten problems of consciousness.* Cambridge, MA: MIT press.

Umilta, C. (1988). The control operations of consciousness. In A.

Marcel & E. Bisiach (eds), *Consciousness in contemporary science*. Oxford: Clarendon Press.

Vallacher, R.R., & Nowak, A. (1997). The emergence of dynamic social psychology. *Psychological Inquiry, 8*, 73–99.

Van Geert, P. (1994). *Dynamic systems of development: Change between complexity and chaos.* London: Harvester Wheatsheaf.

Van Geert, P. (1997). Time and theory in social psychology. *Psychological Inquiry, 8,* 143–51.

Van Gulick, R. (1992). Understanding the phenomenal mind: Are we all just armadillos? In M. Davies & G. Humphreys (eds), *Consciousness: A mind and language reader*. Oxford: Blackwell.

Varela, F.J., Thompson, E., & Rosch, E. (1992). *The embodied mind: Cognitive science and human experience.* Cambridge: MIT Press.

Von Neumann, J. (1966). *Theory of self-reproducing automata*. Urbana, IL: University of Illinois Press.

Waldrop, M. (1992). *Complexity*. New York: Simon & Schuster.

Weiskrantz, L. (1986). *Blindsight: A case study and implications.* Oxford: Oxford University Press.

Weiskrantz, L. (1988). *Thought without language*. Oxford: Oxford University Press.

Weiskrantz, L. (1997). *Consciousness lost and found*. Oxford: Oxford University Press.

Weiss, F.G. (ed.) (1974). *The essential writings of Hegel*. New York: Harper & Row.

Wheeler, J. (1994). *At home in the universe*. New York: American Institute of Physics Press.

Wheelis, A. (1958). *Quest for identity*. New York: Norton.

Wigner, E. (1961). Remarks on the mind-body question. In I.J. Good (ed.), *The scientist speculates*. New York: Basic Books.

Wilber, K. (1982). Odyssey: A personal inquiry into humanistic and transpersonal psychology. *Journal of Humanistic Psychology, 22,* 62–3.

Wilber, K. (1996). *A brief history of everything*. Boston: Shambhala.

Wilkes, K.V. (1988). –, yishi, duh, um, and consciousness. In A.J. Marcel & E. Bisiach (eds), *Consciousness in contemporary science*. Oxford: Clarendon Press.

Wittgenstein, L. (1953). *Philosophical investigations* (3rd edn). New York: Macmillan.

Wundt, W. (1896). *Lectures on human and animal psychology.* New York: Macmillan.
Wundt, W. (1907). *Outlines of psychology.* London: Williams & Norgate.
Wundt, W. (1916). *Elements of folk psychology.* London: Allen & Unwin.
Zohar, D. (1991). *The quantum self.* London: Flamingo.
Zohar, D., & Marshall, I. (1994). *The quantum society.* London: Flamingo.
Zoltan, T. (1999). *The crucible of consciousness.* Melbourne: Oxford University Press.

Index

Compiled by Auriol Griffith-Jones

active reason, Aristotle, 31–3, 56
agency–sentience separation, 5–8, 16, 22, 125, 162, 225, 227
analytic philosophy, 8, 69–70, 72–4, 166–7
apperception, 47, 129
Aquinas, Thomas, 7, 59–60
Aristotle, 7, 31–3, 55, 59, 60, 166
    active reason, 31–3, 56
    De Anima, 3, 32
    final cause, 18, 69
    potentialities, 31, 56, 69
    rational soul, 31–3, 38, 56
    reason through sensing, 34
atomism, 28, 43, 55
Augustine, St, 7, 59, 165
awareness, 82, 169, 178
    self-awareness, 25, 47, 73, 82–3
    subjective, 206
    see also nonqualia

Baars, B., workspace model of consciousness, 16, 83–5, 181–2
behavior, self-determined, 145
behaviorism, 40, 52, 149, 152, 163
Bell, John, 103
Berkeley, George, 45, 61
binding, 89–91, 95, 212, 215
    among quantum objects, 101–6
    attention and, 178
    coherent oscillation and, 89–90, 105
    implicit information and, 171, 177–8
    system-level, 90, 91, 178
    see also coherent oscillation
blindsight (visual agnosia), 81, 189, 194–5, 204–5

Chalmers, D., 225
    information-state model of consciousness, 1, 9–10, 51, 167, 168–72, 173
change, 17–18
chaos theory, 11, 91, 93, 98, 113–21, 175–6
    application to biological and social systems, 119–21
    application to consciousness research, 210
    attractor, 18, 117
    dynamic features, 17
    emergence, 16–19, 115–16
    entropy, 118, 213
    feedback, 121–2
    Mandelbrot set, 113–14, 115, 121–2
    in neurophysiological research of consciousness, 98, 121–4
    nonlinearity (sensitivity to initial conditions), 114–15
    peaked potentiality, 116–17
    period doubling, 118
    self-organization, 17, 117–20, 213–19
    variability, 116–17, 120
cognitive agency, 6, 221
cognitive closure, 227
cognitive tradition, cognitive schematic approach, 140–1
cognitive unconscious, 13, 81, 82–5, 182, 205
coherent oscillations, 90, 178, 215, 217
    BEC-type coherence, 104–5, 106, 110, 111, 112–13, 176–7, 215, 217
    EEG recordings, 88, 109, 110, 112–13, 122, 214
    gamma range, 89, 90, 111–12

giga Hz, 110–11
see also synchronized oscillations; system-dynamic oscillations
complementarity principle, 11, 179–80
Comte, Auguste, 34
consciousness, 1–2, 13
  chaos-systemic approach, 113–21
  cognitive models of, 79–88
  a complete notion as the unbound mental workspace, 127, 150, 201–3, 207, 219–24
  cosmic, 214
  levels of, 157–8
  mapping or locating, 79, 89, 92–4
  methods of enquiry, 20–3, 219–24
  models of, 15, 22–3; Baars, 16, 83–5, 181–2; Chalmers's, 1, 9–10, 51, 167, 168–72; Johnson-Laird, 82–3; Shallice's, 80–2, 86
  neurophysiological approaches to, 87, 88–98
  quantum-systemic approach, 98–113
  'stream of' (James), 131–2
  transcendental, 154–5
  two-tier theory of, 218–19
  Wundt's view of, 129–30
conscious–unconscious divide, 204–8
constrastive analysis, 205–6
constructive alternativism, 142
constructivism, 138, 151
Crick, F., 92, 94–5
cross-sensory association, 190–1

Darwinian evolution theory, 45, 128
deconstructionism, 70, 148
deconstructionist turn, 76–8
Democritus, 7, 28–9, 39–40
Derrida, Jacques, 77
Descartes, René, 8, 13, 35–9
  nonconscious excluded from *psyche*, 8, 13, 36–7, 125
  philosophical responses to, 39–51
determinism, 152
dialectic, 139–40, 141
dissociation, 189, 206, 208
dogma, 225, 226–7
dream research, 186–9, 192

dreaming, 133, 205
dual-aspect theories, 17, 39, 46–9, 67, 133, 170–5
  see also Chalmers
Durkheim, Emile, 160

Eccles, Sir John, 97
Edelman, G.M., 93, 95–6
ego, 25, 150, 151, 157–8
  pure ego, 132, 134
  superego, 135
Einstein, Albert, 103
eliminative materialism, 9, 29, 39, 40–2, 75
emergence, 16, 17, 18–19, 97, 115–17, 121, 174, 201, 216
  emergent properties of consciousness, 173–4, 216, 217–19
  self-organization: of subminds, 215–16, 218; of subselves, 18, 215
  wave function, 105–6
emotions
  in nonconscious, 184
  subjective, 37
empirical psychology, 8
empiricism, 34–5, 41, 42–4, 51, 128, 166, 220
  James's, 130, 131
  see also Hume; Locke
Enlightenment, 7, 46, 61, 64, 161
Epictetus, 57
epiphenomenal materialism, 9, 29, 39, 44–5, 85
Erasmus, Desiderius, 60
Erikson, Erik, 151
ethics, 34
existence, purpose of, 68–9
existentialism, 67–8, 70–2

frame-freezing (consciousness stopping), 14, 197
free will, 35, 85, 134
Freud, Sigmund, 47, 128, 134–7, 149–50
  dreams, 187
  theory of mind, 204
  see also unconscious, Freudian
functionalism, 52

generative assembly device (GAD), 215, 217
Gergen, K., 148–9
Goldman, A.I., 194–5

Hardcastle, V., 93–4, 96, 175–6
Hegel, Friedrich, 7, 45, 50, 62
   absolute idealism, 69
   dialectic, 139–40
hemispheric specialization, 92, 106, 109–10, 179–80, 184–6, 216
Heraclitus, 7, 17, 27, 54–5, 126, 203
Herder, Johann, 66, 67
hermeneutics, 16, 21, 23, 220–4
   and experimentation, 221–4
hippocampus, 93, 94, 191
Hobbes, Thomas, 40, 135
Horgan, John, 226
humanism, 55–6
humanistic psychology, 152, 155–6
Hume, David, 8, 43–4, 48, 61
   associationism, 43, 51–2, 53, 130
   personal identity, 17, 125, 132
Huxley, Thomas, 45
hypnosis research, 189–90

id, in Freud, 135, 136
Idea, 7, 29–30, 48, 56, 64, 183
idealism, 28, 39, 45–6, 125
   Hegel's, 69
idealistic monism, 45
identity materialism, 39, 42–4
information processing, 11–12, 143–5, 180, 197
   in cognitive models of consciousness, 79–88
   in dreams, 186–8
information-state model of consciousness, 1, 9–10, 51, 168–72, 173
   coherence principle, 169–70
   consciousness and brain, 171–2
   dual-aspected reality, 51, 170–1
intention, 83, 85
interaction
   interpersonal, 151–2
   symbolic, 142–3, 152
intralamina nuclei, 92

intuitions, 64

James, William, 50, 52, 128, 130–4, 136, 226
   mediumship, 191, 206
   neutral monism, 168, 171
Jaynes, Julian, 183–4
Johnson-Laird, P., model of consciousness, 82–3
joined sensation, 190–1
Jung, Carl, 137
   collective unconscious, 64, 67
   view of self, 150–1
   see also unconscious, Jungian

Kant, Immanuel, 47–9, 54, 63–4, 68, 72, 161
   Absolute Whole, 69
   noumenon, 18, 48–9, 63–4
Kelly, George, 141–2
Kierkegaard, Soren, 70
knowledge, 166–7

Lacan, Jacques, 77
language, 143, 144
Leibnitz, Gottfried Wilhelm
   apperception theory, 47
   monad, 18, 28, 54, 67
Lewin, Kurt, 142
life processes (Wundt), 128
linguistic turn, 70, 74–6, 162
linguistics, 15
Locke, John, 42–3, 61, 64–5, 68, 130, 166

Markus, Hazel, 143–4
Marx, Karl, 159, 160
Maslow, Abraham, 154–6
materialism, 29, 39–40, 52, 131, 166
   identity theories, 42–4
Medieval philosophy, 7, 35, 58–60
memory
   amnesia, 197
   explicit semantic, 94
mental conclusions, 180–1, 194–5
   fitting a parallel mind to a serial world, 123, 198

parallel to serial transition, 195–200
role of qualia, 11–12, 179–200
mental modules, 18, 20–1, 75, 211
mental workspace, 11, 20, 23, 181, 200–24
  activating information within, 181–2
  Baars's model of consciousness, 16, 83–5, 181, 213
metacognition, 204–7, 208
  and blindsight (visual agnosia), 81, 189, 194–5, 204–5
  and recovered memory, 207–8
metaphysics, 34
Mill, John Stuart, 72
mind, 8
  Classical philosophers' conceptions of mind, 26–33; legacy of, 33–5
  as in contemporary models of consciousness, 79–124, 210–11, 215–18
  Descartes' dualism, 35–9; philosophical responses, 39–51
  empirical psychology, 51–2
mind architecture, 23
mind bondage, 13, 202–3, 213, 226–7
mind–body problem, 2, 30, 33
mind–mind problem, 3, 6, 22, 30, 33–5, 38, 225
  mind–mind division, 6
monad, 18, 47, 54, 67, 69
monism
  idealistic, 45
  neutral, 39, 46, 50, 130, 132–3, 167–8
  substance, 27–8
multiple personality disorders, 207
multiplicity, 16, 19, 148, 201
  covert multiplicity, 17–19, 209; evidence of, 210–12; implication of, 212–13
  as covert property of consciousness, 210–13
  and self-organization, 209
mythology, 67

narrative gravity, 15, 18, 75
narrative interpreter, 185, 215
naturalism, 1, 168
  nonreductive, 50–1, 63
need-hierarchy theory, 154

neo-Platonism, 58
neuralnet models, 210
neutral monism, 39, 46, 50, 130, 132–3, 167–8
Nietzsche, Friedrich, 71–2
nihilism, 71
nonconscious, 12, 13–16, 23, 54, 64, 72
  activation of, 181–2
  in James's stream of consciousness, 133
  and *psyche*, 13, 15, 36–7, 125
  time-transcending, 196
  see also unconscious
nonqualia, 7, 11, 23, 30, 38, 45, 220
  defined, 4–5
  function, 12, 182, 200
nonreductive naturalism, 50–1, 63
notion self, 15–16, 88, 127
  and system dynamics, 163–4
noumenon, 18, 48–9, 54, 63–4

panpsychism, 10, 62–3, 133
parallelism, 39, 46–9, 123, 130
  psychophysical, 128–9
parapsychology, 206–7
Parmenides, 7, 27–8, 203
part-whole, 17, 21, 75–6, 127, 202, 213
Pascal, Blaise, 65
Peirce, Charles Sanders, 130
Penrose, Roger, 176–8
personal construct theory (Kelly), 141–2
Petrarch, Francesco, 60
phenomenology, 48–9
Piaget, Jean, 140–1
Planck, Max, 99
Plato, 55, 59, 69, 139, 184
  dualism, 36, 38
  Idea, 7, 29–30, 48, 56, 64, 183
Plotinus, 58, 69
positivism, 5, 41, 53, 166
  analytic philosophy, 8, 72–4, 166–7
  Comte's, 34, 53, 72, 166
  logical, 74
postmodern philosophy, 22, 76–8, 148
potentialities, 212
  Aristotle, 31, 56, 69

pragmatism, philosophical, 130, 131
prehistory, 25–6
preverbal processing, 185
Protagoras, 7, 55–6
protomentality, 62–3
psyche
   Descartes' exclusion of nonconscious from, 8, 13, 36–7, 125
   Enlightenment reduction of, 161
   holistic, 6, 7, 26–7, 54–5, 125, 165
   and model of consciousness, 15–16, 165
   spiritus, 6, 26, 202
   unbounded, 202–3, 221
psychic mediums, 133
psychology, as discipline, 52

qualia, 79, 80, 130, 225
   activation of nonconscious mental workspace, 181–4, 193–4, 220
   causal role, 10, 11
   constraints of cognitive approach, 85–7
   defined, 2–5, 49
   eliminative reductionist view of, 41–2, 44
   existence, 8–10, 43, 86, 95–7
   'flagging the present', 199
   function, 10–12, 179–200; dealing with the seriality problem, 14, 20, 21, 123, 195, 196–200, 220
   in a historical context, 5–8
   model of, 10, 50–1, 168–72
   monitoring covert processes of mental-conclusion construction, 195–7
   and nonconscious, 182–3
   and nonqualia, 37–8
   problem of, 166–7
   relationship with nonqualia, 4–5, 37–8, 45, 167–78
   'spiritual self', 132
quantum theory, 16–17, 99–106
   behaviour of quantum particles, 99–101
   Bose-Einstein condensate (BEC), 104–6, 112–13
   collapse postulate, 100, 101
   entanglement, 105, 219
   Heisenberg's uncertainty principle, 100, 101
   interaction and binding of quantum objects, 101–6
   neural activities, 107–8
   in neurophysiological research of consciousness, 98, 106–13
   objective collapse, 108–9, 177
   particle-wave duality, 10–11
   photon bunching effect, 102
   and qualia–nonqualia superposition, 176–8
   quantum non-locality effect, 103–4
   Schrodinger equation, 17, 100–1, 167
   standard model, 101–2
   subjective collapse, 108, 177
   wave-function collapse, 106, 107–9, 176
   wave-merging interaction of quantum systems, 105–6

rational soul, Aristotle, 31–3, 38, 56
rationalism, 33–4
rationality, 34
recovered memory, 189
   and metacognition, 207–8
reductivist materialism, 29
relativism, 55, 60
Renaissance, 35, 60–1
Rogers, Carl, theory of self, 153–4
Romanticism, 7, 45–6, 57, 61–9, 125, 134, 221
Rousseau, Jean-Jacques, 65–6
Russell, Bertrand, 50, 70, 73–4, 126, 171

Schelling, Joseph, 45–6, 50, 62
Schlegel, Friedrich von, 67
Schopenhauer, Arthur, 68, 135
science, 34
scientific paradigms (Kuhn), 53, 166
scientism, 37, 221
Searle, J., 173–5
self, 25–6
   in Baars's model of consciousness, 86–7

as cognitive agent, 125, 127, 136, 137–49, 216
dialectical or social-constructivist approaches, 139–47; cognitive-schematic, 140–1; information processing, 143–5; motivating and regulatory, 145–7; personal construct, 141–2; social-systemic, 142–3
director-self, 16, 83–4, 215
expressivism, 67–8
exteriorization of, 161–3
finite, 73, 74
fixed self, 137, 138–9
Humean (personal identity), 17, 125
key issues in recent research, 161–3
material and social, 133
multiple selves, 163, 211–12, 216
neurophysiological correlates, 163–4
in phenomenological, existential and humanistic theories, 152–7
possible selves, 143–4, 163, 211
proto-self, 18, 144
self-awareness, 25, 47, 73, 82–3
as sentient experiencer and humanistic guide, 125–7, 136, 149–52, 155
social constructionism, 138, 147–9
subsystems of, 140, 164
universal, 73–4
see also psyche; self, conceptualizations
self, conceptualizations
in analytic philosophy, 18, 69–70, 72–4, 166
Classical philosophy, 56, 57–8
contemporary philosophy, 62–3, 69–76
contemporary socio-political and cultural-historical analyses, 158–61
existentialism, 67–8, 70–2
founding psychologies, 127, 128, 162; Freud, 134–7; James, 52, 128, 130–4; Wundt, 47, 49, 52, 66–7, 128–30, 136
medieval philosophy, 58–60
postmodern philosophy, 22, 76–8, 148
Renaissance, 35, 60–1

Romanticism, 45–6, 61–9
self-integration, 214–15
self-organization, 17, 117–19, 121
as a dynamic process of consciousness, 17, 213–19
emergent properties of, 17–19, 215–17
of subminds, 215–17
of subselves, 145–6, 164, 213, 214–15
see also multiplicity
self-transcendence, 70–1, 126–7, 154–5, 156, 207
Senses, 7, 29
sentience, 6, 18
seriality and capacity, 14, 20, 21, 123, 195, 196–200, 220
Shakespeare, William, 165
Shallice, T., model of consciousness, 80–2, 86
social constructionism, 138, 147–9
social constructivism, 151
Social Darwinism, 130
sophism, 55
soul, 58
nature of, 3, 29–30
rational (Aristotle), 31–3
Spencer, Herbert, 130
Sperry, Roger, 97
Spinoza, Benedict, 46–7
spiritus, 6, 26
Stoicism, 57
strange attractor, 18, 121
subjective emotions, 37
subjective experience, 184
subjectivity, 15, 21, 69, 76, 84–5, 131, 216
substance, and form, 31
substance dualism, 30, 35, 38
substance monism, 27–8
suicide, 160
superposition, 17, 28, 50, 167–8, 201, 212, 219
psyche and, 202–3
in quantum theory, 20, 100, 101, 104, 108–10
system-dynamic notion, 10–11, 23
superposition of qualia and nonqualia, 172–3

superposition of qualia and nonqualia, *continued*
  biological perspective, 173–5
  chaos and systemic perspective, 175–6
  information theory perspective, 173
  quantum perspective, 176–8
symbiogenesis notion (Margulis), 119
symbolic interaction, 142–3, 152
synaesthesia, 190–3
  subcortic limbic system, 191–2
synchronized oscillations, 89–91, 110, 178, 209
  see also coherent oscillations; system-dynamic oscillations
system dynamics, 10–11, 16–20, 23, 88, 192–3
  and chaos theory, 120–1, 213
  consciousness as property of, 209
  self and, 163–4, 213
system-dynamic oscillations, 94, 122–4, 175
  see also synchronized oscillations

thalamus, 92–3
theology, 34, 59–60
time, 36, 50, 73, 96
  in dynamic systems theory, 123
  frame-freezing, 14, 197
  permanent present, 197
  temporal binding hypothesis, 91
  time-transcending, 14, 196

trait theories, 138–9
transpersonal psychology, 155–7

unconscious, 12, 77, 181–200, 207–8, 219, 223, 225
  in Baar's model, 83
  cognitive, 13, 81, 82–5, 182, 205
  as mental workspace, 20, 23
unconscious, Freudian, 13, 14, 37, 47, 64, 134–7, 163, 186
unconscious, Jungian, 13, 14, 37, 64, 150, 163, 186, 196, 204
unconscious–conscious divide, 201, 204–8

Vico, Giovanni, 66

Weber, Max, 159–60
Whitehead, A.N., 62–3, 72–3
Wilber, Ken, levels of consciousness, 157–8
will
  free will, 35, 85, 134
  power of, 68
  self-will, 71–2
  subjective, 57, 67–8
Wittgenstein, Ludwig, 41, 74–5
workspace model of consciousness, Baars, B., 16, 83–5
Wundt, Wilhelm, 47, 49, 52, 66–7, 128–30, 136